Jesus

AND

Captain Kirk

*The relevance of faith for today
and the future*

Michael Manto

Franklin Street Press

All Scripture quotations are taken from The Holy Bible,
English Standard Version (ESV), unless otherwise noted.

ISBN 978-1-7779102-1-1 (Paperback)
ISBN 978-1-7779102-2-8 (Electronic book)
ISBN 978-1-0688152-3-2 (Hardcover)

First paperback edition January 2022

Cover & interior book design by Franklin Street Press

**

3rd Edition

for all our grandkids

CONTENTS

Jesus and Captain Kirk

Introduction

MANY PEOPLE QUESTION what relevance the Bible could possibly have today, dismissing it as old and outdated, or even repressive and hate filled.

But the opposite is true. The New Testament presents an ethical vision for society that is far superior to our present-day culture. It is more relevant and needed now than at any time in the past. It's not the Bible, *but our society* that is backwards.

Our society not only tolerates but encourages an economic system in which the real buying power of minimum wage workers has dropped by over 30% since the 1960's, because wage increases have not kept up with inflation. Pay for the typical worker has only increased by 12% since 1978, while CEO compensation has jumped 940% during the same time.[1] Ironically, business leaders will resist increasing pay for workers on the grounds that corporations can't afford it. There seems to be no issue, however, with affording obscene executive pay and millions of dollars for 15-minute joy rides into space.

Business leaders complain that the economy cannot afford raising worker's wages. Disturbingly, prior to the Civil

---

[1] Lawrence Mishel and Julia Wolfe, *CEO Compensation Has Grown 940% Since 1978: Typical Worker Compensation Has Risen Only 12% During That Time* (Economic Policy Institute, August 2019).

War, slaveowners used the same "we can't afford it" logic to defend slavery. Wealthy pro-slavery advocates claimed that the economy could not afford the higher wages that would have to be paid workers if Blacks were set free. *The reality, however, was that they needed the cheap labor to maintain their wealth and privileged position.*

Just like today.

Raising the minimum wage is resisted with such ferocity, you'd think our freedom depends on keeping the working-class poor. Unions are broken up and attempts by workers to organize are vilified as a form of "communism."

Governments have been complicit by enacting legislation that hinders workers from organizing, hinders social assistance and affordable health care for the working poor, and supports big business in their tight-fisted approach to dealing with employees, who – thanks to the law – are relatively powerless. As a result, the 'land of the free' has one of the lowest standards of living in the developed world.

With tragic consequences. The middle class is shrinking; the ranks of the low income and poor are swelling; the wealth of the richest nation on earth[2] is being concentrated into the hands of fewer and fewer people. The top 10% receives half the national income.

Evangelicals today are relatively silent on these issues. The majority of evangelical Christians have been duped into thinking this perverse economy aligns with the gospel.

Historically, Evangelical Christians were known for their social activism. They led the charge to end child labour and

---

[2] For the moment, perhaps. But it's questionable how much longer that will last given the growing divide between rich and poor and the shrinking middle class.

slavery in the 19th century, ran soup kitchens and established organizations for the relief of the poor and disadvantaged.

Unfortunately, much of the modern evangelical church has forgotten this, and has abandoned its historic mission to hold a mirror up to society and keep it accountable for its treatment of the weak and powerless.

Evangelicals now are more known for reflecting worldly power interests and extreme right-wing politics than the words and deeds of Jesus Christ. At the same time, many of these same churches still do not allow women – on the basis of gender – to hold senior leadership positions. The Christian faith in general comes under attack because of these things.

In the past, traditional apologetics has focused primarily on the various logical, philosophical and scientific arguments for the existence of God, and hasn't had much to say about gender equality and social justice.

But I do not believe the Church can afford to remain silent on these questions, because for most young people today gender equality is a given, and achieving a just society is no more debatable than ending slavery.

I completely agree.

Any serious defense of the Gospel must address these things head on, otherwise the Church risks irrelevance. This book will present a serious examination of what the *meta-narrative* of the Bible has to say on these topics.

The compatibility of faith with science is another concern to be addressed in these pages. Anti-intellectual and anti-science-fact segments have grown vocal and entered the mainstream of many evangelical churches, in the form of 'young earth creationism'. This needs to be tackled directly, because a young earth is no more scientifically defensible than a flat earth. Does the Bible really teach, as many seem to think, that the Earth is only six thousand years old?

This is where I attempt to take things further than apologetics books typically have in the past, and where this volume is different.

My hope is to show that Christians can fully embrace modern scientific knowledge and remain faithful to Scripture without turning their brains off, while joyfully pursuing the superior vision for social justice that the Gospel presents. Faith in Jesus Christ is, in fact, entirely rational on grounds of science, logic and morality.

The first *Star Trek* series of the 1960's was original and ground-breaking. It dared to point out many of the flaws in societal assumptions of the day. It dared to portray women as intellectual equals and placed Black men in senior leadership positions within Starfleet, challenging the racist and sexist orthodoxy of the 60's.

In the context of the Vietnam War, in which the majority of people viewed 'signing up' as an unquestioned patriotic duty, *Star Trek* dared to point out the stupidity of using violence to solve our disagreements, even in the name of patriotism.

Star Trek was – and in many ways still is – years ahead of its time. It envisions a future where poverty is abolished. People don't go without food, medical treatment and education for lack money.

Star Trek portrayed a vision for a future society that reminds me of the New Testament. The same kind of social idealism in *Star Trek* echoes strongly throughout the New Testament. This is the subject of chapter 1.

One of the perennial arguments atheists continue to recycle, which sound hollower as time goes by but still needs to be addressed, is that there is some sort of inherent incompatibility between faith in God and science. This is the subject of chapters 2 and 3, in which I show there is no actual conflict, and a very deep compatibility.

Chapter 4 looks at the topic of slavery. While slavery is no longer a debatable issue, an attack often leveled against Christianity is that the Bible endorses slavery. Does it?

Chapter 5 looks at the biblical doctrine of gender equality. Tragically, on the basis of how they interpret a few Bible verses, some Christian denominations still do not allow women to hold leadership positions.

Fortunately this is not true of all churches, and many support full gender equality. They also have their Bible verses. So what does the Bible say?

There are some archaic commands in the Old Testament. Not everything in the Bible was meant for all people for all time. Chapter 6 attempts to show that such passages were meant for the original audience, meeting them where they were culturally, but pointing them in the right direction.

Chapter 7 discusses the morality of God's judgment on nations. Chapter 8 covers a smorgasbord of questions and accusations often brought against the Christian faith. Chapter 9 looks into the foundational event in history of Christianity, the resurrection of Jesus Christ.

Chapter 10 examines the scientific evidence for God.

Chapters 11 and 12 look at the philosophical arguments for the existence of God, drawing heavily on the reality of *objective* moral values. If we take the time to really think it through, such philosophical arguments can be as compelling as the physical evidence in science.

Faith in God makes complete rational sense, both on scientific and philosophical grounds. There is an overwhelming amount of evidence for God, and in particular the God of the Bible.

In fact, not only is it entirely reasonable to believe in God, but the New Testament presents an ethical worldview that is, like *Star Trek*, light-years ahead of modern Western culture or anything atheism has to offer.

1

Is the Bible Still Relevant?

"There's another way to survive – mutual trust and help."[3]

IT'S VERY EASY TO LOOK BACK at previous generations and see their injustices, but it's not so easy to see our own. As Jesus pointed out in Matthew 7:1-5, we tend to be blind to our own faults, but have perfect 20-20 vision when looking at the faults of others.

This happens at social and cultural levels, as well as personal. We've abolished slavery and we look back at history and wonder how people back then could have ever supported it. We say to ourselves that, had we been alive in those days we never would have tolerated such horrible injustice.

But what injustices around us now do we tolerate?

I often wonder what future generations may say of us, when they look back upon the 21st century. We no longer accept slavery, but we tolerate an economic system that keeps lower income people effectively trapped in poverty with little hope of bettering themselves. The education needed to get a better job is unattainable for many.

Almost 38 million Americans live in poverty, 11.5% of its population.[4]

---

[3] Captain James T. Kirk, Captain of the *USS Enterprise*.
[4] https://www.debt.org/faqs/americans-in-debt/poverty-united-states/

More than 30% of single parent homes – mostly women – are poor.

Wages earned by those in the lower income groups are barely enough to live on. Once rent is covered, there is precious little left over for anything else, like groceries, medicine and childcare. Forget about college courses to learn new skills.

The vast majority of low-income workers do not get paid sick time. Finances at lower-income levels are so tight, a day or two off due to illness often means bills won't get paid. So low-income people will go to work sick, or send a child to school sick, because they cannot afford the time off. Yet business executives making millions will resist pay increases and paid sick time for workers.

We tolerate this injustice. It's not ideal, we tell ourselves, but it's just reality. We justify our injustices the same way previous generations justified child-labour and slavery.

While corporations get rich and CEO's make millions, efforts to improve conditions for workers are resisted by the wealthy who benefit from the status quo. They will argue that the economy cannot afford it. They issue dire warnings of impending economic doom. They warn that raising wages will lead to huge price hikes and mass unemployment.

These arguments are eerily similar to what pro-slavery advocates said prior to the Civil War. The U.S. economy was very dependant on cheap slave labour, just as our economy depends on low-cost workers today.

Defenders of slavery argued that freeing the Blacks would lead to economic calamity. They wouldn't be able to afford the higher labor rates. The price of cotton would rise, sugar would become unaffordable, and tobacco would rot in the fields, unharvested. Plantation owners (read business owners) would go bankrupt, and many Whites would be ruined.

Pro-slavery advocates of the status-quo accused the abolitionists of being overly naïve; they argued that they didn't understand the economic complexities involved. But we can all see that ending slavery was a moral imperative, regardless of the difficulties and economic risks. The economic risks attending change is no argument for keeping people trapped in an unjust system.

Like individuals, entire cultures have their blind spots: things the dominant culture accepts as normal that to people of some future time will be painfully, obviously wrong. It's easy for us to look back and sneer at the flaws we see in previous generations. It's not so easy to recognize our own for what they are. It will take a future generation to do that, but by then it may be too late for us.

However, with some effort, hard work and study we can rise above our cultural location and try to be better than merely creatures of our time and place. It can be done. Every generation has had a few courageous people who saw the evils embedded within their cultural norms and rose up to challenge them.

In response to people who assert that the Bible is backwards and irrelevant, I will show the opposite is true. Not only is the Bible extremely relevant, in many respects it is ahead of us socially; it's our modern Western culture that's getting it wrong.

The Bible commands justice for the poor, the elimination of poverty and the cancellation of debt. We are to generously provide for the needs of others; feed the hungry, heal the sick, take care of other people and not expect that they be able to pay for it.

9

Jesus warned against the dangers of materialism. He said that we are not to be greedy or selfish; *that we are to love people, not money.*

Interestingly, the Bible is also very clear in its commands that the rich and powerful are not to be favoured, and not to be allowed to use their power, influence and money to pervert the system to their own interests. However, that's exactly what we see going on around us now.

Biblical commands like this may strike us as too idealistic and Pollyanna, but that only reflects a problem with our society and the norms we've come to accept, *not the Bible.*

Here are some criticisms and questions future generations may have for our so-called 'enlightened' western society today:

Why were young people sent to prison for years over minor, non-violent, offenses?[5]

Why were Black people convicted at far higher rates than Whites for the same crimes?[6]

Why was executive pay 265 times that of the average worker? The average worker made $33,000 a year compared to the $8.7 million average for CEOs.[7]

In the early 21st century the U.S. justice system was sending thousands of people to jail for minor, non-violent crimes – often without a fair trial due to plea bargaining –

---

[5] The '3 Strikes' and 'habitual offender' laws in many states results in long prison sentences, even life, for minor offenses.

[6] The likelihood of imprisonment for a Black man is 1 in 3. For White men it is 1 in 17.

[7] https://www.statista.com/statistics/424159/pay-gap-between-ceos-and-average-workers-in-world-by-country/

resulting in the highest incarceration rate in the world.[8] Why was this tolerated?

The vast majority of the prison population came from poor households. Why didn't they make college accessible and affordable for everyone, so that low-income kids could have a better chance?

Why was there little money for better inner-city schools, but they had billions of dollars to build new prisons?

Better education was denied people who didn't have the funds, regardless of intelligence and aptitude, making it extremely difficult to break the cycle of poverty they were born into. This is effectively a class system, keeping people trapped in the lower classes. Why was that tolerated?

Why was it a huge political battle just to make health care more available to lower income families?

Getting justice in court was much more difficult for poor people. That's because they couldn't afford better lawyers. Why didn't they recognize that as a form of bribery that favored the rich and perverted justice for the poor?

The rich were allowed to send thousands of high-priced lobbyists to Washington, meaning the interests of the rich got preferential treatment over everyone else. Why wasn't this recognized as the systemic bribery that it was?

Why did they worship the beautiful and talented, and shower them with obscene amounts of money? Why were famous actors and singers paid better than nurses, police officers and fire-fighters?

---

[8] As of June 2020, the U.S. incarceration rate was the highest in the world, with 25% of the world's prison population. It enjoys sharing the top 5 with such enlightened countries as El Salvador, Turkmenistan, Thailand and Palau.

The Gospel tells us that all people, regardless of race or skin colour, are our brothers and sisters. It commands us to love other people as we love ourselves. To treat the stranger and foreigner in our midst as family. To shelter and protect those fleeing oppression. It means the end of hate and racism. This is extremely relevant to our present-day culture that worships money, and is consumed with greed, racism, materialism, violence and injustice for the lower class.

When those who believe in the Bible take its core message to heart and act accordingly, then those who don't believe, or at least aren't so sure, may be more inclined to listen when Christians talk about Jesus.

The moral and ethical truths in the New Testament are timeless and apply to all cultures because it addresses the underlying human condition that we all share.

So let's have a look at how the Bible is ethically and socially ahead of our society.

Social Security is a Biblical Mandate (and so is hard work)

"When you reap the harvest of your land, you shall not reap the field right up to the edge, neither shall you gather the gleanings … you shall not strip your vineyard bare, neither shall you gather the fallen grapes. You shall leave them for the poor and for the sojourner: I am the Lord your God" (Lev. 19:9-10; 23:22; Deut. 24:19-21).

This legislates a very practical social welfare system appropriate for the 2nd millennia B.C. In that culture the vast majority of people were farmers who lived off the land. Farmers were not to strip their fields bare during harvest, nor

12

were they to reap up to the edges. Whatever fell to the ground, they were to leave. The poor were allowed to go into the fields and collect whatever they needed.

In our culture, the same principle may take the form of providing funds to buy groceries for those in need, and helping lower income people get a good education so they can get better jobs.

Concern for the poor and eliminating poverty is a biblical principle[9], light years ahead of us with practical guidelines on how to make that happen. Yet there is balance as well. When it comes to assistance to the needy, the biblical intention is *not* to underwrite a lazy lifestyle.

Scripture makes a very clear distinction between the legitimately needy who are willing to work, yet need help to get on their feet, from those who are poor because they indulge in an indolent and lazy lifestyle.

The virtues of hard work and thrift are encouraged, and we are strongly warned against laziness. In contrast to the diligent who are "richly supplied", the lazy man "gets nothing" (Prov.13:4). A slack hand causes poverty, while hard work brings wealth (Prov. 10:4-5).

Poverty comes upon the lazy man like a thief (Proverbs 6:6-11; 24:30-34). They suffer hunger (19:15) because they won't do what they can to help themselves (19:24). They don't work, and as a result have nothing even in times of plenty (20:4).

We are warned to "love not sleep, lest you come to poverty" (Prov. 20:13; 24:33-34). In contrast to the diligent who rise "while it is still dark" and go to work (Prov. 31:15;

---

[9] Please see *Appendix 1* for a survey of social justice passages in the Bible. There are too many to list here.

20:13), the sluggard makes excuses for not doing the same (Prov. 22:14).

As a result, the lazy person is frustrated in their plans and desires because they don't work at it (Prov. 21:25-26; 13:4). The plans of the diligent, however, lead to abundance (Prov.21:5), the implication being that the diligent are successful due to their perseverance.

The diligent and hard-working individual is personified as a woman in Proverbs 31:10-31. She is willing to work (v.13), gets up early (v.15) and is not idle (v.27). She recognizes the value of her work (vs. 18,19, 24). As a result of her diligence her household is well provided for (vs.15, 21,27). Yet she is not stingy and is willing to assist those in need (v.20).

Scripture encourages hard work and strongly warns against laziness. We are told to "work with your own hands" so that we *won't be dependent on others* (1 Thess. 4:11-12). Hard work and persistence will pay off with wealth and abundance: (Prov.10:4-5; 12:11; 28:19; 21:5; 13:4).

Yet there is a difference made between the lazy, personified as the "sluggard" in Proverbs, and the poor. We are not told to assist lazy people. They often cannot be helped because they won't do what they can to help themselves. Instead, what they need is a change of attitude. The "poor", on the other hand, are willing to work and do what they can, but need some help (for a beautiful illustration of this, see Ruth 2).

The Bible commands us to be generous with those who have fallen on hard times, with the intention to help them get back on their feet and return to a productive lifestyle in which they can support themselves. But sometimes people need help to get there. This generous spirit towards the poor is tightly linked with justice and righteousness:

"If among you, one of your brothers should become poor...you shall ... lend him *sufficient for his need, whatever it may be*...you shall give to him freely, and your heart shall not be grudging" (Deut.15:7-10).

While the Bible says that laziness will lead to poverty, that is not at all the same as saying the poor are lazy.

This is an important distinction to make. Jesus said: "When I was hungry, you fed me. When I was naked, you clothed me. Whatsoever you did for the least of these, you did for me" (Mat. 25:40).

This would have fallen like thunder on the ears of his first century listeners. In the first century, class structure was rigidly enforced. People believed that the rich and upper classes were favored by God. They were better than everyone else and had God's blessing – their wealth was evidence of that. The lower classes were not as blessed by God. That's why they were poor.

Of course, there must be a reason why God decided not to bless the poor. So the poor were suspected of being in their condition due to some character flaw. God didn't favor them like he did the upper crust.

Sound familiar? The US has much the same problematic attitude, with its overweening concern that so-called 'free giveaways' to the poor creates a 'moral hazard' that only encourages laziness. We are suspicious of the poor, as if it is somehow their fault, and blame them for their perceived 'failings'. So we are reluctant to help the poor but have no problem helping the wealthy.[10]

[10] https://www.theatlantic.com/ideas/archive/2020/04/the-us-should-just-write-checksbut-wont/609637/

Our myth is that the rich are rich because they've worked harder than the rest of us, and the poor are poor because they've made bad decisions or aren't trying hard enough. We are suspicious of the poor, and suspect that on some level they deserve it. So we resist helping them, but will happily bailout the rich.

These are destructive myths. As Martin Luther King Jr. once said: "In this country, we have social welfare for the rich, and rugged free market capitalism for the poor." It's almost as if he foresaw the 2008 bank bailouts.

Quakers often cited Matthew 25:40 (quoted above) in their resistance to slavery, using it to make the argument that, "whatever you do to the least of these, you do to me. So when you enslave a black man, you are enslaving Christ." It can be applied just as well today in the fight against economic injustice. However we treat the disadvantaged, we treat Christ.

In our culture, poverty can become a trap that is extremely difficult to escape. Many low-income people have to work long hours and juggle more than one job just to cover rent and groceries. They are forced to use credit cards, and the debt piles up becoming another anchor that holds them down.

There is no time or money left over for anything that might help them improve their situation, such as go to college to learn a trade. This biblical principle and others we will review in this chapter would help people break out from their low-income trap.

The Bible does not fit neatly within our modern political categories of "Left" and "Right". It clearly supports traditional liberal values of social assistance and caring for the poor, the needy and the lower classes.

And yet the traditional conservative values of self-reliance, thriftiness and working hard to provide for yourself are also strongly endorsed by the Bible.

However, Americans today have little patience for such nuance, and are growing more polarized between "Left" and "Right", with each side unwilling to listen to the concerns of the other.

Rather than demonizing and dismissing the concerns of the other side, we would all be better off trying to understand each other. Both liberals and conservatives have legitimate concerns that find their place in Christian and Jewish scripture, and deserve to be listened to.

Pursue Justice, and Only Justice

"You shall not pervert justice. You shall not show partiality, and you shall not accept a bribe, for a bribe blinds the eyes of the wise and subverts the cause of the righteous. *Justice, and only justice, you shall follow*" (Deut. 16:18-20).

Pretty clear. Wouldn't it be nice if we actually did this? If it sounds Pollyanna, it's only because we've become so jaded by the injustice of our system that we've lost hope.

There can be no mistake that this justice is to be for everyone – not just the rich, but for the most vulnerable in society, for the poor, and for foreigners living among them.

This effectively levels the playing field and blocks the wealthy from using their power and money to influence court cases, legislation and the course of justice.

The Bible is filled with stark warnings for the rich who "oppress the poor, who crush the needy" (Amos 4:1). Amos refers to them as "fat cows" and threatens them with divine judgement. He strongly denounces religious hypocrisy and economic inequality.

According to Amos, God wasn't pleased with their religious observances while they took bribes, oppressed the poor, imposed unfair taxes, and perverted justice. God isn't interested in their songs and religious observance if it is not accompanied with justice. He condemns the rich and powerful – not for being rich and powerful, but for how they used it – for turning justice into 'wormwood' (i.e. *bitterness*) for the poor.

"But let justice roll down like waters, and righteousness like an ever-flowing stream" (Amos 5:24).

This verse is quoted by Martin Luther King in his famous *Letter from a Birmingham Jail*. Reverend King wrote that letter to white clergyman who supported him in principle but were reluctant to take a public stand in support of civil rights.

The context of Amos is fitting. The prophet Amos was confronting the rich *and the religious* for their hypocrisy.

Lutheran scholar Samuel Thomas writes:

"All the Hebrew prophets exhibit moral outrage, but Amos seems to be downright hopping mad... Throughout Amos 5-6, the prophet lashes out against those who have become rich at the expense of the poor, and against public – but hollow – displays of piety. According to Amos, God says, "I hate, I despise your festivals, and I take no delight in your solemn assemblies" (Amos 5:21). Religious devotion is meaningless if it is accompanied by unfair taxes on the poor, backdoor bribes, and working against those in need (Amos 5:11-12).

Because of these sentiments, this passage has become an important source for some observers of contemporary American religious and political culture. I think Amos would disapprove of the concentration of wealth and the corresponding increase in poverty, and he would rage against the displays of self-importance and exceptionalism in some quarters of American life.

According to Amos, a nation is exceptional by the measure of how it cares for the lowest members of society; and a nation of religious hypocrisy and economic injustice is one that will perish."[11]

Those who are at ease, who have it good, who "lie on beds of ivory", will be the first to be taken away in judgement because they forgot the plight of the poor. "Because they sell the righteous for silver and the needy for a pair of sandals – who trample the heads of the poor into the dust and turn aside the way of the afflicted" (Amos 2:6-7).

While I've focused on Amos, this theme is found throughout the Bible. In Isaiah's day, the people were wondering why God seemed so far away, even though they were very religiously devout. They went to church on a regular basis and observed all the right rituals. But God wasn't impressed with their religiousness because they oppressed their workers (Isaiah 58:3).

Instead of religious observance and ritual fasting, God would prefer they practice social justice: "Is not this the fast that I choose: to loose the bonds of wickedness, to undo the

---

[11] Samuel Thomas, "Let Justice Roll Down Like Waters (Amos 5-6)", [cited 12 Jun 2020].
https://www.bibleodyssey.org/en/passages/main-articles/let-justice-roll-down-like-waters-amos-5--6

straps of the yoke, to let the oppressed go free, and to break every yoke? Is it not to share your bread with the hungry and to bring the homeless poor into your house; when you see the naked, to cover him?" (Isaiah 58:6-7).

The same theme is carried through into the New Testament. "Religion that is pure and undefiled before God and the Father is this: to visit the orphans and widows in their affliction, and to keep oneself unstained from the world" (James 1:27). James is saying that we are to take care of the vulnerable and poor in our midst.

> "What good is it my brothers if someone says he has faith but does not have works? Can that faith save him? If a brother or sister is poorly clothed and lacking in daily food, and you just say, 'Go in peace, be warmed and filled', without giving them what they need. What good is that?" (James 2:14-16).

A few more samplings: "You shall do no injustice in court", "You shall not be partial to the poor or *defer to the great*, but in righteousness shall you judge…", "You shall not oppress your neighbor or rob him." (Lev. 19:13,15).

"You shall not curse the deaf or put a stumbling block in front of the blind." In other words, do not take advantage of the other people's weaknesses and vulnerabilities.[12]

"You shall not mistreat any widow or fatherless child" (Exodus 22:22). In that society at the time widows and the fatherless were the most vulnerable members of society. We are to apply that same principle to those who are vulnerable

---

[12] Lev. 19:14. I can't help but point out that this is exactly opposite of the preeminent principle of Darwinian evolution, which entirely depends on the strong taking advantage of the weak.

and struggling in our society, such as single mothers and low-income earners.

In a message to the king, Jeremiah says: "Do justice and righteousness, and deliver from the oppressor him who has been robbed; do no wrong to the resident alien, the orphan or widow, nor shed innocent blood." If they do that, it will go well with them (Jeremiah. 22:1-5). Desolation is promised to the king that does not do these things (v.5).

The king and his court were the form of government at the time. Clearly, government is expected to take an active role in defending the welfare of the poor and powerless.

Woe is pronounced on those who expand their fortunes at the expense of others, who oppress workers by keeping their wages down. The good king (i.e. good government) defends the cause of the poor and needy (Jer. 22:13-16). Leaders not interested in doing that are warned of harsh judgement (v.17). The Bible warns that a society that has gone too far into systemic corruption and injustice is bound for self-destruction.[13]

Throughout the Bible (especially Isaiah, Jeremiah, Amos, Micah), desolation is pronounced, *not on the poor or working class for any lack of personal piety*, but upon national leaders and the rich (in other words, the elite upper class in control), for failing to assist the poor sufficiently.

It is therefore obvious that in Scripture, society and government are expected to take an active role in ensuring social assistance, through the means available to it: fair tax policy, legislation, and the court system.

Let's wrap up this section with a thought from the Psalms. The Supreme Ruler of the universe is high and

---

[13] This is the primary warning of the biblical prophets, notably Isaiah, Amos, and Micah.

exalted, exalted above even the stars and the heavens. He looks down on the earth, and what catches his attention? Who does he notice? Kings and princes? The rich, powerful and talented? Attractive movie stars? No, but the poor and the needy, the lowliest members of society, and he raises them out of the ashes (Psalm 113).

Regular Debt Forgiveness

In one of the most advanced laws of the Old Testament, all debts were cancelled every seven years. This debt write-off did not require any sort of bankruptcy, in which debtors had to give up their assets. Debts were simply erased:

> "At the end of every seven years you shall grant a release. And this is the manner of the release: every creditor shall release what he has lent to his neighbor (fellow Hebrew). He shall not exact it of his neighbor, his brother, … for there will be no poor among you" (Deut.15:1-3).

The release applied to everyone within their nation. This command is quickly followed by commands to lend generously to the needy, and to not use the approach of the seventh year as an excuse not to lend.

> "If among you, one of your brothers (i.e. *countrymen*) should become poor…you shall not harden your heart or shut your hand against your poor brother, but you shall open your hand to him and lend him *sufficient for his need, whatever it may be*. Take care lest there be any unworthy thought in your heart and you say, 'The seventh year is approaching', and you look grudgingly

22

upon your poor brother...you shall give to him freely, and your heart shall not be grudging" (Deut.15:7-10).

Along these lines are other OT laws which outlawed loaning money to 'brothers' (i.e. anyone within the nation of Israel) at interest. They could charge interest on loans to foreigners living outside the country (incredibly risky in the ancient world), but not within their country.

Taken together, these laws, along with other passages we've looked at, lay the foundations for a society in which people won't get trapped by debt, and that endless cycles of poverty can be broken.

I imagine that many in our culture today would resist such an idea, but that has more to do with our cultural location and outmoded ideas of a finance economy than on any real principle of humanitarianism.

In the US, there is over a trillion dollars in outstanding student loans that crush millions of graduates and keep them locked down in poverty. Many of them postpone home buying and marriage because they have to service the debt.

Detractors argue that no one told the students they had to borrow the money. But what real choice did they have? In our society a good education is necessary to get the better paying jobs. We resist the idea of making education free, yet good jobs are only available with an education. In our perverse economy, we think it is better to keep people weighed down with a crushing load of debt. *The Bible says set them free. Forgive the debt.*

Of course, there is not just the debt of student loans, but massive levels of consumer debt. Many people have been forced to borrow just to make ends meet, to keep a roof over their heads and food on the table.

It's a complex issue and not at all black and white. While taking on debt for legitimate purposes – like an education – is understandable, a lot of our consumer debt is harder to justify. We live in a very materialistic society, the desire for more stuff is seen as a good thing (ancient cultures simply called this 'greed') and we've become intoxicated with easy credit. Combine this with ridiculously low interest rates (as of this writing) and a society that encourages excessive consumption, and we have a recipe for financial Armageddon. Easy credit and low interest rates have allowed us to live beyond our means.

Many point out that it would be better for the real economy if these student loans were forgiven. Their money could then go towards buying things they need, with all the economic activity that would generate, rather than servicing debt. It would be good for Main Street, but maybe not so much for Wall Street.

The biblical principles of outlawing interest on loans, and of forgiving outstanding loans every seven years would also serve another important function. It would keep the finance sector of an economy from becoming disproportionately large. It would keep the focus of the economy where it matters most: on real goods and services, on actually making things, in short - on jobs - rather than trading pieces of paper that represent a gamble on some monetary device.

In 1947, the finance sector of the US economy, as a percentage of GDP, was only 10%. That meant more jobs for more people on Main Street America, and a healthier middle class.

By 2016 it had doubled to 20%.[14] Manufacturing shrunk dramatically, and with it increased job losses and a host of other economic problems such as increased household debt, slow growth, increased income inequality and greater instability as manifested in 2008.

The finance economy doesn't make anything real. It only pushes virtual paper around, makes a few people very rich and more people poor. Most of the finance sector has become little more than casino, in which the bankers bet the life savings of the working and middle class. If they win, they get rich. If they lose, they get bailed out and the rest of us are left holding the tax bill to pay the national debt.

The result of our finance economy is that 90% of the wealth in the US is now concentrated in the hands of 20% of the population. How can this be a good thing? *How does this end well?*

Deut.15:1-3 and other biblical principles would keep such a perverse economy from developing. It is not for nothing that most ancient cultures discouraged if not outlawed the practice of loaning money at interest.

A law that eliminates debt on a regular basis would force people to think long and hard before loaning money.

Remember, this biblical law doesn't forbid making loans. It only stipulates that whatever is left unpaid will be forgiven after seven years. This will cause people to be careful with their lending practices. They can still make loans if they want to help someone out, but it would prevent the growth of the kind of perverse, grotesque finance sector we have today. We would not see the rise of a class of

---

[14] https://www.washingtonpost.com/news/monkey-cage/wp/2016/03/29/how-wall-street-became-a-big-chunk-of-the-u-s-economy-and-when-the-democrats-signed-on/

billionaires getting rich from the easy money that can be made in a credit driven economy.

This biblical principle is light years ahead of us. If followed, it would make for a much more sound, robust economy founded on real goods and services instead of debt and financial instruments, and less vulnerable to the vagaries of fickle stock speculators.

Foreign Immigrants Are to be Treated Like Family

"When a stranger sojourns (i.e. immigrant) with you in your land, you shall not do him wrong. You shall treat the stranger who sojourns with you as a native among you, and you shall love him as yourself" (Lev. 19:33-34). We read elsewhere that "You shall not wrong a sojourner or oppress him" (Exodus 22:21; repeated in 23:9).

Israel was surrounded by pagan nations. In fact, none of the other nations had a religion like the Jews. Foreigners coming into their country would almost always have a different religion, different politics, values and customs. They would have looked and dressed very differently from the Jews.

Yet, this is how God commands them to treat the immigrant. "Perfect love casts out fear" (1 John 4:18). Rather than being afraid and suspicious of immigrants and foreigners, we are to love and accept them.

No Preferential Treatment for the Rich

"You shall not...defer to the great" (Lev.19:15). According to the superior ethic we find in the Bible, the rich don't get special treatment, they don't get to buy justice and favorable legislation – unlike modern society which worships and fawns over them and showers them with favors.

Instead, in words carefully crafted not to give the rich any sense of comfort or entitlement, Jesus warned them that it was easier for a camel to pass through the eye of a needle than for a rich man to get into heaven.

He also said: *"What good is it if you gain the whole world yet lose your own soul."*

In a starkly chilling parable, Jesus tells the story of a rich man who dies and goes to hell (Luke 16:19-31). The reason for his punishment? Ignoring Lazarus, the poor beggar who laid at his gate every day. According to James 2:1-9:

> "My brothers and sisters, show no partiality as you hold the faith...for if a man wearing a gold ring and fine clothing comes into your assembly, and a poor man in shabby clothing also comes in, and you pay attention to the one in fine clothing, and [ignore the poor man], have you not made distinctions among yourselves and become judges with evil thoughts? ...has not God chosen the poor of this world to be rich in faith and inherit the kingdom...But you have dishonoured the poor man. Are not the rich those who oppress you and drag you into court? ... if you fulfill the royal law according to Scripture, 'You shall love your neighbor as yourself,' you are doing well. But if you show partiality, you are committing sin..."

The poor and the rich are to be treated equally in church, in society and in court. Along those lines we find in Deuteronomy this command:

"You shall not show favoritism, and you shall not accept a bribe, for a bribe blinds the eyes of the wise and subverts the cause of the justice…" (Deut. 16:19-20; Exodus 23:8). Also, "You shall not pervert the justice due to the poor in his lawsuit. Keep far from a false charge" (Exodus 23:6-7).

Now isn't this interesting? Here we have an iron-age society in the 2nd millennia B.C. with a clearer understanding of the basic rules of fair play, justice and equal treatment than what we are practising in our 'modern' society.

In our system people who can afford better lawyers have a better chance in court than those who can't. Not exactly bribery, in the strict sense, but how is this situation materially different?

The justice system in America favors the rich. You are treated better if you are rich and guilty than poor and innocent. Justice is often denied if you can't afford it. Thousands of men and women are sitting in prison – even for minor offenses – for no other reason than they couldn't afford the bail. They are too poor to get out. The course of justice is perverted for the poor because they can't afford it.

According to the Bible, justice is not something you should have to pay for or be denied if you can't afford it. This biblical worldview strikes me as much more just than what we typically see in our modern society.

You Don't Have to Go to War if You Don't Want To

When I was a teenager I spent a summer hitch-hiking across Canada from my home in London, Ontario to Vancouver, B.C. This was in the early 70's when the U.S. was still in the Vietnam war. The roads were packed with hitchhikers, and there were almost as many Americans as Canadians. The vast majority of the Americans I met were draft dodgers or had already served a tour of duty and had run to Canada to avoid going back.

At the time many Americans criticized draft dodgers for being cowards and shirking their duty to their country. I travelled with many of them across the country and listened to their stories. It never occurred to me that they were cowards. They were simply refusing to kill or be killed for an unjust war they didn't believe in. Many of them could not go back home because they would be jailed.

I wasn't a Christian then and didn't know the Bible, but if I had I may have thought of Deuteronomy 20:5-9.

It provides a long list of exemptions from military service. You were exempt if you'd been married in the last year, so that you could stay home and "make your wife happy." You were exempt if you'd just built a house or planted a vineyard. Finally, my favorite: you didn't have to go if you were afraid.

Rather than berate them for cowardice and not giving their all to their country, it just says 'okay, you don't have to go if you are afraid.' No shame. This also recognizes the simple fact that not everyone is cut out for military duty, regardless of how just the cause, without shaming them for it.

This is much more compassionate and humanitarian than anything we see today. The Bible is extremely lenient and liberal in its exemptions for military duty.

In the NT we find passages such as: "Put your sword away. He who lives by the sword dies by the sword" (Mat.26:52). "Love your enemies" (Mat.5:43-48; 1 Peter 3:9). "Repay no one evil for evil...if your enemy is hungry, feed him...Do not be overcome by evil, but overcome evil with good" (Romans 12:9-21).

These biblical principles add up to: you don't have to go to war if you don't want to. The implications are that as thinking people we should not be blindly devoted to our leaders. No mindless obedience to flag and country. No 'my country, right or wrong.'

Don't get me wrong. I'm not a pacifist. I am proud of my family's rich military history. My father-in-law served in the US Army during WW2 in Africa and Italy. My grandfather was an army instructor during WW2, and I had two uncles in the Canadian army fighting on the European front.

Sometimes we have to fight. Sometimes a cause is just and joining up is the right thing to do. World War 2 is, of course, one of the best examples of that in recent history.

Many Christian traditions have the concept of a 'just war.' The idea behind that is essentially: sometimes joining up is the right thing to do, but we are to be discriminating about it. It carries with it the idea that we are not to participate if the cause isn't just. We are to put our thinking caps on, do our research, double check on what our leaders are telling us, and think for ourselves whether or not a particular war is just or not.

All too often our political leaders get us involved in wars for the wrong reasons, for national pride, personal ego, to save face, to gain territory, make money, enrich the corporations building the machines of war, for oil, for business profits and natural resources.

In the early 20th century the US fought many wars in Central America because a national government wanted to kick out a big American business. Do I even need to mention the territorial wars of France (1790-1815) and Germany (1939-1945) to extend their national borders?

I could go on, but it's hardly necessary. I don't think I'm going out on a limb when I say that the vast majority of wars have been started by an aggressor for unjust reasons.

Whether or not a war is just largely depends on which side you are on. The Japanese attack on Pearl Harbor wasn't just, but the American response to defend themselves was.

More recently, Russia's barbaric, naked aggression against a smaller, peaceful neighbor cannot be justified. However, Ukraine is entirely within its rights to stand up to such aggression and defend itself.

Defending ourselves against wonton aggression is one thing. But when our political rulers ask us to join up, we need to make sure we are not on the wrong side, the aggressor in an unjust cause. No one nation is always in the right, and we have to be humble enough to recognize that. This is, essentially, what the American draft dodgers during Vietnam were doing. Setting aside blind loyalty to country and thinking for themselves.

We are to judicially decide for ourselves when to fight. People need to stop blindly obeying leaders. Great progress would be made in the cause of peace if people everywhere, on both sides of a potential conflict, started thinking for themselves rather than goose-stepping off to war every time our 'fearless leaders' tell us to.

Overcome Evil with Good

When armed men came to arrest Jesus, Peter picked up a sword in self-defence and struck back, wounding one of the attackers.

Peter's response was very human and very understandable. Yet Christ has a better way: he said to Peter, "Put your sword away. They that live by the sword will die by the sword." Christ then healed the man that Peter wounded – one of the very thugs who was there to take him away to be crucified.

In a world filled with hatred, racism and injustice it's easy to get angry. In fact, we should get angry. God does.[15] We would need to be lobotomized not to feel angry.

But rather than lashing out and seeking revenge,[16] we are instead to work towards eliminating hatred, racism and injustice.

The Bible does not endorse passivity or indifference in the face of wickedness – quite the opposite, actually. Another theme we find through the Bible is God's anger at those (usually the rich) who are indifferent.

Yet in our anger we must not respond with violence – thus becoming part of the problem instead of the solution.[17]

> *"Repay no one evil for evil ... Do not be overcome by evil, but overcome evil with good."[18]*

Gun sales have sky-rocketed in the United States, reaching all-time new highs. More than 5 million Americans bought weapons for the first time in 2020 alone. Gun manufacturers can't keep up with the demand and their

---

[15] As already discussed, God's anger at economic and legal injustice towards the vulnerable is a constant theme through the Prophets.

[16] Mat. 5:39 "If anyone slaps you on the cheek, turn to him the other also"; v.44 "Love your enemies"; Ro. 12:17 "Repay no one evil for evil."

[17] Ephesian 4:26, "In your anger do not sin." The Bible does not say don't get angry. It just reminds us to respond justly, not with violence or hatred.

[18] Romans 12:17-21

profits are surging.[19] We live in a world where gun makers get rich, but food banks are struggling to keep up with growing demand.

We must find a better way. It's too bad Bibles weren't flying off the shelves instead of guns: "Love drives out fear" (1 John 4:18).

If we respond to fear and evil with violence, then we are allowing evil to get the better of us, and we end up little better than those we are angry with. Instead, we are to overcome evil with good: "Love your enemies and pray for those who persecute you" (Mat. 5:43-47).

Apparently, Peter learned his lesson. A few years after the incident in the garden Peter was leading the early Church. He wrote to one of the churches: "Do not trade insult for insult, evil for evil, but on the contrary bless" (1 Peter 3:9).

Punishment Should Be Proportional to the Crime

In 2020 a 63-year-old man, Fair Wayne Bryant, was released from prison after serving 23 years for the unarmed, non-violent theft of a pair of hedge clippers.[20] Kalief Browder spent 3 years in jail, without trial, after being accused of stealing a backpack by a single witness. He was only 17.

These are not isolated incidents. The justice system in America is sending tens of thousands of people to jail for minor, non-violent offenses.

This excessive punishment has resulted in America having the highest incarceration rate on the planet.

---

[19] https://www.cbsnews.com/news/gun-sales-record-high-2020/
[20] https://www.cbsnews.com/news/louisiana-man-fair-wayne-bryant-who-spent-23-years-in-prison-for-stealing-hedge-clippers-granted-parole/

Many states have a '3 Strikes' law that requires mandatory life sentencing, with no chance of parole, for people convicted three times regardless of how minor the crimes may be. This results in people going to jail for the rest of their lives even for minor offenses.

"In an open letter to the Washington State voters, more than 20 current and former prosecutors urged the public to vote against the '3 Strikes' proposal. To explain why they opposed the law's passage, they described the following scenario:

> "An 18-year old high school senior pushes a classmate down to steal his Michael Jordan $150 sneakers -- Strike One; he gets out of jail and shoplifts a jacket from the Bon Marche, pushing aside the clerk as he runs out of the store -- Strike Two; he gets out of jail, straightens out, and nine years later gets in a fight in a bar and intentionally hits someone, breaking his nose -- criminal behavior, to be sure, but hardly the crime of the century, yet it is Strike Three. He is sent to prison for the rest of his life.""[21]

"An eye for an eye"[22] is often maligned because it is misunderstood to be an endorsement to seek revenge. But this biblical law was intended to limit punishment to be in proportion to the crime.

It means that if you are guilty, you get to make *fair* restitution and move on with your life. If you steal a loaf of bread, a backpack or a gardening tool, you return the item or

---

[21] www.aclu.org/other/10-reasons-oppose-3-strikes-youre-out
[22] Lev.24:20; Ex.21:24; Deut.19:21.

repay its value and it's over. You don't get your hand amputated[23] or spend years locked in a cage.

It means that the punishment is not to be in excess of the crime, which must also mean that it does not brand you for the rest of your life. This biblical law allows for a second chance. According to the ACLU:

> "Eliminating the possibility of parole ignores the fact that even the most incorrigible offenders can be transformed while in prison. Countless examples are on record of convicts who have reformed themselves through study, good works, religious conversion or other efforts during years spent behind bars. Such people deserve a second chance that "3 Strikes" laws make impossible."[24]

The biblical principle is that if you are guilty of a crime, you make restitution, and then you get to move on. This ethic of extending forgiveness includes forgetfulness. When something is forgiven, it is *forgotten as if it never happened*. There is no further punishment. You are not branded for life. It is not something that dogs you forever.

In America, criminals are marked for life. Even after they are released it follows them forever. It is never forgotten. Finding a decent job or a place to live becomes extremely difficult because all applications have that question about prior convictions. They are not being given a second chance. They may no longer be sitting in prison, but

---

[23] Many ancient cultures typically amputated hands, even for something as minor as stealing an apple. We may not cut off limbs – instead we just send them to prison for years.

[24] www.aclu.org/other/10-reasons-oppose-3-strikes-youre-out

they are still being punished for the rest of their lives, even for minor offenses.

The accusation against Kalief Browder turned out to be false. He was completely innocent, but still spent 3 years in jail before authorities figured that out.

But even if Kalief had stolen the backpack – *so what?* Why jail? Since when is a backpack worth years in jail and destroying a young man's life over?[25] An eye for an eye... a backpack for a backpack.

In the case of Fair Wayne Bryant, the hedge clippers he stole were worth maybe $25. At minimum wage, that's about 4 hours of work. A half day of community service at most if he didn't have the cash to make restitution. Certainly not 23 years.

We can take this even further. This biblical principle is meant to place limits on punishment, but it's not a command that we *have to punish.* Listen to what Jesus had to say about it: "You've heard it said, 'an eye for an eye, a tooth for a tooth'. But I say unto you, do not resist the one who is evil. If someone slaps you on the cheek, turn to him the other also. If anyone sues you for your tunic, let him have your cloak as well...Give to the one who begs of you, and do not refuse the one who would borrow." (Matthew 5:38-42).

This ethic is reflected throughout the New Testament. In 1 Peter 3:9 we find: "do not trade insult for insult, evil for evil, but on the contrary bless." In Romans 12:17-21 we read: "Repay no one evil for evil...do not be overcome by evil, but overcome evil with good."

---

[25] Kalief never recovered from the trauma and committed suicide two years after his release.

This may be too progressive even for many in the liberal extremities of the Democratic Party. Turn the other cheek. If someone wants to take your shirt, let him have your coat too.

See that kid trying to take your backpack? Give him some school supplies to go with it, and send him on his way.

Rather than criminalize minor, non-violent offenses, let's address the underlying structural problems in our society. Instead of building more prisons, spend the money on schools and subsidize lower income kids to get a good education so that they can have a realistic alternative to working for minimum wage for the rest of their lives. Pay for them to become lawyers, architects, engineers and auto mechanics. Or do we just keep building more prisons?

This is where the message of Christ takes us, if we'd pay attention. Why is it we are willing to spend the money to incarcerate people for non-violent offenses, but not on schools to educate them?

The End of Racial Division

On June 13, 2020, Patrick Hutchinson was participating for the first time in a peaceful Black Lives Matter march through London, when he came across a white man laying on the road being beaten by an angry mob. He was badly injured, and Mr. Hutchinson could see that his life was in danger. He went over and picked him up and started to carry him away from the mob.

The angry mob followed and continued to hit at the injured man, but with the help of some friends Hutchinson was able to get him safely to the police. One of the most powerful images of 2020 will no doubt be the photograph of that large Black man with the injured White man over his shoulders.

Hutchinson didn't stop to inquire into the white man's politics. There was a group of anti-protesters demonstrating against BLM. Was he one of them? Was he a white supremacist? A Republican? A vegan?

It would be difficult to find a more fitting real-life example of the parable of the Good Samaritan, one of the most famous stories ever told by Jesus (Luke 10:25-37).

During a discussion with the crowds about the commandment in Lev. 19:18 to "love your neighbor as yourself", a lawyer stood up and said, "And who is my neighbor?" Jesus told the parable of the Good Samaritan in response.

Most of us are no doubt familiar with how it goes. A Jew is beaten and robbed by thieves and left to die on the road. A priest comes by later, sees him, decides that he has better things to do than help the dying man, and passes on by. A Levite also comes by, likewise sees the injured man and continues on his way. Finally, a Samaritan comes by and seeing him, brings him to an inn and takes care of him.

Jesus concluded the story with a question: which of these three was a neighbor to the man who fell among the robbers? The lawyer answered: the Samaritan.

Jesus said, "You have answered correctly. Go and do likewise."

The good Samaritan and the injured Jew were complete strangers. Not only were they strangers, but Samaritans had different religious and political views than Jews.

Samaritans were a racially mixed group of partly Jewish and partly Gentile (non-Jew) ancestry. Jews and Samaritans despised each other and there was a lot of bigotry between them. Tensions often ran high and intense fighting had at times broken out between the two groups in the past.

The Samaritan didn't inquire into the injured man's politics, his stand on social issues, or his moral life. The Samaritan simply saw someone in need and helped him. Jesus said, "Go and do likewise."

By using a Samaritan who comes to the rescue of a Jew, two strangers with different ethnic, racial and religious backgrounds, Jesus is in a very dramatic way telling us that a neighbor is anyone in need, regardless of politics, religion and race.

This is infused throughout the entire New Testament. In Galatians 3:28 we read that "There is neither Jew nor Greek, there is neither slave nor free, there is neither male nor female, for you are all one in Christ."

On a similar note, Colossians 3:11 states: "Here there is no Greek or Jew, circumcised or uncircumcised, barbarian, Scythian, slave or free, but Christ is all, and in all."

These passages cover all the major boundaries that humanity typically separates along: "Jew or Greek" – meaning racial differences. "Circumcised or uncircumcised" – religious outlook. "Slave or free" – social class. "Male or female" – gender. We are not to be divisive along these lines. Instead, we are to see them all as neighbors, brothers and sisters.

One of the most vivid passages in the New Testament is the vision of heaven in Revelation 5:9. In this vision we see people from all races, languages and cultures gathered around God in heaven.

A Warning to the Church in America

Jesus makes another subtle point in his story of the Good Samaritan. Before the Samaritan finds the injured Jew, two other men come across him, a priest and a Levite. Both the priest and the Levite would have been Jews. Priests and Levites were highly respected religious leaders that the Jews gathered around Jesus would have looked up to.

Jesus could have chosen anyone instead of a priest and Levite as the 'bad guys' in his story. He might have used characters from the lower class: a farmer, a fisherman or a tradesman. Or better yet, someone from those classes of people that Jews at the time despised: sinners, tax-collectors, Roman oppressors, adulterers. Someone from one of these groups would have been much more appropriate as villains in the story as far as his Jewish audience was concerned.

Instead, Jesus used highly respectable religious leaders from the upper class. It's hard not to conclude that Jesus' choice was intentional.

The Old Testament basis for the Good Samaritan story is Leviticus 19:18, "Love your neighbor as yourself."[26]

Interestingly, in another passage, Jesus referred to Lev. 19:18 as only *the second* greatest commandment, which he said is "like the first" (Matthew 22:37-40). And what's the first and greatest commandment? "Love God with all your heart" (Deut. 6:5).

Jesus states that the "second is like the first" in Matthew 22. How is that? They go together because even the greatest commandment to love God must fit within the rubric of loving people, because *we show our love for God in our love for others:*

> "If anyone says, 'I love God', yet hates his brother, he is a liar, for he who does not love his brother cannot love God. And this commandment we have from him:

---

[26] This is one of the most cited Old Testament passages in the New Testament: Mat. 19:19; 22:39; Mark 12:31; Luke 10:27; Romans 13:9; Galatians 5:14; James 2:8.

whoever loves God must also love his brother" (1 John 4:20-21).

How we treat other people is how we treat God. When we ignore the plight of those in need, we ignore God: "Truly I say to you, what you *did not do* for the least of these, you *did not do* for me" (Mat. 25:45).

The priest and the Levite, representatives of a respected Jewish religious class, not only failed to love the injured stranger they left to die – breaking Lev. 19:18 – but by doing that they also failed to love God, breaking the greatest commandment in Jewish religion.

Some might think there could potentially be a conflict between the first commandment to love God, and the second to love our neighbor, as if the greatest commandment to love God could supersede our obligation to assist the needy, providing a loophole that allows them to religiously adhere to a so-called 'love for God' that mitigates their obligation to assist the needy.

Like the Levite and the priest in the story of the Good Samaritan, religious people can sometimes be cold, distant and uncaring, yet feel they can rest secure in their religious devotion and church going activities.

The Bible, however, doesn't leave room for that kind of religion.

The prophet Isaiah warned against the type of religious devotion towards God that was bereft of compassion towards people: "They seek me daily and delight to know my ways, as if they were a nation that did righteousness." Yet God wasn't interested in their show of religion because "in the day of your fast (religious rituals) you do as you please and *oppress all your workers*" (Isaiah 58:2-3).

The prophet called on them to "take away the yoke (of oppression)," to "pour yourself out for the hungry and satisfy the desire of the afflicted," then they would be a righteous nation, and the Lord would be with them (Is. 58:9-12).

"This is the fast I choose: loose the bonds of wickedness, undo the straps of the yoke, to let the oppressed go free and to break every yoke", "share your bread with the hungry, bring the homeless poor into your house, to cover the naked" (Is. 58:6-7).

In other words, true religion is practised in how we treat "the least of these", not in religious activity detached from compassion and concern for others. We cannot love God without loving people. "When I was hungry, you fed me. When I was naked, you clothed me. Whatsoever you did for the least of these, you did for me" (Mat. 25:40).

The vast majority of the evangelical church has morphed into the very sort of religion that Isaiah and Jesus warned of:

A religion that is no longer interested in "picking up the cross and following me," rather it curries the favor of the rich and powerful for political gain.

A religion that is pro-rich and pro-gun, and shows little concern for the things that Jesus was most concerned about.

A religion that is happy with giving to the rich in the form of overly generous tax breaks and bailouts and preferential treatment in Washington and the courts, but is against increasing aid to the poor, against assisting lower income kids to get a good education.

A religion that dismisses welfare programs for the poor as "socialism".

No wonder its lost credibility in the eyes of those outside, and as a result is losing an entire generation.

"Woe to you, scribes and pharisees, hypocrites! For you tithe mint and dill and cumin, and have neglected the weightier matters of the law: justice and mercy and faithfulness" (Mat. 23:23).

People who change the world for the better are men and women like Patrick Hutchinson, not those striking blows in the name of "righteousness" – regardless of how justified their views may be.

Conclusion

Many people today dismiss the Bible as irrelevant, but the problem is with us. It's our society that is getting it backwards. Could it be that the words of Christ are simply *too far ahead of us*, and we just aren't willing to make the necessary structural changes in our society? Future generations may well judge 21st century American attitudes as archaic and irrelevant, not the biblical message.

In the fictional world of *Star Trek*, money is obsolete. Hunger and poverty have been eliminated. Children don't go without food or education just because they don't have the cash. In the words of Jean-Luc Picard, Captain of the Enterprise:

"The acquisition of wealth is no longer the driving force of our lives. We work to better ourselves and the rest of humanity."

I think the creators of *Star Trek* were on to something, but Jesus was already talking about this two thousand years ago. He said, "Whatever you wish that others would do for you, do also for them, for this is the Law and the Prophets"

(Mat.7:12). This has been referred to as "The Golden Rule", and for good reason.

It would certainly solve a lot of the world's problems in short order if we took this simple command to heart. Taken together with other biblical precepts, such as 'don't be greedy', and 'be generous to the poor', we could eliminate much of the poverty and suffering in the world.

Some of the more practical implications are pretty straightforward. For starters, we would consider the welfare and betterment of others in our decision making, rather than enrich ourselves at their expense.

Wealthy corporations and shareholders might be more willing to make a little less (and still be rich), and share more of the profits with their workers, so that they could earn a decent living wage.

We would likely not see corporate executives getting paid, on average, 265 times the average worker.[27] Think about that: the average worker has to labor 265 years just to earn what the typical CEO gets in one year.

In stark contrast to the values of our society, Jesus taught that we should not chase money and possessions; that it was more blessed to give than to receive. He taught against materialism and greed.

Jesus said rich people were going to hell, not because they were rich, but because they ignored the plight of the poor. The prophets warned the rich that God's judgment was coming upon them because they enriched themselves at the expense of others, and robbed workers of fair wages.

Yet, as Ron Sider says, advertising companies spend billions of dollars every year "to convince us that Jesus was

[27] https://www.statista.com/statistics/424159/pay-gap-between-ceos-and-average-workers-in-world-by-country/

wrong about the abundance of possessions," and that greed and materialism really is the true path to happiness.[28]

Modern Western culture has enshrined business success at almost any cost and places profits ahead of people. In glaring contrast we find that there is no tolerance in Scripture for bettering ourselves at the expense of others. As the Bible points out, "love does no wrong" (Romans 13:8-10). This is much needed in today's world torn with greed, racism, strife, and inequality.

Many people may be offended by the biblical message. They may argue that it's naïve and unrealistic, and could never work. But that's just a reflection of the entrenched values and attitudes within our twisted culture, not a reflection of moral truth.

Whether or not we believe in the Bible doesn't change what the biblical view is, which carries an ethic that is superior to our culture reeking with greed and self-centeredness.

If the Bible is the word of God, then we could rightly expect it to be superior to our society in many respects. Which means it will run counter to our culture in those areas where our culture has gone wrong. Any God who is worthy of the title is going to pose a cosmic authority problem for any society.

While there are a few archaic passages in the Old Testament that were relevant for the original iron-age audience, but no longer apply to us today (discussed in Chapter 6), what's amazing is how modern and advanced its overall message is.

---

[28] Sider, *Rich Christians in an Age of Hunger*, p. 27

Further Reading

Lewis, C. S. *The Abolition of Man* (1943).

Hendricks, Obery. *Christians Against Christianity: How Right Wing Evangelicals Are Destroying Our Faith* (2021).

Pearcey, Nancy. *Total Truth*: *Liberating Christianity from its Cultural Captivity* (2005).

Sider, R. *Rich Christians in an Age of Hunger* (6thEdition 2015).

2

Does Evolution Disprove God?

THE FIRST NOVEL I EVER READ was about a caveman. I still have vivid memories of my experience reading that novel, how it drew me in so that I could forget where I was, and felt like I had entered that paleolithic world, fighting off wild beasts and Neanderthals. I was only about 9 or 10 years old, and it was the novel that got me hooked on reading. I've been fascinated by the history of ancient humanity ever since.

There is, of course, good evidence that evolutionary processes have been at work in our history. There is strong support for common descent in DNA, since humans share about 95% of their DNA with chimpanzees.

Many people today carry Neanderthal DNA, including some relatives of mine. When I learned from them that they had some Neanderthal DNA, I sent in a sample of my own DNA for testing, hoping there'd be something cool like that in my background.

I must admit to feeling slightly disappointed when the results came back, and the most exotic DNA I carried was a bit of Swedish mixed in with a mostly Scottish and German heritage.

Early ancestors of modern humans can be found in the fossil record going back millions of years. Australopithecus appeared some 3-4 million years ago, and are known to have made sophisticated stone tools. Homo erectus lived 2 million years ago and used fire. Whatever else these amazing creatures may have been, they were human-like, intelligent and anatomically very close to us.

The fossil record shows that our human lineage goes back millions of years, and our close DNA match with primates is evidence of some form of evolutionary development. Reptiles and aquatic animals go back even further in the fossil record, hundreds of millions of years.

Militant atheists see this as evidence that there is no God. In their worldview, evolution *means* life is an accident, developed through strictly natural forces without any divine assistance. Since, in their view, evolution can account for the existence of life without the need for a Creator, there's no need to believe in God.

The assumption behind this is that evolution also means *unguided*. However, they're getting science confused with their philosophical assumptions. Evolution as a strictly biological process says nothing about guidance and need not be a problem for faith any more than the discovery that oak trees grow from acorns ought to be. We are surrounded by natural processes, none of which are a defeater of, or challenge to, faith.

It is entirely acceptable that God may have used some sort of physical process that took millions of years to bring about human and animal life on Earth. The main point for theistic faith is that God is the author and designer of our world and the universe. Exactly how He did it, what kind of natural processes He put in place, or how long it took, is beside the point. A lot of very prominent theologians and Christian scientists are very comfortable with evolution.

No Conflict: The Compatibility of Faith and Evolution

Many scientists who accept evolutionary theory are also believers. One such well-known scientist is Francis Collins, a biologist who led the project that mapped the entire human genome. As such, he knows DNA better than most people and accepts evolution as a physical process. He is also a devout Christian. His arguments for the existence of God and compatibility of evolution can be found in his excellent book, *The Language of God*.[29]

Stephen Jay Gould, an atheist, also sees no reason for conflict. He acknowledged that a large percentage of his fellow scientists were believers, and that this was not a contradiction: "Either half my colleagues are enormously stupid, or else the science of Darwinism is fully compatible with conventional religious beliefs, and equally compatible with atheism."[30]

Francis Collins quotes this statement from Gould at length, and upon reflecting on it, says: "So those who choose to be atheists must find some other basis for taking that position. Evolution won't do."[31]

As Timothy Keller points out: "... if 'evolution' remains at the level of scientific biological hypothesis, it would seem there is little reason for conflict."[32]

Evolution as a physical process is no more a defeater for theistic faith than the knowledge that the oak tree in my backyard started out as an acorn. Through a completely

---

[29] Francis Collins, *The Language of God*. (2006)
[30] Scientific American 267, No.1 (1992).
[31] Francis Collins, *The Language of God*, p. 167
[32] Keller, *The Reason for God*, p. 98

natural process the acorn sprouted, took root and gradually, over time, grew into a tree.

As a believer I accept that ultimately God is the original author of nature and natural processes responsible for the existence of that tree, and at the same time I can study in detail, as I remember doing in grade school, how seeds germinate and grow. To believe in God as the creator of life does not require me to think that God came down, waved a magic wand and *poof!*... made the tree instantly appear.

Faith does not short-circuit our curiosity and investigation into the natural world. In other words, being the Creator means he is the author of the existence and processes of nature, but that does not mean that everything in existence has to be the result of a miraculous special act of creation.

Let's look at it another way: Henry Ford invented cars, but he also invented the assembly line – which at the time was a radical new approach to producing cars. Does the existence of the assembly line mean that Henry Ford never existed?

Suppose the fame of Henry Ford has spread throughout the galaxy. While assembly lines are not in doubt, the existence of such a person as Henry Ford is. Many aliens believe in Ford, but some doubt. A pair of aliens from Alpha Centauri decide to travel to Earth looking for evidence of Ford to settle the question once and for all. One is a 'believer' in Ford, the other a skeptic.

They arrive in Detroit and find a Model T in a museum. The 'believer' points to the car and says, "Look, here's a car. It has clearly been designed by an intelligent agent. This is proof that Henry Ford existed."

The skeptic is still not convinced. They cross the road and find a factory used to build cars. It has a series of complex assembly lines. The skeptic gloats triumphantly. "See, here is an assembly line that produces cars. There is no need to believe in your imaginary Henry Ford! The assembly line obviously puts 'Ford' out of a job."

But as us Earthlings are aware, the discovery of a physical process, in this case the assembly line, does not disprove the existence of Henry Ford.

As a Christian, like many believers including many scientists, I have no problem with evolution as a natural process. Timothy Keller summarizes this position very well in *The Reason for God*:

> "Many Christians believe that God brought about life this way...Christians may believe in evolution as a process without believing in 'philosophical naturalism' – the view that everything has a natural cause, and that organic life is solely the product of random forces guided by no one. When evolution is turned into an All-encompassing Theory explaining absolutely Everything we believe, feel and do as the product of natural selection, then we are not in the arena of science, but of philosophy."[33]

Evolutionary theory as a process is one thing and is scientific in so far as the facts support it. But claiming that it means there is no God, and that evolution requires that we abandon faith, is a leap out of science into philosophy.

It may very well be that God used natural processes like evolution to bring about life on Earth, just as we see natural processes going on around us all the time. Many Christians throughout history have seen no conflict between evolution

---

[33] Keller, *The Reason for God*, pp. 90-91

and faith.[34] The Catholic Church officially accepts that evolution is compatible with faith.[35]

It's worth pointing out that when the general public first became aware of Darwin's theory in the mid 19th century, it was not generally seen to be in conflict with Christianity. The idea that there was an inherit conflict between religion and Darwinian theory didn't arise until much later, after militant atheists lobbied for years to push the idea that science was incompatible with faith.

"When The Origin of Species was published, it aroused immense interest, but initially it did not provoke antagonism on religious grounds... Although many criticized his lack of evidence, none raised religious objections, even as Stephen Jay Gould has acknowledged."[36]

Several prominent biologists at the time even saw Darwin's theory as supporting the divine design argument. "The initial response [to Darwin's theory of evolution] from those involved in Natural Theology was extremely favorable. Asa Gray, the distinguished Harvard botanist, hailed Darwin for having solved the most difficult problem confronting the Design Argument – the many imperfections and failures revealed in the fossil record."

Gray simply interpreted the theory as showing that "God has created a few original forms and then let evolution proceed within the framework of divine 'law'."[37]

---

[34] Theologians BB Warfield, Charles Hodge, for example.
[35] John Paul II, 1992
[36] Stark, For the Glory of God, p. 185
[37] Ibid, p.185

That about summarizes it all very nicely. The theory of evolution, as a description of biological processes, does not require atheism and is not in conflict with faith in God. There is only a *perceived* conflict by those who have taken on board certain philosophical assumptions.

It is this perceived conflict and its roots that we'll look at next.

Some Areas of Superficial Conflict

Many of you reading the opening pages of this chapter may have been thinking something along the lines of – *Hey, wait just a minute! Don't Christians believe that the Earth was made in six days? Doesn't the Bible say the Earth is only six thousand years old? Of course that's in direct conflict with established science! So Christianity must be incompatible with evolution!*

There are two small but very vocal groups who claim that the 'Bible says' the Earth was created in six days, just six thousand years ago: militant atheists and young earth creationists (YEC).

Atheists and creationists make odd bedfellows, in that they both insist on a literal interpretation of Genesis 1 and 2.

Militant atheists delight in claiming the Bible says the Earth was created only six thousand years ago. They say this, of course, not because they believe in the Bible but because it serves their purpose in trying to make Christians look stupid.

In this they have an unwitting ally in young earth creationism. Young Earth Creationists also believe 'the Bible says' that the earth was created in six days, six thousand years ago. YEC advocates a literal interpretation of Genesis 1 and 2.

The problem with YEC is two-fold: first, the Bible nowhere actually says the earth is young, much less only six thousand years old (we will discuss shortly how they arrive at this conclusion). Simply put, the Bible is very clear on the fact that God created the earth. How long ago He did it, or what the process might have looked like in empirical terms, is open for interpretation.

But the second problem with YEC is much more insidious and damaging to the faith, especially for young people raised in a Christian home in which they were taught YEC.

In recent decades young earth creationists have grown very militant in insisting that a literal interpretation of Genesis 1 and 2 is *the only way* it can be interpreted faithfully. This requires them to try to shoe-horn science into a text that was never intended to be read as science.

As a result, YEC is very hostile to evolutionary theory. Because they believe that their literal interpretation is 'what the Bible says', they feel the need to leap to the defense of the Bible by proving the earth is really just a few thousand years old, and they go to great lengths trying to disprove evolution. This takes them down a rabbit hole of pseudo-scientific nonsense.

This often results in a tragic loss of faith for young people raised in homes and churches which teach YEC. Their faith becomes closely intertwined with a literal interpretation of Genesis, and then they go off to college and are presented with solid proof that the earth is 4.5 billion years old.

The evidence for an earth that is billions of years old is as irrefutable as the evidence that it is round, not flat. It is no more open for debate than the orbit of the Earth around the sun. As a result, because their personal Christian faith was so tightly linked with the belief that 'the Bible says' the earth is young, their faith is deeply shaken and as a result, many feel compelled to reject the Bible, and with it their Christian faith.

This is tragic because it is wholly unnecessary; the Bible teaches no such thing. These young people were not properly instructed in the various ways the Bible could be legitimately interpreted.[38]

St. Augustine warned us against taking a stand on certain interpretations of obscure passages:

> "In matters that are so obscure and far beyond our vision, we find in Holy Scripture passages which can be interpreted in very different ways without prejudice to the faith we have received. In such cases, we should not rush in headlong and so firmly take our stand on one side that, if further progress in the search for truth justly undermines this position, we too fall with it."[39]

In other words, there are passages in the Bible that can be interpreted differently without making any difference to the Christian faith. St. Augustine wrote these words in his commentary on Genesis sixteen hundred years ago, and they are still significant for us today because young earth creationists are making precisely the mistake Augustine warned against.

---

[38]This is also a key difference between education and indoctrination. A proper education will do a decent job of presenting different views on a topic, and why people who hold different views have arrived at those views. Indoctrination presents only one view as valid and dismisses any evidence to the contrary.

[39] St. Augustine. Quote from *The Language of God*, p.83.

The YEC position is unfortunate. First, they are in complete denial of well-established science, and second, none of it matters to the Christian faith. It makes no difference to the faith how old the earth is, and it makes no difference whether the flood was local or global.

More importantly, these passages can be interpreted differently without denying the faith or the inspiration of the Bible. You can be a good Christian and believe the earth is 4.5 billion years old, as current science understands it, and that the biblical flood was local. Yet YEC plays right into the hands of militant atheists who are all too happy to make Christians look foolish and anti-intellectual.

Tragically, the anti-intellectual and anti-science stand taken by YEC sets up an impossible barrier for thinking people to overlook, who may otherwise be interested in exploring the faith. When presented with a version of Christian faith that appears to be asking them to turn off their minds and leave their brains at the door before entering the church, many decide to walk away.

I would if that was the only option for faith presented to me.

> "The tragedy of young-earth creationism is that it takes a relatively recent and extreme view of Genesis, applies to it an unjustified scientific gloss, and then asks sincere and well-meaning seekers to swallow this whole, despite the massive discordance with decades of scientific evidence from multiple disciplines. Is it any wonder that many sadly turn away from faith concluding that they cannot believe in a God who asks for an abandonment of logic and reason?"
>
> ~ Francis Collins

The Age of the Earth

So how do young earth creationists arrive at this idea that the "Bible says" the earth is six thousand years old? There is only one way this can be derived from the biblical text: the same way Bishop Ussher did it 400 years ago. By using the genealogies found in Genesis.

It was James Ussher (1581-1656), Bishop of Armagh in Ireland, who first popularized the idea of a young earth. He calculated that the earth was created in 4004 B.C., making it only 6,000 years old, by counting the genealogies in Genesis backwards. It was a popular idea for a while. Even the famous Isaac Newton believed it at one point.

But by the mid 1800's this date was largely forgotten, "and the prevailing view among theologians as well as geologists was that the earth was very old. It was the evolutionists who claimed that Ussher's date was the representative Christian view, the better to discredit their opponents."[40]

In modern times the young earth view was revived and given new life by Henry Morris in the 1960's and 70's. He took on a stridently dogmatic tone that his interpretation was the only true interpretation a faithful Christian could take. Unfortunately, this dogmatic tone has become part of the DNA of the modern YEC movement.

Young earth creationists base their argument on some genealogical listings found in Genesis. That's a big problem because biblical genealogies can't be used that way, nor were they ever intended to be.

In Jewish tradition, from the days of Moses right on up to the Christian era when the New Testament was written,

---

[40] Rodney Stark, *Glory of God*, p.190.

genealogies were never intended to give an exhaustively complete list of every single ancestor in a family lineage.

The purpose was to establish ancestral heritage with a particular tribe or ancient figure. Listings were often 'important person' only. Unimportant names were often dropped in order to reach an aesthetically pleasing number, usually 10 or a multiple of 7. This is referred to as telescoping.

Moderns like to include every person in a genealogical listing, but most ancient genealogies were telescoped. Telescoping was common and everyone expected this. This is not an error – the genealogies were still historically accurate and provided what was intended: establish ancestral lineage to an important person or tribe, often King David, Abraham, Aaron or one of the fathers of the twelve tribes.

The Bible itself makes it clear that genealogies can't be used the way Bishop Ussher and Creationists claim. For instance, the genealogy of Christ in Matthew 1:3-17 is compiled in a suspiciously neat arrangement of 3 listings of 14 generations each, Abraham to David, David to the exile, and the exile to Christ. The names as provided are accurate, but a comparison to the Old Testament will show that many names were omitted in order to arrive at the desired number of 14 generations each.

A comparison of genealogies in the Old Testament demonstrates the same practise of telescoping. There are numerous such listings, many of which overlap. In other words, they cover the same family tree or portions of the same tree, and they often differ. Some have huge gaps that others fill in, and vice versa. That's not a problem, nor does it mean the Bible is in error. That was the common custom and it was understood that genealogical listings would be telescoped.

The Genesis genealogies state that 'so-and-so begat so-and-so', or became 'the father of'; or that so-and-so was 'the son of'. The Hebrew words for son, *ben*, didn't only mean son, but also grandson, great grandson or any descendant. The Hebrew word for bear or begat, *yalad,* can mean 'became an ancestor of' and does not necessarily mean 'the immediate father' – but a 'father' anywhere back down the line.

Biblical genealogies clearly cannot be used to determine the years from Christ back to the creation of the world, nor was that ever the intention.

Richard Dawkins and other atheist writers are correct in stating many Christians believe the Earth is six thousand years old. However, many more Christians don't. It's an area of biblical interpretation that Christians are not all agreed on, but this need not be a cause for concern because the age of the earth is quite simply not central to the faith. Refuting a peripheral belief held by some Christians does not disprove Christianity.

Militant atheists delight in ridiculing Christians along these lines, often focusing their attack on the position held by young earth creationists. A typical example of this approach can be found in Bill Nye's book, *Undeniable.*[41]

Nye simply asserts that "the Bible says" the earth is six to ten thousand years old, and then proceeds to demolish that belief – which of course is extremely easy since the science on the age of the earth is solid.

Nye makes several glaring errors: assuming the Bible says the earth is young, when it does not; assuming that YEC is representative of historical Christianity and biblical interpretation, when it isn't; and limits his dialogue on the

---

[41] *Undeniable*, pages 9-13.

topic with Ken Ham, a Christian whose blundering irrationality makes for an easy target. Conveniently for Nye, Ham is a fundamentalist who believes Genesis is literal history and the earth is six thousand years old.

Not once in his book does Nye interact with serious Christian thinkers and scientists who accept the science of evolution and the age of the Earth, such as Nancy Pearcey, John Lennox, Alister McGrath, Richard Swinburne, Alvin Plantinga, Michael Behe, Hugh Ross, Francis Collins, Robin Collins, to name just a few.

After scoring a cheap victory over such an easy target, Bill Nye goes on to give himself a pat on the back for his apparent intellectual triumph over the Bible and so-called unscientific believers. This is the sort of classic straw-man argumentation we find filling the pages of books written by militant atheists like Nye and Dawkins.

Militant atheists and Creationists both get it wrong by thinking Genesis was meant to be literal history. So how do we get it right?

Yahweh is Better

One of my favorite books is *Animal Farm*, written by George Orwell in 1945. It's a story about talking animals who conspire together to wage a rebellion against the cruel human owner of the farm they live on. After successfully driving the humans out, the animals take over management of the farm. It's not long however before the animals soon find themselves under the yoke of new, even crueler task masters – the pigs.

Animal Farm is of course an allegory, but it has an important point. To properly appreciate the story you have to know its historical context.

It was written in 1945, just after World War Two and during the dramatic rise of the Soviet Union and its autocratic ruler, Joseph Stalin, one of the most repressive autocracies in history. Orwell wrote *Animal Farm* as a satirical critique of autocracy in general, and of Stalin in particular.

Now imagine that sometime in the distant future, say five thousand years from now, an archeologist discovers a copy of *Animal Farm* in the ruins of a 21st century library that's been dug up.

After carefully translating it and submitting it for peer review among his fellow historians and archeologists, he publishes his interpretation of the story.

The original social and historical context of *Animal Farm* is no longer understood by the people of the 71st century. World War Two and the Soviet Union have been long forgotten.

Unfortunately our archeologist doesn't bother to do his homework on the cultural and historical setting of the 20th century. To make matters worse, people in the 71st century don't use allegory as a literary device and no longer understand that genre.

As a result, the people of the future don't understand the allegory, or even that it was intended as an allegory. So they make a lot of erroneous assumptions, concluding that the primitive peoples of the 20th century must have been pretty stupid. *They believed in talking animals, for heavens sake! And clearly they didn't understand science. After all, there's nothing in the text about quantum physics and faster-than-light space flight! How primitive and stupid they were!*

Not just *Animal Farm*, but all literature has a context. Every book ever written was written by someone who lived within a social, historical and cultural environment – and you cannot understand *any* book without an understanding of its context.

Even though *Animal Farm* was written as an allegorical fantasy, that doesn't mean it's false. It used allegory to convey an important truth about the real nature of autocracy which we would all do well to heed.

Genesis is like that.

Understanding context is an axiom of good biblical interpretation. Failure to grasp context will always lead to misunderstanding. It's for this reason Genesis is one of the most misunderstood and abused books of the Bible.

Just as a future reader of *Animal Farm* would need to understand the mindset of 20th century readers for whom it was written, we need to understand the mindset of the Hebrews in the 15th century B.C. for whom Genesis was written.

The original audience Genesis was written for were Hebrew slaves recently escaped from Egypt, following Moses across the desert to freedom. Ancient people at the time, not just Hebrews but all people groups, viewed the cosmos as being filled with thousands of gods with a variety of different powers and realms of influence.

There were gods of the sky, gods of the rivers and seas, gods of different valleys, hills and mountains. The presence and activities of these gods is how ancient people explained natural and human events.

Furthermore, these gods were for the most part petty, vicious, lustful and competitive with each other, and constantly at war with one another. Human battles were seen as an extension of wars between competing gods. The creation of the world, in fact, was the result of one god killing another god in a cosmic battle. The world sprang from the body of the slain god who lost the war.

Within this pantheon of jealous, competitive gods, from a human viewpoint it was therefore critical for survival to choose the right god. Pick the wrong god, and you might fall victim to another tribe or nation with a stronger god.

As a result, ancient people often switched gods the way we switch internet service providers. This explains why the Ten Commandments starts with: *I am Yahweh your God. You shall have no other gods before me.* In other words, don't switch gods like the pagans do. Stick with Yahweh, he's the only God that matters.

This is one of the major themes we find throughout the Old Testament. Yahweh is the only true God, and the only God worthy of worship. The gods of the pagans are nothing, don't be afraid of them. Remain true to Yahweh, and have nothing to do with the gods of the pagans. Obey Yahweh, and only Yahweh.

This is the big point that Moses constantly tries to drive home into the minds of his people through the entire Pentateuch (The first 5 books of the Bible, starting with Genesis, that Moses is traditionally credited with writing.)

We must also bear in mind that these ancient Hebrews did *not* have a fully formed Jewish theology at the time of the Exodus, when Genesis was written. They'd been slaves for 400 years, and the vast majority of them would have been illiterate and uneducated. They likely didn't know much about this new god 'Yahweh' that Moses kept talking about.

After a series of dramatic events and miracles, these Hebrews find themselves following the prophet Moses out of Egypt and across the desert to a new land populated by hostile pagan gods.

What these Hebrew slaves needed to know was *who* their God was. They needed to know that the God they were following wasn't just another petty little god like the gods of the pagans, but the Supreme Ruler of the Universe, who was more powerful than all the other gods, and therefore they didn't have to be afraid of anything.

Moses tells them this through a story that starts with, "In the beginning, God (Yahweh) created the heavens and the earth."

The story moves on through the six days of creation describing how God created light and dark, the heavens, seas and dry land, and everything in them.

The six days are a structure used to organize God's creative activities. In the first 3 days, God makes various 'spaces': Day and Night (day 1); the sky and heavens above (day 2); the seas and dry land below (day 3).

The last 3 days are about filling those spaces with good things: Day and Night are filled with various lights (the moon, sun and stars in day 4); the seas are filled with fish and 'sea creatures', and the sky is filled with birds, (day 5); finally, the land is filled with animals and people (day 6).

People often get hung up on the six-day format, especially literalists like young earth creationists, who try to extract some literal scientific significance from the six days, or worse, insert science into it. This often leads to tangential debates about the precise meaning of the term 'day'. That's a waste of time. The Hebrew word translated as 'day' in our English Bibles did not mean a 24-hour period. The Hebrew term for day is extremely elastic, and simply means a period of time of any length.

Throughout the Old Testament the same word is used in different places to denote a literal day, or various periods of time ranging from months to years to eons of time. The word could be used to describe any length of time from 24 hours to millions of years.

Therefore, trying to divine some sort of literal scientific meaning out of the six days, or figure out if it's really a six-day period within a week or some sequence of events over eons of time is unhelpful. It results in expecting information from the text that the text never intended to provide.

Features in the text itself make it clear that it's not intended to be taken literally. For instance, at the end of each 'day' of creation, it concludes with "there was evening and there was morning, the *Nth* day…"

Yet the sun isn't said to be created until the fourth day, so obviously there can be no literal evening and morning. Also, light ('Day') is created on the first day, well before the fourth day in which the sun is created.

We must either assume the writer of Genesis was extremely stupid and not paying attention to his own words, or he was using poetic license to say something. Either way, a literal interpretation is clearly not the intention of the writer and entirely out of court.

Hebrew literature commonly used literary structure to organize the ideas and message of the text. The six days in Genesis is just that, and nothing more. They're there to provide a literary structure, not an attempt to convey scientific facts in an ancient language.

The six-day structure is used to organize the creative activities of God, who first creates various spaces (the heavens, oceans and land), and then fills them with good things.

At the end of each day, God declares the created things as *good*. Significantly, at the end of the sixth day in which he created humans, God declared humanity as *very good*.

Days 1-3	Days 4-6
God creates various 'spaces'	**God fills the spaces with good things**
God creates Day and Night (light and dark)	God fills Day and Night with lights (the sun, moon and stars)
God creates the sky and heavens above	God fills the waters with sea creatures and the sky with birds
God creates and seas and dry land	God fills the land with animals and people

Table 1: Days of Creation

Here are the salient points that the ancient Hebrews could not have missed:

Genesis 1 & 2 states that humans – not just Hebrews but all of humanity – were created in God's image, *both male and female*. This would have come as a shock to the original audience. It may be acceptable to us now, but the ancient world had no such concept of a general equality between different races, tribes, people or genders.

Men and women were certainly not equal, let alone in the image of God. Slaves were barely human, little better than animals. To say that a slave, let alone a slave *woman,* was equal, and in the image of God, was absolutely ludicrous to the ancient mind.

In the ancient world, only Kings were said to be in the image of the gods. Genesis is telling them that everyone, all of humanity, from the least to the greatest, bear the image of God. Including slaves such as themselves recently escaped from Egypt.

After intentionally creating the world and humanity, God said it was good. This was in stark contrast to the common pagan belief that the material, physical world was inherently evil and inferior to the spiritual realm in which the gods dwelt.

According to pagan belief, humans were unimportant, hardly worthy of notice by the gods. Pagan gods considered common people, if they considered them at all, as good only as slaves to do the menial work the gods didn't want to do.

Pagans believed that humanity and the world was an afterthought, an accidental by-product, not the result of an intentional creative act in which we were the goal.

For instance, one of the common pagan beliefs was that the world came into existence as a result of the gods fighting and killing each other, and the earth sprang from the dead body of one of the slain gods. In other words, humanity was an accident.

In this regard, pagan and atheistic worldviews are much closer than atheists may care to admit. They both believe that humanity is an accidental by-product of much larger forces, and therefore insignificant within a vast uncaring cosmos.

Genesis tells a different story: People are the intentional result of the Ruler of the Universe, who created us in his own image, therefore all human life has immense value and significance.

In the Genesis story, Yahweh creates the *entire cosmos*: the sky and heavens above, the oceans, land and all the rivers, hills and mountains. Yahweh is responsible for the entire structure of the cosmos, and everything in it.

No other god makes such an audacious claim. The gods of the pagans only created parts of the world and only ruled over those limited portions. Yahweh, however, rules over the whole show.

The pagans worshipped local deities who moved within limited boundaries of influence. They had gods of the sea, gods of the hills, gods of the sky, gods of the stars, gods of the sun. Genesis specifically states that God created all these things: the rivers, stars, seas, land, sky and sun – the entire cosmos.

The significance of this is that each of these things were gods of the Egyptians. They worshiped the Nile River as a god. Ra was the sun god. The constellation Orion and other stars were a part of their pantheon of gods.

Yet Genesis claims that the Hebrew God created all these things. The point would not have been lost on the ancient Hebrews: their God ruled over all other gods. Their God was the Creator of all, and therefore greater than all the other gods put together. The gods of the pagans were not gods at all, but mere created things.

The message to the Hebrews was that they were not following just some petty little deity with limited power, but the all-powerful God who ruled above all other gods, the King of the Universe. Therefore they could trust their God to take care of them and see them safely through to the Promised Land.

That's what Genesis is all about. It's not a scientific description of creation. It's not a science text and was never meant to be. It is literature making a *theological statement about God*, who He is and humanities relationship to Him in theological terms that the original audience would have appreciated, elevating humanity – even former slaves such as themselves – to the image of God.

It is that understanding of God that led to the scientific revolution. Our God created the universe and everything in it, and his original creation was good. He created us in his image, and we still bear that image, tarnished as it may be as a result of sin.

That's what Genesis is saying. It doesn't matter how long ago he did this, and the Bible doesn't say. The idea that the earth is six thousand years old is not only bad interpretation, but an interpretation not required by the biblical text nor necessary to the faith.

Timothy Keller, pastor of a large midtown Manhattan church, has this to say: "I think Genesis 1 has the earmarks of poetry and is therefore a 'song' about the wonder and meaning of God's creation. Genesis 2 is an account of how it happened. There will always be debates about how to interpret some passages – including Genesis 1. But it is false logic to argue that if one part of Scripture can't be taken literally then none of it can be. That isn't true of any human communication."[42]

Being poetry doesn't mean it's a myth. We all know that poems and songs aren't meant to be taken literally, but they can still, like *Animal Farm*, express important truths using the artistry of human language.

Genesis is like that. It's a poem or song expressing the central truth at the heart of the Jewish faith: Yahweh is not like the gods of the pagans.

Our God, the same God whom Jesus also said is our Father, is the Supreme God, the creator and ruler of all, and the only person or thing worthy of our allegiance and worship.

This is the wonderful truth at the heart of the creation story in Genesis, a truth that has echoed down through history and still resonates with us today. As Christians we

---

[42] Timothy Keller, *The Reason for God*, p.97

answer to a Higher Authority, higher than any government, state or autocratic dictator that may demand our obedience. We owe our allegiance to God, and only God, and Him alone are we to obey.

Noah's Ark and the Flood Story

The problem for YEC is that the earth gives every indication of being extremely old. They attempt to get around that by something known as 'Flood Theology'.

According to Flood Theology, the apparent age of the earth is the result of a catastrophic global flood that completely covered the entire world, including Mount Everest and all the highest mountain ranges. The titanic pressures and forces of the massive amounts of water covering the earth during the flood resulted in making the earth look old. All that water pressure, in other words, accelerated the aging process and resulted in the earth only appearing to be old, when in fact it isn't.

As a result, it's crucial to YEC proponents that the flood story in Genesis be interpreted as a global flood, not just a local regional flood. This goes hand in hand with their literal interpretation of Genesis chapter 1.

As science, flood theology is highly suspect and is, at most, a pseudo-science. I won't bother disputing it on scientific grounds, because the real science behind the age of the earth is solid and irrefutable.

For our purpose here, it's not necessary to try and prove the earth is billions of years old. That's not in dispute. What we need to determine is whether the biblical story really teaches a *global* flood or not. Does a faithful interpretation of the flood story require us, if we want to

70

remain faithful to Scripture as inspired by God, to believe in a global world-wide flood?

There are the three Hebrew words which are key to our understanding of the biblical flood story:

Erets: land, country, nation.
Kasah: covered, residing upon, running over, falling upon.
Har: hills, mount or mountain.

Hebrew has a much more limited vocabulary than English, so many Hebrew words do double duty. The Hebrew word *erets* is one of them. It can mean land, country or world, but more often means land or country. For instance, Abraham is asked by God to leave his *erets*. Obviously, he wasn't being told to leave the planet.

The Hebrew word translated "covered" in Genesis 7:19 is *kasah*. It can mean residing upon, running over or falling upon. Twenty feet of rainwater falling on the hills is quite different from that amount covering them.

The Hebrew word translated "mountain" is *har* and also means hills. It is more usually translated as hill or hills in the Old Testament.

We can easily translate Genesis 7:19 as: "all the high hills in the country (or region of the Mesopotamian Valley) were covered with water to a depth of twenty feet." Or, twenty feet of water fell upon the hills. This is very different from the usual rendering that all the highest mountains of the earth were covered.

Bradley makes an important point regarding the biblical text: "Further evidence for a local flood is found in Genesis 8:5, where it is noted that the water receded until the tenth month when the tops of mountains (or hills) became visible for the first time. The reference here seems to be what Noah could see, not the entire world. In Genesis 8:11, the dove returns with an olive leaf. Since olive trees don't grow at higher elevations, a flood that covered all the mountains of the world would not give this type of evidence of receding."[43]

There is no scientific evidence of a global flood. A flood that covered all the mountains of the Earth would require 4.5 times the total water resources that exist on planet Earth.[44] Which, obviously, isn't available. However, "While evidence for a worldwide flood is clearly missing, there is considerable evidence from both geology and archeology of one huge and several smaller floods in the region of Mesopotamia during the time period of Noah's flood."[45]

The story in Genesis lines up quite well with other ancient stories of a catastrophic local flood that inundated the Mesopotamian Valley. Noah's flood was regional, and the biblical text does not claim a global flood. It can be read just as easily as a local flood, and details in the passage itself, as already noted, indicate a widespread local flood. The Christian faith simply does not require a global flood.

Conclusion

Once we step out of our modern mindset and into the mindset of the ancient world in which the Hebrews lived, Genesis really isn't all that hard to understand and actually makes a lot of sense. Genesis isn't a science report, it's

---

[43] Walter Bradley, "Why I Believe the Bible is Scientifically Reliable" in *Why I Am a Christian* (2001), p. 179
[44] Ibid, p. 179
[45] Ibid, p. 179

literature with a purpose, and its purpose is to make one major point: *The Hebrew God, Yahweh, is better than all the other gods of the pagans put together.*

Bill Nye, Jerry Coyne, Richard Dawkins, et al, spill a lot of ink arguing for the truth of evolution, but fail to show why it need be a problem for believers beyond the limited purview of creationism. Instead, they make the superficial and unfounded assumption that evolution and fossils and such are proof that God does not exist. But this is an overly simplistic assertion. The theory of evolution is not in dispute and is entirely compatible with religious faith.

The scientific theory of evolution, as far as natural, biological processes go, says nothing about guidance. Nor does it undercut or remove the ample evidence for God we see in the fine tuning of the cosmos, in the world, or in biology. There are a lot of good reasons to believe, scientifically, that the universe is the intentional result of a super-intelligence. This is the theme of chapter 10.

A close examination of evolution, evolutionary morality and our own inner 'moral compass' provides powerful evidence for the existence of God that is rationally hard to avoid. We will look into that in Chapters 11 and 12.

Whatever else evolution may be responsible for as a purely natural process, atheism does not logically follow. Extending the science of evolution to the conclusion that there is no God is a non-sequitur.

Furthermore, it would seem that far from being a problem for Christianity, evolutionary theory poses a greater problem for atheism than it does for theism. We'll look at that in the next chapter.

Further Reading

Collins, Francis. *The Language of God* (2006).

Coyne, Jerry. *Why Evolution is True* (2009).

Denton, Michael. *Evolution: A Theory in Crisis* (1986).

Enns, Peter. *Genesis for Normal People* (2022).

_____ . *The Evolution of Adam: What the Bible Does and Doesn't Say About Human Origins* (2021).

Lennox, John. *Seven Days That Divide the World: The Beginning According to Genesis and Science* (2011).

3

Is Science and Christianity in Conflict?

WE OFTEN HEAR that there is some sort of ongoing conflict between Christianity and science. You can believe in God, or you can be a rational, scientifically minded person – but not both.

The idea that there is an inherent conflict between faith and science is a modern myth, invented in the late 1800's. Up until then few people thought there was any conflict. Scientists and theologians generally believed that faith and science were entirely compatible, taking the view that science was the investigation into the workings of the world God had created for us to explore. Indeed, many of the great scientists through history were Christian.

In this chapter we will have a look at the apparent warfare between Christianity and science. First, a definition of science might be in order, taken from a popular online dictionary:

"The observation, identification, description, experimental investigation, and the theoretical explanation of phenomena."[46]

From this definition of science, it's hard to see why there should be any tension between faith and the investigation of the natural world. For two millennia

---

[46] "Science," The Free Dictionary, www.thefreedictionary.com/science

Christians have believed that God has given us two books, which we are free to study. The Bible and the Book of Nature. The Bible itself encourages us to study the natural world and learn from it (Psalm 19:1).

When Darwin's book on evolution first came out in the mid 1800's, it was criticized for its lack of evidence, but it was not resisted on religious grounds and most theologians saw no issue with it. But this happy compatibility between science and religion didn't sit well with dogmatic atheists of the day, who felt that science should be their exclusive domain.

In the late 1800's atheism started becoming more fashionable, and a movement began to promote the theory of evolution. Led by T.H. Huxley, the leaders of this movement were not content to simply argue the case for evolution. They insisted that 'science' was incompatible with Christian faith and that therefore a scientist could not also be a Christian. They pushed the idea that Newton and Darwin had "evicted God from the cosmos...[and as a result] forced religious leaders to respond."[47]

Huxley in particular promoted the idea that the creation account in Genesis should be interpreted literally – the earth was created in six days just six thousand years ago – not because he believed it, but because he knew it would force a wedge between science and faith.

The myth of a warfare between Christianity and science can be traced back to two books that came out in the late 19th century. The *History of the Conflict between Science and Religion,* by John William Draper, was published in 1871. Then Andrew Dickson White came out with *A History of the Warfare of Science with Theology in Christendom* in 1896.

---

[47] Rodney Stark, *For the Glory of God*, p. 185

Both of these books, though largely forgotten now, were very influential in their day. They also had a clear agenda, as their titles suggest, to promote the idea that Christianity is reactionary, adverse to science and reason, and there is an inherit conflict between the two. Up until then the idea hadn't occurred to most people and in fact it was thought by most that science and Christianity were entirely compatible.

Draper wrote:
"The history of science is not a mere record of isolated discoveries; it is a narrative of the conflict of two contending powers, the expansive force of the human intellect on one side, and the compression arising from traditionary faith and human interests on the other."[48]

The two books by Draper and White were packed with lies and have since been discredited. Alister McGrath is a trained scientist and a prolific writer on the history of science. He has this to say: "The idea that science and religion are in perpetual conflict is no longer taken seriously by any major historian of science, despite its popularity in the late nineteenth century. One of the last remaining bastions of atheism survives only at the popular level – namely, the myth that an atheistic, fact-based science is permanently at war with a faith-based religion. Not only is this caricature clearly untrue in the present day, but historical scholarship has now determined it to be misleading and inaccurate in the past. Yet the myth still lives on in popular atheistic writings, undisturbed by the findings of scholars. At least in the minds

---

[48] John William Draper, *History of the Conflict between Science and Religion,* 1871.

of some atheist propagandists, science is the supreme champion of atheism."[49]

There are two common stories which people think confirm the popular notion that Christianity is opposed to science: Galileo and Columbus.

You can't get too far into a conversation about God with an atheist before they bring up Galileo. Everyone knows that Galileo got in trouble with the Catholic Church because his scientific ideas questioned the Bible. The trouble is, almost everything we think we know about that whole affair is wrong. What most people don't know is that Galileo was a devout Christian and that he wrote a vigorous defense of the Bible.[50]

His trouble with the church had more to do with a personality conflict with the Pope at the time. Galileo unwisely compared the Pope to a simpleton, even after the Pope had been a great supporter and benefactor, and that's when he attracted the ire of the Pope.

Nothing Galileo said was particularly new. Much of what Galileo wrote had already been taught by other scientists (almost all Christian) for a couple of hundred years without incurring the wrath of the church, and in fact in full support by the church. Also notable of the whole affair is that it is pretty much the only such affair one can find over the span of several centuries of a very harmonious relationship between the Church and scientists, most of whom were Catholics anyway.

---

[49] Alister McGrath, *The Twilight of Atheism*, p.87
[50] "Letter to the Grand Duchess Christina of Tuscany" https://web.stanford.edu/~jsabol/certainty/readings/Galileo-LetterDuchessChristina.pdf

The reason we hear so much of Galileo is that atheists can barely find any other example in which a scientist got in trouble with the church over its long history. Even then, it wasn't because of his science. Galileo wasn't actually saying anything new. Copernicus had already outlined the broad strokes of heliocentricity a century before, with the full support of the church.

Copernicus is well known for publishing his book *Revolutions,* in which he described how the sun was at the center of the solar system, and the planets revolved around it.

Copernicus was a devout Christian, educated in several of the best Christian universities in Europe at the time. Most of what he wrote in his book was not new either — it was already being taught in the Catholic Universities in which he gained his education. Nothing Copernicus taught about heliocentricity was resisted on religious grounds, nor was it considered in conflict with the Bible. Galileo himself never considered his scientific views to be in conflict with Christian faith.[51]

Another such story involves Columbus. We all 'know' that everyone in 1492 thought the Earth was flat because that's what the Bible said, except Columbus, who figured out it was round and wanted to sail around the world to prove it. But the Churchmen, obscurantists that they are, resisted this because they felt threatened by it.

The Church resisted Columbus, but not on religious grounds. The church leaders who opposed Columbus knew the earth was round, as did all educated people of the time. They opposed him because they worried that Columbus had

_____

[51] See his *Letter to the Grand Duchess*.

greatly underestimated the distance to Japan and feared that he and his crew would die at sea.

Scientists within the church calculated the distance from the Canary Islands to Japan to be about 14,000 miles. Columbus thought it was only 2,800 miles.

Turns out the Church was right and Columbus got it wrong, and if it hadn't been for the North American continent – which Columbus didn't know existed – he and his men would have died at sea. But when Columbus arrived in the western hemisphere, based on his erroneous calculations he thought it had to be India. Columbus was still lost, he just didn't know it, and that's how native Americans came to be called Indians.

The church had it right. But that fact doesn't serve the interests of hardline atheists or Hollywood script writers more interested in drama than historical accuracy.

It was Andrew White in particular who made up the myth that before Columbus everyone thought the earth was flat. But as Rodney Stark relates: "almost every word of White's account of the Columbus story is a lie. Every educated person of the time, including Roman Catholic prelates, knew the earth was round. The Venerable Bede (673-735 AD) taught the world was round, as did Bishop Virigilius of Salzburg (720-784)."[52]

So here we have two leading Christian bishops in the 8th century, 600 years before Columbus, teaching the earth was round. Other leading Christians through history also taught the earth was round: Hildegard of Bingen (1098-1179) and Thomas Aquinas (1224-1274). One of the most popular science textbooks of the Middle Ages was titled *Sphere*,

---

[52] Rodney Stark, *For the Glory of God*, p. 122

published in the 1200's. It taught, as the title suggests, that the earth was round.

"Medieval people knew the earth was a sphere and even its approximate size. You couldn't get a decent education in the Middle Ages without knowing this."[53] The flat earth story of Columbus is a myth, but a myth which serves atheists well in promoting the idea of a historical conflict between the church and science.

This stereotype of the so-called conflict between faith and science is still promoted by militant atheists more interested in making Christians look bad than they are in accurate historical scholarship. Fortunately, no credible historian of science takes their views seriously.

Here are a few more quotes from scientists on the compatibility of faith and science. In speaking of Richard Dawkins and hardline atheists, Alister McGrath had this to say:

> "...the view that the natural sciences are an intellectual superhighway to atheism is rejected by most scientists, irrespective of their religious views. Most unbelieving scientists of my acquaintance are atheists on grounds other than their science; they bring those assumptions to their science rather than basing them on their science."[54]

> "The point is simple: nature is open to many legitimate interpretations. It can be interpreted in atheist, deist, theist and many other ways – but it does not demand to be interpreted in any of these. One can be a 'real' scientist without being committed to any specific

---

[53] ibid, p. 122
[54] McGrath, *The Dawkins Delusion*, p. 44

religious, spiritual or antireligious view of the world. This, I may add, is the view of most of the scientists I speak to, including those who self-define as atheists. Unlike dogmatic atheists, they can understand perfectly well why some of their colleagues adopt a Christian view of the world. They may not agree with that approach, but they are prepared to respect it."[55]

"I actually do not believe that there are any collisions between what I believe as a Christian, and what I know and have learned about as a scientist."
Francis Collins

"Either half my colleagues are enormously stupid, or else the science of Darwinism is fully compatible with conventional religious beliefs, and equally compatible with atheism."
Stephen Gould

"Faith is not the opposite of reason. Faith rests squarely upon reason,"
Francis Collins

According to Canadian astronomer Hugh Ross:
"The community of believers has no reason to fear and every reason to anticipate the advance of scientific research into the origin and characteristics of the cosmos. The more we learn, the more evidence we

---

[55] ibid, p. 46

accumulate for the existence of God and for his identity as the God revealed in the Bible."[56]

Not only is there no inherit or real conflict, but there's a growing interest among scientists in spiritual questions. According to science writer Alister McGrath:

"Today, this stereotype of the warfare of science and religion lingers on in the backwaters of Western culture. Yet it has largely lost its credibility. The surging interest in the spiritual aspects of the natural sciences has been complemented by a new interest in the positive interaction of science and religion, evident in courses with titles such as 'Science and the Spiritual Quest.' The growing realization that even many scientists who are Nobel laureates are interested in issues of faith has severely dented the case for a necessary link between science and atheism, or for the outdated stereotype of the perpetual war of science and faith. The simple fact is that there is no *necessary* connection between them: some scientists are religious and some are not."[57]

Great Scientists in History

The great scientists of the past, those men responsible for laying the groundwork of modern science, who proved that the earth was a sphere, that it revolved around the sun,

---

[56]Hugh Ross. "Why I Believe in the Miracle of Divine Creation" in *Why I Am a Christian*, edited by Norman Geisler and Paul Hoffman (2001), p. 142
[57] McGrath, *Twilight of Atheism*, p. 89.

who first mapped the orbits of the planets in our solar system, who first looked through telescopes to make accurate calculations of planetary orbits, were almost all devout Christians, mostly Catholic, educated in the great Christian universities of medieval Europe.

Copernicus (1473-1543)
Francis Bacon (1561-1626)
Galileo (1564-1642)
Kepler (1571-1630)
Pascal (1623-62)
Boyle (1627-91)
Newton (1642-1727)
Faraday (1791-1867)
Babbage (1791-1871)
Mendel (1822-84)
Pasteur (1822-95)
Kelvin (1824-1907)
Clerk Maxwell (1831-79)

This is a fairly short list of some of the better-known names. Rodney Stark compiled a rather extensive list of the scientific stars of history, noting their religious devotion or skepticism. Only two can be regarded as skeptics.[58]

Some might well ask: what about today? It's all fine and good to talk about scientists in the past who believed in God, but don't we know better today?

In 1914 James Leuba sent questionnaires to a random sampling of people listed in the American Men of Science. They were asked to select from one of three questions. It's worth noting that Leuba's definition of faith in God was so

---

[58] Stark, *For the Glory of God*, p. 198-199

stringent that many clergy would not qualify as believers. However, despite his narrow definition of faith, 41.8 percent responded that they believed in God. 41.5 percent said that they do not, and another 16.7 percent indicated agnosticism. This was not what Leuba had been hoping for, and he expressed confidence that in the future the levels of faith would drop.

Interestingly, Leuba's survey was exactly repeated in 1996, with no change in results.[59]

The Christian Roots of Modern Science

We've talked about the baseless assertions hardline atheists have made about faith and science and dispensed with the notion that there is a necessary conflict. But we can go one further: modern science arose within and was fostered by the medieval church. Far from being in conflict with science, Christianity gave birth to the modern scientific method. Modern science grew out of the medieval Catholic church and Catholic universities.

Historian Rodney Stark summarized it well: "Science arose only in Europe because only medieval Europeans believed that science was possible and desirable. And the basis of their belief was their image of God and his creation...science developed in Europe because of the widespread 'faith in the possibility of science...derivative from medieval theology.'"[60]

This of course will strike the modern mind as outrageous, having been immersed in popular Hollywood caricatures of Columbus bravely fighting for his idea of a

---

[59] Ibid p. 193
[60] Stark, *The Triumph of Christianity*, p. 284

round earth against an entrenched Church blinded by religious superstition, and of Galileo heroically resisting a Church fearful of science.

But it's true. And the reason? Because medieval theology made it possible. "Christianity depicted God as a rational, responsive, dependable, and omnipotent being and the universe as his personal creation, thus having a rational, lawful, stable structure, awaiting human comprehension."[61]

In other words, Christians started to study the world, planets, stars and solar system for governing laws because they believed it could be done, and that God, being a God of order, had established a universe of order with laws that could be relied upon and studied. Furthermore, they were convinced that God wanted us to do so.

One of the scriptural passages most frequently cited by medieval scholars was from the Wisdom of Solomon (11:20). "Thou hast ordered all things in measure and number and weight." They took this to mean, and quite properly, that the universe was rational, intelligible, and could be accessed and understood by human reason with enough study.

Throughout the early and medieval church, scholars and theologians felt it was our duty to study the world and the universe, because it was God's handiwork.

As CS Lewis sums it up: "Men become scientific because they expected law in nature and they expected law in nature because they believed in a law giver."

One of the most famous astronomers in history, Kepler, studied the solar system to learn how the planetary orbits really worked, precisely because he believed in a rational God of order who would have established orderly laws for the universe.

---

[61] Stark, *Glory*, p.147

Kepler discovered the laws of motion that governed planetary orbits. He was a devout Christian who believed God was a rational being who created the universe according to an intelligible plan that could be understood through the natural light of reason.

Pagan cultures did not have this concept of God. Their idea of god or the gods did not allow for science. Their gods were erratic, irrational, and cared little for humanity. Anything that occurred in nature might have been due to the fiat of an irrational divine despot, and not according to any regular law of nature that could be studied.

As a result, pagans had no reason to suppose that nature functioned according to rational laws that could be studied and understood. The very idea was ludicrous to pagan thinking, if not impertinent and irreverent.[62]

There is a deep harmony and compatibility between science and Christianity. Not only is there no real conflict between the two, but the medieval Catholic church gave birth to modern science.

The same cannot be said for *naturalism,* however.

The term 'naturalism' has generally come to mean that nature is all there is. As a philosophy naturalism rejects any possibility of anything transcendent above the physical world.

According to naturalism, there is nothing beyond or outside the physical universe (or multiverse). There is no 'spirit' or 'soul'. Everything can be explained in terms of physical properties and processes. It was best expressed by Carl Sagan when he introduced his series 'Cosmos' with these

---

[62] For a detailed study of why science arose in Christian Europe, see Rodney Stark, *For the Glory of God*, Chapter 2. That chapter alone is well worth the price of the book.

oft quoted words: "The Cosmos is all there is or was or ever will be."

Naturalism is for all practical purposes synonymous with materialism and atheism. Naturalism, and atheism for that matter, is not science: it is a philosophy; a worldview that assumes nothing non-material exists.

Atheists are by definition, therefore, also naturalists. There is no immaterial spirit, no God or gods, and for the atheist, evolution is entirely accidental and survival the only criteria that ultimately matters, because only survivors get to pass on their genes – regardless of what they may have done to survive.

What often gets overlooked, however, is that naturalism has some very serious implications for rational thought – and by extension science. We will look at this next.

What Are Your Genes Fooling You into Believing?

Daniel Dennett boasted that the theory of evolution was a "universal solvent", an acid, which eats away and removes purpose, structure, and teleology. Its explanatory power even destroys religion, as it suggests evolutionary origins for all religions and ideas of God, and therefore we need not be bothered to think that any religion is true.[63]

I suppose Dennett, being an atheist, thought this was very clever, but I think his boasting was a bit short-sighted, if not poor philosophy. If Dennett is right, evolution provides an explanation for *all* our ideas – not just religious.

---

[63] *Darwin's Dangerous Idea: Evolution and the Meaning of Life*, 1995.

So then if our religious ideas are false because of their evolutionary origins, then so is everything else we might think and believe.

Put another way, if evolutionary origins are the basis for asserting that religious ideas are false, then why suppose it doesn't make all our ideas false? We can use the same argument to assert any and all of our ideas are false, religious or otherwise, since everything about us is, supposedly, the result of evolution.

It therefore calls into question everything our minds produce. If everything our minds produce is questionable, then the *rational capability of our mind* is itself highly dubious.

As Thomas Nigel puts it: "If we came to believe that our capacity for objective theory [true beliefs, e.g.] were the product of natural selection, that would warrant serious skepticism about its results."[64]

This puts the naturalist in an absurd position: if our rational mind is in doubt, we can't solve the problem by thinking it through. C.S. Lewis said:

"The [Naturalist] gives...a history of the evolution of reason which is inconsistent with the claims that he and I both have to make for inference [to the truth] as we actually practise it ... This imposes on [the Naturalist] the very embarrassing task of trying to show how the evolutionary product which he has described could also be a power of 'seeing' truths. But the very attempt is absurd...Inference itself is on trial: that is, the Naturalist has given an account of what we thought to be our inferences which suggests that

---

[64] Thomas Nigel, *The View from Nowhere* (Oxford University Press, 1989), p. 79.

they are not real insights at all….If the value of our reasoning is in doubt, you cannot try to establish it by reasoning."[65]

A Mind Is a Terrible Thing to Waste

Darwin himself saw the problem in 1881. "But then with me the horrid doubt always arises whether the convictions of a man's mind, which has been developed from the mind of the lower animals, are of any value or at all trustworthy. Would any one trust in the convictions of a monkey's mind, if there are any convictions in such a mind?"[66]

Evolution only selects for survival; it does not select for truth. To survive we need to act in certain ways, but, as Patricia Churchland points out:

> "Boiled down to essentials, a nervous system enables the organism to succeed in the four F's: feeding, fleeing, fighting and reproducing. The principle chore of nervous systems is to get the body parts where they should be in order that the organism may survive … [a more powerful brain] …. is advantageous so long as it … enhances the organism's chances for survival. Truth, whatever that is, definitely takes the hindmost."[67]

The implications for rational thought are serious: If our minds are just the result of adaptive behavior that has survived only because of its survival benefit, then why trust its rational capacity to reason, to perceive and grasp truth?

---

[65] CS Lewis, *Miracles*, pp.31-33
[66] Darwin, in a letter to a friend, 1881
[67] Churchland, Journal of Philosophy (October 1987), p. 548.

That's not the 'purpose' of our brain – if evolution can be said to have a purpose. Its only 'purpose' is survival. So why trust it for any purpose beyond mere survival?

By extension, why trust any of its conclusions or thoughts – including the theory of evolution? Evolution can only be trusted to give us cognitive faculties that help us survive, *not* to provide us with reliably rational minds that can accurately perceive abstract truth.

If any of the beliefs formed by such a mind also happen to be true, that's just an accidental aside to their primary survival benefit. This is, as C.S. Lewis calls it, "the cardinal difficulty of Naturalism."[68]

Alvin Plantinga develops this point fully in *Where the Conflict Really Lies*. In this well-argued book, Plantinga shows that there is no real conflict between science and faith. The real conflict is between science and naturalism because, given naturalism, we have no good reason to trust our minds.

Thus, naturalism undercuts rational thought, the very basis of science:

> "This underlying neurology causes adaptive behavior … but it also determines belief content. As a result, these creatures have beliefs, which of course have a certain content. And here's the question: what reason is there for supposing that this belief content is true? There isn't any. The neurology causes adaptive behavior and also causes or determines belief content: but there is no reason to suppose that the belief content thus determined is true. All that's required for survival and fitness is that the neurology cause adaptive behavior (for survival)."[69]

---

[68] CS Lewis, *Miracles*, p.17
[69] Alvin Plantinga, *Where the Conflict Really Lies* (2011), p. 327.

Atheists claim that we are the result of an accidental evolutionary process, and that what we believe is also a result of this accidental process. Since this provides an explanation for religious belief, we need not be troubled to think that any of our *religious* ideas are true.

Therefore if someone happens to be a believer, it is a result of an accidental combination of chemicals, DNA and perhaps social conditioning. If we are *inclined* to believe in God, it is only because of these things. Our genes are just fooling us into thinking there is a God, when in fact he doesn't exist.

The same must also be said of the atheist, however, if we are going to be consistent. The person who is *disinclined* to believe does so for the same reasons: an accidental arrangement of DNA. Whatever belief system an atheist happens to hold is just as much an accident. Their genes are also just telling them what to think and believe, just like everyone else. They are, therefore, atheists by accident.

Atheists are just dancing to their DNA as much as anyone else, it would seem.

So naturalism, it turns out, amounts to a theory that is self-refuting. Like making an argument that no argument can be valid. A philosophy that no philosophy is true.

"[Naturalism] is really a theory that there is no reasoning... [this is] what Naturalism is bound to do. It offers what professes to be a full account of our mental behavior; but this account, on inspection, leaves no room for the acts of knowing or insight on which the whole value of our thinking, as a means to truth, depends."[70]

The acid burns both ways. If we are going to be consistent and intellectually honest, then the 'universal solvent' of evolution *must* also be applied to all our ideas, beliefs and philosophies – not just religion.

What atheists can't do is apply this universal solvent to our beliefs about God, and not to other beliefs, including naturalism. When Darwinian scientists apply their evolutionary scalpel to what our minds tell us about God, but not to anything else, they are not being intellectually honest or consistent. Nancy Pearcey summarizes this beautifully:

> "The logical flaw in the theory, however, is that it undercuts itself. For if all of our ideas are products of evolution, then so is the idea of evolutionary psychology itself. Like all other constructs of the mind, it is not true but only useful for survival... Once the very possibility of objective truth has been undermined, then Darwinian evolution itself cannot be objectively true... If all ideas are products of evolution, and not really true but only useful, then evolution itself is not true either. And why should the rest of us pay it any attention?"[71]

Christianity holds that there is a rational Mind behind the existence of the universe, who established the universe to be intelligible and accessible to our minds. Christianity also holds that humanity was created by this Mind in its own

---

[70] CS Lewis, *Miracles*, p.27
[71] Pearcey, *Total Truth*, p. 216

image, which includes our mind and rational capacities. This belief was the foundation of the modern scientific movement that arose within the medieval Christian church.

There is therefore no *real* conflict between science and Christianity. Science fits quite nicely into a theistic worldview, in fact, because of theism's support for a rationally intelligible universe. Given theism we have every reason to be confident in our rational minds, and no reason to fear whatever science may discover about our evolutionary past. Christianity is very compatible with science and therefore *evolutionary science*.

Far from being incompatible with faith, science can be an integral part of our relationship with God. Francis Collins is one of the world's top scientists. He used to be an atheist. His book, *The Language of God*, tells the story of his journey from atheism to faith as a result of his study of science.

It doesn't work out so well for naturalism, however. Darwinian (unguided, strictly materialistic) evolution calls into question the reliability of our rational minds, thereby undercutting the very foundations of science. Given naturalism, and by extension atheism, we have no good reason to trust in our rational minds.

It would seem, then, that while there is no genuine conflict between science and God, there is a very deep and profound conflict between science and naturalism – the philosophical pillar upon which atheism relies.

The argument we still so often hear from militant atheists at the popular level that science has disproved God, and that 'scientific' thinking requires atheism, is not only historically inaccurate, but also just plain bad philosophy – not to mention superficial, tiresome and boorish.

Stephen Jay Gould, world famous paleontologist, evolutionary biologists, and science advisor to the White

House, was also a self-described atheist. He had this to say about his fellow scientists who insisted that science required disbelief in God:

> "To say it for all my colleagues and for the umpteenth million time: science simply cannot by its legitimate methods adjudicate the issue of God's possible superintendence of nature. We neither affirm nor deny it; we simply can't comment on it as scientists. If some of our crowd have made untoward statements claiming Darwinism disproves God, then I will find Mrs. McInerney and have their knuckles rapped for it."[72]

I'll finish with a quote from David Bentley Hart:

> "A culture could remain quite contentedly Christian in all its convictions and still achieve space travel. The mass manufacture of nerve toxins and nuclear weaponry, court mandated sterilizations, lobotomies, the miscegenation of human and porcine genetic materials, experimentation on prison populations, clinical studies of untreated syphilis in poor black men, and so on: all of this required the scientific mind to move outside or beyond Christian superstitions regarding the soul and the image of God within it."[73]

---

[72] Quoted in *Twilight of Atheism*, p. 109. Mrs. McInerney was Gould's 3rd grade teacher who was in the habit of rapping knuckles when their owner said something stupid.
[73] David Bentley Hart, *Atheist Delusions*, p. 232

Further Reading

Berlinski, David. *The Devil's Delusion: Atheism and Its Scientific Pretensions* (2009).

Hart, David Bentley. *Atheist Delusions* (2009).

Lennox, John. *God's Undertaker: Has Science Buried God?* (2009).

_____. *God and Stephen Hawking: Whose Design is it Anyway?*

Plantinga, Alvin. *Where the Conflict Really Lies: Science, Religion, and Naturalism* (2011).

Stark, Rodney. *For the Glory of God: How Monotheism Led to Reformations, Science, and the End of Slavery* (2011).

4

Does the Bible Endorse Slavery?

"Let my people go."[74]

RECENTLY I WATCHED A LATE-NIGHT talk show host tell his audience – gleefully smiling in evident delight – that "the Bible is a handbook for how to keep slaves."

It's a common assertion, and there are a handful of passages that can easily leave us with the impression that the Bible does indeed condone slavery, such as: "When you buy a Hebrew slave, he shall serve six years, and in the seventh he shall go out free, for nothing." (Exodus 21:2-6).[75]

When coming across a verse like this that uses words such as 'buy' and 'slave', it's very natural for the modern reader to assume that the Bible is endorsing slavery as we understand it today, and stop reading at that point.

The issue is not helped by the fact that in the early 19th century there were pro-slavery Christians who believed the Bible endorsed slavery, and quoted verses to support their convictions. Interestingly, atheists use the same verses today, although for wildly different reasons.

Pro-slavery 'Christians' appealed to these passages precisely *because they believed* in the Bible and sought to prove that God was in favor of slavery. Today's atheists, of

---

[74] Exodus 5:1
[75] See also Lev. 25:44; Ex. 21:20-21; Eph.6:5; 1 Tim. 6:1-2.

course, quote them *because they don't* believe in the Bible and seek to discredit and ridicule it.

Anti-slavery abolitionists also appealed to the Bible, claiming it was the moral grounds for ending slavery. They firmly believed that the Bible condemned slavery, and that genuine Christianity could not in any way be compatible with it.

When they confronted pro-slavery Christians, they did not call on them to ignore the Bible and become more secular; rather, they called on them to be more true to the Christian faith and to realize what the Bible really teaches.

Christians in the abolition movement had their Bible verses, and white pro-slavery churches in the South had theirs. As Lincoln said in his second inaugural address: "Both (Confederacy and Union) read the same Bible and pray to the same God, and each invokes His aid against the other."[76]

So is it just a matter of picking and choosing what verses we like? If, as Lincoln implied, the Bible is ambivalent about slavery and can be used to support either position, then it would be rather useless as any kind of moral guide. It would also be difficult to accept the Bible as the Word of God, if indeed the God of the Bible was okay with slavery. In which case the atheists would have a point.

In order to properly grasp the biblical teaching on the topic, it is necessary to go beyond a few isolated verses and read the entire Bible.

James W.C. Pennington was a slave who escaped to the north. Once free, he found employment, got an education and became a preacher and Presbyterian minister. As a former slave he struggled mightily with the same 'slavery'

---

[76] Abraham Lincoln, Second Inaugural Address, March 4, 1865.

texts cited above. I will use his words to summarize what I seek to accomplish in this chapter:

"My sentence is that slavery is condemned by the general tenor and scope of the New Testament. Its doctrines, its precepts, and all its warnings are against the system. I am not bound to show that the New Testament authorizes me in such a chapter and verse to reject a slaveholder. It is sufficient for me to show, what is fully acknowledged by my opponents, that it is murdering the poor, corrupting society, alienating brethren, and sowing the seeds of discord in the bosom of the whole church, and covering all missionary ground with the blasting fires of controversy. Let us always bear in mind what slavery is, and also what the Gospel is."[77]

The Voice of the Abolitionists

Pennington is saying that when the entire Bible is taken into consideration so that the over-all meta-narrative of Scripture is grasped, there can be no confusion: *It's very clear that the Bible explicitly condemns slavery and all forms of human oppression.*

This is the approach that abolitionists took with their understanding of the Bible. They argued that rather than fixating on just a few particular verses, we must take into consideration the entire "tenor and scope" of Scripture. Any interpretation of a particular verse and passage of scripture must fit within this overall spirit; if it doesn't, if the conclusions drawn from a verse do not agree with the spirit of the overall biblical message, then it's very likely that the interpretation of the verse under consideration is wrong.

---

[77] Pennington, *Two Years Absence, or A Farewell Sermon*, preached November 2, 1845. Page 27.

I'm convince that this is the mistake that pro-slavery Christians fell into – the same mistake modern atheists make.

It would be all to easy, of course, for me or any modern-day theologian to interpret the Bible in a favorable light, now that the slavery question is settled and, fortunately, we live in a society that no longer tolerates it.

So in this chapter I will make use of, as much as possible, the work of some of the leading 19th century biblical interpreters.

Albert Barnes, ardent social reformer and Presbyterian minister. In 1857 he wrote a 384-page book, *An Inquiry into the Scriptural Views of Slavery.* It was hugely influential for abolition.

Fredrick Douglass, an ex-slave who became a well-known leader in the abolitionist movement. He was a prolific writer and fiery orator.

James W.C. Pennington, a former slave who became a minister in the Presbyterian church.

George Bourne, outspoken Presbyterian minister in Virginia and courageous anti-slavery pioneer. In 1845 he wrote *A Condensed Anti-Slavery Bible Argument*. In 1816 he published a fiery treatise condemning slaveholders as oppressors and thieves: *The Book (Bible) and Slavery Irreconcilable.* This treatise influenced many abolitionists.

Theodore Weld was a Christian evangelist, social reformer, and one of the key architects of the abolition movement. Well known in his day, he published *"The Bible Against Slavery"* in 1837.

Slavery Legislation in the Bible

One of the main contentions brought against the Bible by critics is that it contains laws on governing slaves. From this they assume that the Bible therefore supports and endorses *slavery* as we understand the usage of that term today. After all, if Scripture has laws telling slaveholders how to keep slaves, then it must be okay with it.

Fair enough. So let's have a look at the biblical laws governing the care and 'ownership' of 'slaves'.

1. A 'slave' entered into service voluntarily, usually out of financial hardship to pay off debts (Lev.25:39-43; Deut.15:12). Translations can sometimes be a challenge. For instance, some English Bibles translate Deut.15:12 as "If your brother... is sold to you,". The Hebrew word for "sold" means "sells himself", as per the NIV English translation: "If a fellow Hebrew, a man or woman, *sells himself* to you and serves you six years, in the seventh year you must let him go free." The buying and selling of slaves in a slave trade, as we would understand it, is not in view here.

2. Slaves had equal legal protection as masters (Lev. 19:15,33-34; 24:22).

3. A 'slave' could be released from service at any time by family who put up the money to pay off their debts (Lev. 25:47-52).

4. A 'slave' could leave at any time. Biblical law required that runaway slaves were to be sheltered, protected, and *not* returned to their masters. Thus, slaves were protected from abusive masters. (Deut. 23:15-16). Therefore, a slave only stayed in service with his 'master' if he wanted to, effectively

101

making service voluntary.[78] This law also applied to foreigners and fugitive slaves from other countries, making Isreal a safe haven and refuge for slaves fleeing oppression. George Bourne noted that this one law alone "would put an end to the practice of human slavery in a week."[79]

5. All people, including 'slaves', the poor and foreigners, were entitled to the same civil and religious rights as masters (Lev. 24:22; Num. 15:15-16, 29, 9:14; Deut. 1:16-17).

6. Hebrew 'slaves' were to be set free after six years of service. When they were released, they were sent on their way with enough money and provisions to get a new start on life. (Ex. 21:2-6; Deut.15:12-15). Masters were to "supply them liberally from your flock", so that they didn't leave empty handed. Masters were admonished to be very generous when releasing their 'slaves', because they were once slaves themselves in Egypt.

7. Slaves could not be abused. (Exodus 21:26-27). If they were, they were to be set free. This applied to foreigners as well. While these passages specifically mention the loss of an eye or a tooth, it is clear these are meant as examples of abuse.

---

[78] This stood in contrast to the US Fugitive law that required runaway slaves to be returned. Even citizens in so-called free states were required to assist in the capture and return of slaves.
[79] Bourne, *Anti-Slavery Bible* Argument, p. 59.

8. The Old Testament strongly forbade kidnapping, an act punishable by death (Deut. 24:7; Ex. 21:16). Abolitionists correctly pointed out that the prohibition against kidnapping was also effectively a prohibition against slavery. Not only was the kidnapper to be put to death, but anyone in possession of a kidnapped person was under the penalty of death. This is clearly a prohibition against *slavery* as well, since chattel slavery involved holding people captive against their will, an obvious form of kidnapping. Also, Blacks were originally kidnapped from their homes in Africa, forced onto slave ships and brought to America against their will. It is clear that slaves in America were kidnapped persons, and their slaveowners were in possession of kidnapped persons.

9. The rules governing Hebrew 'slaves' also applied to foreign 'slaves', with the exception perhaps of the six-year limit rule. However, foreign slaves were still voluntary, as they could leave whenever they wanted and could not be returned to their 'master' as per the rule discussed above for fugitive 'slaves'. Biblical law stipulated that the foreigner in their midst was to be "loved" and treated like a fellow Hebrew, so foreigners enjoyed the same protections (Lev. 19:18, 33-34; 16:29; Deut. 10:18-19; 29:10-14; Ex. 22:21; 23:9; Mal.3:5).

10. Slaves were entitled to all the same religious ceremonies and vacation days. Over a 50-year period this amounted to 23 years and 64 days of

time off (Ex. 12:44; 20:10; 23:12; Lev. 25:4-6; Deut. 12:11-12).

11. Slaves had full and equal membership in the national covenant, and received the same instruction in religion and morality (Deut. 16:9-14; 31:10-13; Gen. 17:12).

12. Slavery is a violation of the eighth commandment: "You shall not steal" (Exodus 20:15). Slavery is kidnapping – the stealing of a human being, as discussed above.

It's worth mentioning here that the Hebrew word translated as 'slave' or 'servant' in our English Bibles is *ebed*. The Hebrew word *ebed* had a wide range of meanings, from *slave* as we would use the term today, to hired hands and voluntary paid servants.

Various English Bibles over the years have translated *ebed* into 'slave' or 'servant', since both are *possible* within the Hebrew meaning. The point here is that *ebed* does not necessarily mean 'slave' in the same sense we use it today.

However, I'm not going to quibble over translations or base my argument on using *servant* instead of *slave* in these passages. There's no need, since the biblical laws listed above effectively define what it means by *ebed*, regardless of how we might translate it into English.

From the biblical laws governing the rights and protections of *ebeds*, we can see that passages using the English word 'slave' are not talking about *slavery* as we think of it, but something else altogether.

We are separated by 3,400 years, and live in a completely different culture than that of the ancient

Hebrews, so an exact parallel is difficult to find with our present-day society, but from the definitions above an *ebed* was roughly equivalent to contract workers today.

They entered into the contract voluntarily for a fixed length of time, were paid for their services, could leave whenever they wanted, and were protected by law from abuse. It was typically done out of financial hardship to pay off debt, but if someone paid the debt for them, they were released from the contract.

Leading abolitionist writers all agreed on the following points regarding biblical 'slavery' legislation. They argued that if these Old Testament laws had been followed, then slavery would have been impossible in America:

- forbidding kidnapping on pain of death,
- forbidding the possession of a kidnapped person on pain of death,
- forbidding abuse,
- abused 'slaves' were to be freed,
- sheltering runaways and forbidding anyone from returning them,
- strict limits of six years of service,
- providing released *ebeds* with enough funds to get a fresh start,

The biblical passages are therefore not an endorsement of *slavery*, but rules protecting the rights of *servants* who entered into service voluntarily for a financial return and who could leave whenever they wanted. Really not so different from employment laws we have today which protect workers from abuse in a power relationship.

In some regards the Old Testament is even better than our modern society, since the *ebed* was released after six years and provided generously with enough funds to get a fresh start on life. People were not trapped into life-long debt and poverty which is all too common today.

A Closer Look at the 'Pro-Slavery' Bible Passages

Leviticus 25:44-46

One of the passages used by Southern pro-slavery advocates was Leviticus 25:44-46, often cited by atheists as 'proof' that the Bible supports slavery: "from the nations around you... you may buy slaves." This covers rules for foreign *ebed* ownership, usually acquired as a result of war.

The Hebrew word for 'buy' (*kana*) also means *acquire* or *hire* and does not condone 'kidnapping' of foreigners. Kidnapping is expressly condemned elsewhere, on pain of death (Deut. 24:7; Ex. 21:16). *Kana,* is more often used to describe free and voluntary service. This verse is not endorsing slavery or slave auctions, but could easily be translated as: "...you may hire servants from other nations."

Foreigners and sojourners in their midst were to be treated as brothers. Laws governing the treatment of Hebrew 'servants' also applied to foreigners (with the one exception of the six-year limit on time of service), including the law that fugitive slaves were to be sheltered, so their service was still effectively voluntary.

What's going on here is something similar to our own modern rules for warfare and treatment of prisoners found in the Geneva Convention. War obviously is not ideal, but we haven't reached the ideal yet. The Geneva Convention is an attempt to regulate this less-than-ideal situation to limit human suffering by setting some rules for the treatment of prisoners. It doesn't mean the framers of the Convention wanted war or were endorsing it.

Leviticus 25 is doing something similar. The biblical ideal is an end to poverty, oppression and war, but we aren't there yet.[80] The purpose of Leviticus 25 is to limit human suffering in a broken world.

Exodus 21:2-6

"When you buy a Hebrew slave, he shall serve six years, and in the seventh he shall go out free, for nothing."

Critics claim this passage supports slavery, but they overlook a key point in this passage: 'slaves' (*ebeds*) were released in six years, men and women. If a man's release happened to come around before his wife's, he had options. He could go free and wait for his wife's six year to cycle to complete, after which she would be freed.

Or, if he loved his master and wanted to stay, he could stay on. In the meantime, all the rules for care and good treatment would apply. The 'slave' only stayed if he wanted to. Clearly this is not slavery as practised in the American south.

Exodus 21:20-21

"When a man strikes his slave, male or female, with a rod and the slave dies under his hand, he shall be avenged.

---

[80] "They shall beat their swords into plowshares, and their spears into pruning hooks; nation shall not lift up sword against nation, neither shall they learn war anymore" (Isaiah 2:4); "There shall be no poor among you" (Deut.15:4); "Do not oppress the foreigner" (Ex.23:9); "You shall not oppress your neighbor or rob him" (Lev.19:13); "You shall not oppress a hired servant" (Deut.24:14).

But if the slave survives a day or two, he is not to be avenged, for the slave is his money." (ESV).

This passage has its difficulties, but a few things should be noted. If a master kills his slave, the slave is to be *avenged*.

While some English translations use 'punished' (NIV), the ESV gets it right. The Hebrew word means avenged, a strong term, which affirms the 'slave' as a human being, completely undercutting any possibility of the chattel principle that prevailed in American slavery.

This passage confirms that the Old Testament did not regard 'slaves' as property. The murder of a slave was just that – the murder of another human being, and the owner's life was forfeit.

This stands in stark contrast to American slavery, in which slaves were mere property, and nothing more, and that slave owners could beat and kill their slaves with complete legal impunity.

Does this passage suggest that a slave could be beaten severely, and that as long as he didn't die the owner wasn't punished? No. Exodus 21:26-27 tells us that an injured slave was to be set free.

The expectation of how the Hebrews were to treat others, including *ebeds* and the oppressed, is indicated in laws repeated throughout Exodus, Leviticus and Deuteronomy: "You shall not oppress a sojourner. You know the heart of a sojourner, for you were sojourners in the land of Egypt" (Exodus 22:21-24; 23:6-9).

Slaves would also be included, since the Hebrews were *ebeds* (slaves/servants) in Egypt: "You shall remember that you were a slave (*ebed*) in the land of Egypt, and the Lord your God redeemed you;" (Deut.15:15).

Obviously, the passage under discussion here has its problems. It may not be perfect, but it was a huge advancement for the ancient world. No other contemporary nation at that time had laws like this, in which a 'slave' was recognized as a human being instead of property.

Just like America, ancient pagan nations surrounding Isreal viewed slaves as mere property, like an ox or any farm implement that could be disposed of, even killed, however the owner wished.

The advancements seen in Jewish law points us in the right direct, on a trajectory towards freedom. This theme is covered in Chapter Six, so I won't get into the details of this principle here.

I will close out our discussion of this passage with the words of Esau McCaulley:

"The question I wanted to pursue was whether the biblical texts condoned slavery as good or whether it sought to limit the damages of a broken world. Reading and interpreting these passages as a descendant of slaves remains painful. ... Nonetheless, while we wish that some Old Testament texts would go further, it is to my mind clear that God's very character and the central story of the Old Testament speaks against slavery. ... My ancestors read it that way and so do I."[81]

Exodus 20:17

The Tenth Commandment references servants: "You shall not covet your neighbor's house; you shall not covet your neighbor's wife, or his male servant, or his female servant, or his ox, or his donkey, or anything that is your neighbor's." (ESV).

---

[81] McCaulley, *Reading While Black*, 151.

Male and female servants in this passage have been translated in some English Bibles as slaves, from which some critics infer that there is an implied endorsement of slavery, since the commandment is not forbidding the practice of slavery, or the keeping of slaves, only that we must not covet other people's slaves.

Such an argument is stretching things quite a bit, and like all the other so-called pro-slavery arguments, overly rely on an interpretation isolated from the rest of scripture. The observations and conclusions made for the discussions of the other slavery texts will also apply here.

Abolitionists noted that it was "wickedly absurd" for pro-slavery advocates to use the tenth commandment in defense of slavery:

"It is certainly a very strange circumstance that the tenth commandment should ever have been pressed into the service of human slavery, because that practice is a direct violation or breach of this as well as the eighth commandment – it being impossible for one person to enslave another, without first 'coveting' or eagerly desiring what he knows is not morally or justly his own ... as he himself would instantly see and acknowledge, were he himself, or his family, or friends, to be themselves enslaved."[82]

Where Do We Go with these 'Slavery' Verses?

We just covered the major passages used by 19th century defenders of slavery, typically cited today by critics of Christianity who also like to argue that God is apparently okay with it.

---

[82] Bourne, *Anti-Slavery Bible Argument*, 87-88.

I've shown that they cannot be used to assert that the Bible supports slavery. Only a superficial reading that stops with those texts would allow us to suppose otherwise.

The 12 points of 'slavery' legislation discussed above do not disappear whenever a passage is used to argue that the Bible condones the practice. They still apply and must be taken into consideration with any slavery text.

There are a few other minor passages that have been used by 19th century defenders of slavery, and might be cited today by critics of the Bible. But they are morally the same as the major passages just covered, and the arguments made here will also apply.

This is not to say that some of these slavery texts aren't without their challenges. They can be difficult to understand in some respects, as mentioned in the discussion of Exodus 21:20-21.

They may not say all we might want them to say today, but as a Christian I do not stop reading at these or any difficult Old Testament passage.

I keep reading. I keep reading through to Isaiah and Amos who railed against the wealthy for enslaving and oppressing the poor. I keep reading on to the Good News of Jesus Christ, who said:

> "I tell you the truth, whatever you do for one of the least of these, you do for me." (Mat. 25:40)

> "So in everything, do to others what you would have them do to you." (Mat. 7:12)

> "Love your neighbor as yourself." (Mat. 19:19)

"A new command I give to you, that you love
another." (John 13:34)

"This is my commandment, that you love one another
as I have loved you." (Jn 15:12)

"No longer do I call you servants, but I call you friends,
for all that I have heard from my Father I have made known
to you." (Jn 15:15)

"Love your neighbor as yourself. All the Law and the
Prophets hang on these two commandments." (Mt 22:39)

There is no room for slavery here. Obedience to the
Gospel removes any possibility of oppressive, unfair, cruel or
unjust treatment of human beings.

Just in case a wooden headed literalist wants to quibble
over what is meant by a neighbor or brother in order to
narrow the scope of these passages and lessen their impact,
Jesus clears that up for us in Luke 10 with the parable of *The
Good Samaritan*. This is covered in detail in chapter 1, so I
won't repeat myself here, but in this parable Jesus says that
our neighbor is anyone in need, across racial, ethnic and
religious lines.

The Bible itself admits that the Old Testament was not
perfect, was less than ideal, and was meant to be superseded
when the perfect came: Jesus Christ. So we need not be
troubled by any Old Testament passage that is less than
perfect. This is the theme of Chapter 6.

The Bible on Human Oppression

When Jesus announced the purpose of his mission at the beginning of his ministry (Luke 4:18), he could have selected any passage from Jewish scripture. He chose to read Isaiah 61:1 - "to proclaim liberty to the captives...to set at liberty those who are oppressed."

Slavery is obviously included. Some have argued that Jesus never did condemn slavery, ergo he must have been okay with it. Clearly such critics have not bothered to read Luke 4, or taken to heart much of anything else Jesus had to say.

Jesus said that "whatever you do to the least of these, you do to me" (Matthew 25:40). Abolitionists noted the direct implication – when you enslave a Black man, you enslave Christ. It's difficult to find a more strident and forceful prescription against *any* form of abuse or slavery.

The Golden Rule

"So in everything, do to others what you would have them do to you, for this sums up the Law and the Prophets," Jesus said in Matthew 7:12, laying down the Golden Rule.

Quakers appealed to the sense of fair play implied by the Golden Rule to argue against slavery: how would you feel if Blacks gained power and enslaved whites?

This one rule alone, if taken to heart, would make slavery and all forms of abuse impossible. As Bourne quipped: "the strongest advocates of human slavery would be convinced of its ... deep criminality ... Let them and their relations and friends be but once enslaved themselves, and

113

they will readily see and acknowledge the natural and moral guilt of the practice."[83]

Take Away the Yoke

The prophet Isaiah warned against a type of religious devotion towards God that was bereft of compassion towards people: "Yet they seek me daily and delight to know my ways, as if they were a nation that did righteousness."

God wasn't interested in their show of religion because "in the day of your fast (religious rituals) you do as you please and *oppress all your workers*" (Isaiah 58:2-3).

The prophet called on them to "take away the yoke (of oppression)," to "pour yourself out for the hungry and satisfy the desire of the afflicted," then they would be a righteous nation, and the Lord would be with them (Is. 58:9-12).

"This is the fast I choose: loose the bonds of wickedness, undo the straps of the yoke, to let the oppressed go free and to break every yoke", "share your bread with the hungry, bring the homeless poor into your house, to cover the naked" (Is. 58:6-7).

In other words, true religion is practised in removing "the yoke of oppression", not in religious ritual detached from compassion and concern for others. As Jesus said, *how you treat the lowliest of people is how you treat me* (Mat. 25:40).

The Book of Exodus.

The story of the exodus was a source of tremendous hope and inspiration for enslaved American Blacks.

---

[83] Bourne, *Anti-Slavery Bible Argument*, page 27.

Esau McCaulley puts it powerfully: "What does the Bible reveal about God's character? Does God appear to take pleasure in slavery? The exodus narrative is definitive in this regard. What is God like? He is a God who hears the suffering of an enslaved people and rescues them (Ex. 3:7-10). This rescue becomes part of his resume (Deut. 7:8; Lev. 11:45). When the Israelites prayed, they prayed to a God whose character was revealed in this liberating activity...The enslaved Black Christians knew. No fancy exegetical moves could convince them that the God who liberated the Israelites didn't care about enslaved persons in this country... The enslaved people read (or heard) in the biblical texts about a God who delighted in liberation, and this gave them hope."[84]

The slaves in America identified with the Hebrew's bondage in Egypt and saw in the story of exodus a promise of freedom.

"Let my people go!" (Exodus 5:1)

"I am the Lord your God, who brought you out of the land of Egypt, out of the house of slavery." (Exodus 20:2)

"You shall remember that you were a slave in the land of Egypt, and the Lord your God redeemed you;" (Deut.15:15).

Some of the favorite verses within the Black community in their argument against slavery were: [85]

"God hath made of one blood all nations" (Acts 17:26 KJV).

---

[84] McCaulley, *Reading While Black*, 143-144.

[85] Swartley, *Slavery, Sabbath, War & Women*, 57-58.

"For in one Spirit we were all baptized into one body – Jews or Greeks, slaves or free – and all were made to drink of one Spirit" (1 Cor. 12:13).

"A new command I give you: Love one another" (John 13:34).

"You are all sons of God through faith in Jesus Christ. For all of you who were baptized into Christ have clothed yourself with Christ. There is neither Jew nor Greek, slave nor free, male or female, for you are all one in Christ Jesus" (Gal. 3:26-28).

"Here there is no Greek or Jew, circumcised or uncircumcised, barbarian, Scythian, slave or free, but Christ is all, and in all" (Col. 3:11).

The Book of Philemon

The book of Philemon lays the groundwork for ending slavery. Philemon was a wealthy slave holder and a member of the church in Colosse. Paul visited Colosse often and had even stayed with Philemon on previous trips. One of Philemon's slaves, Onesimus, stole from him and fled to Rome, where he met the apostle Paul.

Paul sent Onesimus back to Philemon with a letter (the book of Philemon). In this letter Paul tells Philemon to take Onesimus back, *not as a slave, but as a brother*!

Paul reinforces this further, in which he tells Philemon to receive the former slave as he would receive Paul personally. In other words, the social standing of Onesimus was elevated to that of St. Paul's, treated the same way leaders of the church were to be treated. Paul goes on to promise Philemon that he would repay any debts Onesimus owed him for the stolen property.

In sending Onesimus back like this, Paul was setting Onesimus truly free. Onesimus would not have to spend the rest of his life in hiding as a runaway slave (slavery was still legal in the Roman Empire at this time), but would be restored to society as a freeman.

Abolitionists in the 19th century noted the power of this passage: "The principles laid down in the epistle to Philemon...would lead to the universal abolition of slavery. If ... their masters were to treat them 'not as slaves, but as brethren', the period would not be far distant when slavery would cease."[86]

Slavery Ranked Among the Worst of Sins

In 1 Timothy 1:9-11, the apostle Paul lists the sins that are contrary to "the glorious gospel of the blessed God."

"...for those who kill their fathers or mothers, for murderers, for adulterers and perverts, for *slave traders* and liars and perjurers – and for whatever else is contrary to the sound doctrine that conforms to the glorious gospel of the bless God," (NIV).

Slavery is placed in the same category with murder, patricide and matricide. The Greek word translated "slave traders" in this passage is *andrapodistai*, and literally means "slave-owners" or "slaveholders."

The KJV translation of this word is interesting. It translates it as "men-stealing". The ESV uses "enslavers".

Slavery is also kidnapping (men-stealing), since chattel-slavery could not occur without it, so any of these

---

[86] Barnes, *Inquiry*, p. 330.

translations will serve. As already discussed, kidnappers, and therefore slave traders and slave owners, were under penalty of death according to Levitical law. Therefore the Bible condemns the practice of slavery in the strongest possible terms.[87]

Love Does No Wrong

> "Love does no wrong to a neighbor; therefore love is the fulfilling of the law" (Romans 13:9-10).

The New Testament brings us to the high point of the Bible, the Gospel message, in which all men and women are to be seen as brothers and sisters regardless of race and class. The lines of racial division are erased in Christ.

One of the central themes of the New Testament is that love is the supreme command in how we are to treat each other. Quoting Leviticus 19:18, Paul writes that "all the commandments are summed up in this word: 'You shall love your neighbor as yourself.' Love does no wrong to a neighbor, therefore love is the fulfilling of the law" (Romans 13:8-10).

1 Corinthians 13: This entire chapter speaks of love superseding everything else. Love is greater than all other powers or gifts. Regardless of how talented or powerful a person may be, if they are not acting in love, it counts as nothing in God's eyes.

The message of the New Testament, if taken to heart and put into practice, would foster a society in which slavery and any form of oppression and cruelty would be impossible for a culture.

---

[87] Bourne, *Anti-Slavery Bible Argument*, 27-29.

There are a small handful of verses in the New Testament that appear to give an implied endorsement of slavery. Quoting from the ESV, they are:

Ephesians 6:5, "Slaves, obey your earthly masters..."

Colossians 3:22, "Slaves, obey in everything those who are your earthly masters..."

1 Timothy 6:1, "Let all who are under a yoke as slaves regard their own masters as worthy of all honor."

Titus 2:9, "Slaves are to be submissive to their own masters."

1 Peter 2:18, "Servants, be subject to your masters with all respect."

That's it. Out of the entire New Testament, 5 verses. Let's put this into some perspective. The New Testament is a collection of 27 books with 7,957 verses. The dearth of passages that might be used to endorse slavery is striking.

We just concluded an extensive review of the biblical passages which clearly condemn human oppression, showing that the central story and meta-narrative of the Scriptures speaks against slavery.

On the basis of these 5 'slavery' passages then, are we expected to overturn the entire weight and counsel of the New Testament writers and the teachings of Christ? *Hardly!*

But even these 5 verses are not the endorsement of slavery we might think, so let's have a closer look.

The Greek word translated "slaves" in the first 4 verses listed above is *doulos*. It is similar to the Hebrew word *ebed*. It designates a wide range of roles and does not necessarily mean 'slave'. It was often used for household servants. Some English Bibles translate *doulos* as servant, as that is also in view.

119

The Greek word for "servants" in 1 Peter 2:18 is *oiketes*, and has a fairly narrow meaning of household or domestic servant.

Slavery was part of the reality of life and society in the Roman Empire at the time. Estimates put the slave population of the Empire at around 20-25%, and large numbers of slaves and servants of all kinds were entering the church. So it was a reality that had to be faced pastorally by Paul and the Church leaders.

The simple fact that slavery is discussed in the New Testament should not be taken as an endorsement of the institution. The slavery passages are instructing slaves how to conduct themselves in the less-than-ideal social reality they find themselves in, not endorsing slavery.

God's will is reflected in such passages as, "Do not become slaves of men" (1 Cor.7:23). Slavery and the slave trade are severely condemned in 1 Tim. 1:9-10, as already discussed.

It's easy to struggle with Ephesians 6:5, "Slaves, obey your earthly masters..." and the other verses like this, but there is a difference between passages reflecting God's ideal for human society, and instructions to believers on how to live within the imperfect and broken world we live in.

God does not desire that we be slaves of men, but neither does he call us to rise up in violence. The Gospel is not a manifesto for violent insurrection. Believers were to live peacefully, and show love for their masters.

However, within that context Ephesians 6:5 is quickly followed by a command to masters to "do the same"! To act towards their servants as the servants were just commanded to act towards them, reminding them that they too have a "master in heaven," and that he is not partial to them. In other words, masters are to treat their servants the way they

120

would want God to treat them, an obvious allusion to the Golden Rule.

"…as servants of Christ, doing the will of God from the heart, rendering service with a good will as to the Lord and not to man, knowing that whatever good anyone does, this he will receive back from the Lord. Masters, do the same to them, and stop your threatening, knowing that he who is both their Master and yours is in heaven, and there is no partiality with him." (Eph. 6:6-9).

When Paul says, "Masters, do the same to them," he is telling them to also act as servants of Christ, to do the will of God from the heart just like the servants.

Likewise Colossians 4:1 commands masters to treat their servants "…justly and fairly, knowing that you too have a Master in heaven." Again, Paul reminds them that they have a master in heaven, and they are to treat their servants accordingly.

The implication is clear: masters are to treat their servants as they would want God to treat them, again getting back to "do unto others as you would want them to do to you." If taken to heart and followed, the institution of slavery could not survive very long.

Paul and the leaders of the church were not in a position to legislate Roman legal code or civil law. But they could teach and educate people on how to live peacefully; on how to love one another, and over time the change this would bring about in the hearts and minds of people would impact society as well, eventually changing it for the better.

The Gospel fosters a social environment in which all people are seen and treated as equals, regardless of race or gender. This would make the formation of slavery or any kind of oppressive legislation impossible.

1 Cor. 7:21 carries a subtle message: "Were you a slave when you were called? Don't let it trouble you – although if you can gain your freedom, do so." In other words, do not rise up in violence against your masters. If you can gain your freedom peacefully, then do so. But if no such opportunity exists, don't worry about it. Your standing before God is no less.

Some may take offense at Eph. 6:5 and 1 Cor. 7:21, but the Gospel is not a manifesto for violent revolution. Rather, we are to love our enemies, do good to those who spitefully use us and even pray for them. Do unto others what you would have them do unto you.

This is a much more effective way of making the world a better place – not through violent revolt but love. This is what Paul is saying in Eph. 6:5. He is advocating peaceful resistance and social change, not through violence and armed rebellion, but through love and changed hearts.

As Albert Barnes said in 1857: "God asks not for the aid of our vices."[88]

Therefore Ephesians 6:5 and the other passages cited above should not be misconstrued as a biblical endorsement of race based, chattel slavery as practised in recent Western history.

But Didn't Christians Support Slavery?

The sad fact is many Christians in the antebellum South were racist and slaveholders and claimed biblical support for their views.

Of course there have been Christians throughout history who supported objectionable ideas, just as there are

---

[88] Barnes, *An Inquiry into the Scriptural Views of Slavery,* p.267

people from all areas and walks of life who have believed and supported all kinds of objectionable ideas.

However, *just because some Christians have been untrue to the Gospel doesn't make the Gospel untrue.*

The question to be asked isn't whether there were Christians who took objectionable views, but whether they did so *in spite of* the faith or *because* the faith requires it.

Fredrick Douglass was a former slave who had converted to Christianity in his early teens. After escaping to the north he became one of America's most prominent and outspoken abolitionists.

A devout Christian, he distinguished between the "Christianity of Christ" and the hypocritical, perverse, "slaveholding religion of this land," stating that such a religion could not be called Christianity:

"I have, in several instances, spoken in such a tone and manner respecting religion, as may possibly lead those unacquainted with my religious views to suppose me an opponent of all religion. To remove the liability of such misapprehension, I deem it proper to append the following brief explanation. What I have said respecting and against religion, I mean strictly to apply to the slaveholding religion of this land, and with no possible reference to Christianity proper; for, between the Christianity of this land, and the Christianity of Christ, I recognize the widest possible difference… I love the pure, peaceable, and impartial Christianity of Christ: I therefore hate the corrupt, slaveholding, women-whipping, cradle-plundering, partial and hypocritical Christianity of this land. Indeed, I can see no reason, but the most deceitful one, for calling the religion of this land Christianity."[89]

There were a lot of very wealthy white landowners who depended on slavery for their riches. Christianity was the main religion, and most people claimed to be Christian, so it was culturally necessary to try to twist the Christian religion into supporting the institution upon which their wealth depended.

So how do we know who's right? Christians in the abolition movement had their verses, and white pro-slavery churches in the South had theirs. So is it just a matter of picking which verses you want to support your preferred view, like making selections at a salad bar? If that's the case, then the Bible is rather useless, which is the real point behind atheist's arguments that the Bible endorses slavery.

Prooftexting, also referred to as "cherry picking" or "parking", is the practise of lifting a verse out of its context and making conclusions as to its meaning without due consideration of all the relevant passages in the Bible that weigh in on the subject. Prooftexting interprets a verse in isolation from the rest of the Bible.

Pro-slavery advocates used proof-texting when claiming biblical support. They parked on a few passages and insisted on a static interpretation without reference to the rest of the Bible and ignored the overwhelming number of passages which would have corrected their wrong assumptions. Interestingly, Richard Dawkins and other

---

[89] Douglass, *Narrative of the Life of Fredrick Douglass,* 108. See also his sermon, *"What, to the Slave, is the Fourth of July."* Delivered in Rochester NY, 1852.

outspoken critics of Christianity take the very same approach to reading the Bible.

We can know that the abolitionist understanding of the Bible was the correct one because the interpretative approach followed by the abolitionists did a more thorough job of taking all of the relevant passages into consideration throughout the entire Bible.

As a result, their interpretation lined up with the over-all spirit and message of the Bible, the example and words of Christ in the Gospels, as well as how Christ told us to interpret the Old Testament.

The biblical ban on kidnapping alone is a case in point. (Ex. 21:16, Deut. 24:7, 1 Tim 1:10.) The Antebellum South depended on slaves kidnapped from Africa. Yet Southerners claimed divine endorsement of slavery, all the while studiously ignoring those verses which expressly and fiercely condemned kidnapping. According to these Old Testament laws, anyone found in possession of a kidnapped person were to be put to death!

Other key laws in the OT we've covered (release of injured slaves, anti-abuse, servants to be released after six years, commandments to help and shelter runaway slaves) also serve to illustrate this point. If these passages had been taken seriously by 'Bible-believing' Southerners and embraced with the overriding ethic of love found in the New Testament, slavery would not have been possible.

Advocates of slavery 'parked' on a few passages that appeared to endorse their cause and drew the conclusions they wanted in isolation from the rest of the Bible, ignoring anything that would contradict it.

This practise has long been known in theological circles since the beginning of church history as a sure-fire way to end up in serious error and heresy.

125

The Bible is ambivalent and even silent on many things, but on how we are to treat our fellow humans it is stunningly, brilliantly clear. *In fact, according to Jesus, how we treat our fellow humans is the whole point of the Bible.*

"The principles laid down by the Savior and his Apostles are opposed to Slavery, and if carried out would secure its universal abolition."[90]

[90] Barnes, *Inquiry*, 274.

Further Reading

Barnes, Albert. *An Inquiry Into the Scriptural Views of Slavery* (1857).

Bourne, George. *A Condensed Anti-Slavery Bible Argument by a Citizen of Virginia* (1845).

Coren, Michael. *Heresy: Ten Lies They Spread About Christianity* (2012).

Douglass, Fredrick. *My Bondage and My Freedom* (1855).

Douglass, Fredrick. *Narrative of the Life of Fredrick Douglass, An American Slave* (1845).

Hosmer, William. *The Church and Slavery* (1853).

McCaulley, Esau. *Reading While Black: An African American Biblical Interpretation as an Exercise in Hope* (2020).

Metaxas, Eric. *Amazing Grace: William Wilberforce and the Heroic Campaign to End Slavery* (2007).

Stark, Rodney. *For the Glory of God: How Monotheism Led to Reformations, Science, and the End of Slavery* (2011).

Swartley, William. *Slavery, Sabbath, War & Women* (1983).

Weld, Theodore Dwight. *The Bible Against Slavery* (1837).

5

Does the Bible Put Women Down?

ATHEISTS OFTEN ATTACK CHRISTIANITY for the patriarchal position some churches take on gender roles, but there is nothing particularly Christian about patriarchy.

Charles Darwin wrote that evolutionary benefits were "transmitted more fully to the male than to the female offspring... Thus man has ultimately become superior to woman."[91] He doubted women could ever overcome the inferior status evolution had bestowed on them.

Most of the luminaries of the Enlightenment believed men were superior to women physically and intellectually. Jean-Jacques Rousseau argued that higher education was wasted on women because "the search for abstract and speculative truths, for principles and axioms in science, for all that tends to wide generalization, is beyond a woman's grasp."[92] Patriarchy for them was just the natural order of things.

For most of human history, patriarchy has been the norm. The pagan civilizations of ancient Babylon, Assyria, Persia, India, China, Greece and Rome prior to the arrival of Christianity were all extremely patriarchal.

---

[91] Charles Darwin, *Descent of Man*, 1871
[92] Jean-Jacques Rousseau, *Emile*, p.349.

Historian and medieval scholar Dr. Beth Barr researched the history of patriarchy in the Christian church back to its origins in the Roman Empire. As she explains it, "Christians are, historically speaking, pretty late to the patriarchy game. We may claim that the gendered patterns of our lives are different from those assumed in mainstream culture, but history tells a different story...Christian patriarchy mimics the patriarchy of the non-Christian world."[93]

However, the issue of patriarchy in some churches is often used to bludgeon all Christians and Christianity as a whole.

When it comes to the status of women, critics of Christianity typically employ the same tactics used regarding slavery: cherry pick a few isolated verses, and point to some churches that also endorse patriarchy. Because some Christians believe in patriarchy, so the argument goes, the Christian faith itself must be false.

Again we are treated to the tired straw-man logic atheists often employ: some Christians have believed or done something offensive, therefore Christianity must be false.

Women throughout history, however, have had a different view. According to historian Rodney Stark, Christianity has attracted more women than men from the very beginning of church history. He writes: "From the earliest days women predominated...Indeed, the converts of Paul 'we hear most about are women,' and many of them 'leading women.'"[94]

---

[93] Beth A. Barr, *The Making of Biblical Womanhood*, p. 12.
[94] Rodney Stark, *The Triumph of Christianity*, p. 121

"In a Roman world quite short of women, women greatly outnumbered men among the early Christians. This occurred in part because Christians did not 'discard' female infants and Christian women did not have a substantial mortality rate from abortions done in a world without antibiotics or even knowledge of germs. It also occurred because women were more likely than men to convert."[95]

Nancy Pearcey relates that "Christianity was unusually appealing to pagan women because in the Christian subculture women enjoyed a far higher status than in the Greco-Roman world. Christianity recognized women as equal to men, children of God with the same supernatural destiny. The Christian moral code enhanced the dignity and well being of women."[96]

Stark adds: "Recent, objective evidence leaves no doubt that early Christian women did enjoy far greater equality with men than did their pagan and Jewish counterparts."[97]

Infanticide was legal in ancient Rome. They referred to the practice of killing their babies as 'exposure', because the unwanted newborns were left outside on the side of a hill until they died of exposure to the elements. Girls were ten times more likely to be disposed of than boys, because girls were considered an unwanted burden.

Studies have shown that few Roman families ever raised more than one girl, while having numerous boys.[98]

---

[95] Stark, *Triumph*, p.417

[96] Nancy Pearcey, *Total Truth*, p. 441

[97] Stark, *Triumph*, p.124

[98] Of course, this led to an extreme shortage of marriageable women later on for all those boys, a situation that caused serious problems in Roman society.

As Stark puts it, "The superior situation of Christian women vis-à-vis their pagan sisters began at birth."

Christians, along with Jews, considered the practice of exposure murder and refused to follow it. Christians did not expose infants and ended the practice through legislation throughout the Empire in later centuries as their influence grew.

As these Christian girls reached maturity, their advantage continued. Pagans typically married their girls off at an extremely early age, typically 13 or 14 but often as young as 11 or 12. They had virtually no say in who they married, often being given to much older men.

Christians had a different practice. Christian women did not marry until they were much older, usually around 18, and they had much more say in who they married.[99]

The predominance of women in the church has continued through history into modern times. To this day the vast majority of Christians are women. Here are some statistics:

Branch of Christian Church	Male	Female
Catholic	30	70
Liberal Protestant	33	67
Mainline Protestant	34	66
Fundamentalists	35	65
Evangelicals	43	57

Table 2: Percentage of men vs women in church.[100]

---

[99] Stark, *Triumph*, p.128
[100] From a 1996 survey. Cited in *Total Truth*, p. 441

131

Right from the very beginning of the church, women have outnumbered men almost 2 to 1. One of the major points of criticism the ancient Romans leveled against the early church was that "women and slaves" flocked to it. It gave them status, a voice and equality they didn't have in pagan circles.

Romans considered it a waste of time to educate a woman, since she would spend most of her life raising children. Rome and Greece, indeed most pagan cultures, were extremely elitist and sexist, and they were much more patriarchal than anything we've seen in our own recent history in Western culture.

The church ended all that.

However, it needs to be admitted that there are still churches which restrict women from leadership roles, and claim biblical support for it.

First, a few key definitions are in order before we dive into the discussion:

Patriarchy, as Dr. Barr describes, is "a society that promotes male authority and female submission... Both the tradition of male church leaders and the authority of male household heads function within cultures that generally promote male authority and female submission."[101]

Complementarianism is the theological term for the belief that patriarchy is biblically mandated. According to complementarians, God has ordained men to lead and women to follow in the church and home. Women are not allowed to lead or teach men and are banned from senior leadership and teaching positions in complementarian churches. They believe men and women are equal, but have different roles which 'complement' each other.

---

[101] Barr, The Making of Biblical Womanhood, p. 14.

Complementarian is a fancy term coined by modern patriarchs to avoid the negative connotations patriarchy has today, but it's the same thing. "Complementarianism is patriarchy."[102]

Egalitarian is the theological term for the opposite. Egalitarians believe the Bible teaches the full equality of women and men, and places no restrictions on women based on gender. Women, as full spiritual equals to men, can be called by God to teach and lead in the church, including male parishioners, as they are gifted to do so.

According to egalitarians, patriarchy is not divinely ordained but has come about as a result of human sinfulness and imperfection. As such it has been done away with through the redemption we have in Christ and should not be practiced in the church of Christ.

Complementarians find support for their position from a small handful of passages, which fall into two broad categories. First, we have what are known as the 'household codes' which would appear to endorse gender-based hierarchy within marriage: Ephesians 5:22-33, Colossians 3:18-19, 1 Peter 3:1-7.

The second group has a more direct bearing on church leadership, and appear to restrict women from leadership based on gender: 1 Timothy 2:8-15; 1 Timothy 3:1-13 and 1 Corinthians 14:34. While there are a few other highly debatable passages with a tangential bearing to the discussion, these six passages form the foundation of the complementarian position, and their entire argument hinges on how we interpret them. We will have a look at all six in turn, starting with the leadership passages.

---

[102] Barr, The Making of Biblical Womanhood, p. 13.

1 Timothy 2:8-15

"I do not permit a woman to teach or to exercise authority over a man; rather she is to remain quiet."

On the surface of it, this seems pretty clear. Women are not permitted to hold positions of authority over men, nor are they allowed to instruct men. This passage appears to support a patriarchal view of gender roles for women: stay home, raise kids, and let the men do the leading. But does it?

The problematic phrase is in verse 12: "to teach or to exercise authority over a man;" (ESV). The Greek word translated 'teach or to exercise authority' is *authentein*. The entire meaning of this passage hangs on how we translate this word.

The difficulty is that *authentein* is used just once in the New Testament, here in 1 Timothy 2:12. So we have to go outside of the New Testament, to contemporary Roman and Greek sources, to see how the word was used. Fortunately, thousands of texts have survived from the 1st century. A survey of these texts will help us gain a better understanding of this word.

Biblical scholar and New Testament Greek expert Bob Edwards completed an exhaustive survey of first century texts which use the word *authentein* and its variations. His survey shows that *authentein* did not mean simply 'to teach or exercise authority'.[103] Rather, the word carries very dark overtones of oppression, violence and even murder. Here are some representative examples illustrating how writers at the time used *authentein* and its variations: [104]

---

[103] Edwards, *Equality Workbook*, p.53-60
[104] Ibid, p.55-56

Flavius Josephus was a 1st century Jewish historian, well known for his *Wars of the Jews*. He uses the word twice in reference to individuals responsible for murder.

Philo writing in the 1st century uses the word to describe suicide, or 'self-murder'.

Other contemporary texts use *authentein* to describe the following:

"doer of a massacre."

"author of crimes"

"supporters of violent actions"

"perpetrators of a slaughter"

"murderers, slayers, perpetrators of evil"

In the Wisdom of Solomon, found in the Catholic Bible, the noun form of the word is used to describe parents who "slaughtered their own defenseless children." This is referring to parents who had joined secret cults in which ritual child sacrifice was practised.[105]

Charles Trombley also conducted a review of contemporary literature, and determined this word was often used to describe "something both sexual and murderous...it was not until the third or fourth century – Augustine's time – that the word began to be associated with usurping authority."[106]

A deeper understanding of the Greek word *authentein* suggests that a lot more is in view here than simply taking or holding authority over men. It was commonly used to indicate something violent, murderous or suicidal. Verse 12

---

[105] Edwards, *Equality Workbook*, p.53.

[106] See Trombley, C. *Who Said Women Can't Teach? God's Vision for Women in Ministry*, pp. 198-204. Quoted in Edwards, *Let My People Go*, p.39

is more accurately translated as: "I do not permit a woman to teach violence or instigate violence against a man."[107]

Why would Paul choose such a word for this passage, especially when better words for authority are available? Throughout the New Testament the word used for authority is *exousia*. A look at the cultural and religious atmosphere of Ephesus at the time reveals why Paul's use of *authentein* makes perfect sense.

The Historical Context of Ephesus

Paul wrote the letter to Timothy, a young pastor of a church in the city of Ephesus. Paul was very concerned with false doctrines entering the church, and in the letter Paul encouraged Timothy to stand against these destructive teachings. This is the main theme of the entire letter, and the literary context of our passage.

Bob and Helga Edwards investigated the situation in Ephesus at the time Paul wrote his letter to Timothy.[108] The city of Ephesus was dominated by the cult of Cybele (also called Artemis). Syncretism was common in the day. This is the habit of blending parts of different religions together. People would join a cult or religion and retain parts of the old religion that they liked. So as people converted to Christianity, they would bring with them beliefs and practices from other religions and seek to blend it with their new Christian faith. As a result, the cult of Cybele had made its way into the Christian church, and it had some very nasty practises indeed.

---

[107] Edwards, *Equality Workbook*, p.61
[108] See Edwards, *Let My People Go*, Chapter 6

This cult worshiped the mother goddess Cybele, led by female priestesses who took a very dim view of men and anything masculine. They believed that women, because they gave birth, possessed mystical life-giving powers. Violence by women against men and ritual castration was encouraged. Here is a description of one of their rituals:

"On the Day of Blood (March 24), the cult priests, in mourning for Attis, flagellated and castrated themselves, and ran through the streets proudly holding their bloody genitals."[109]

Cultic violence by women against men was pervasive throughout the Roman Empire in Paul's day and into the 2nd century. An early Roman author, Taitian (110-172 A.D.), wrote that in Rome Artemis was still worshipped with the ritual killing of men.

Edwards writes that, "Temple prostitution and the sacrificial murder of men were both part of Diana (Roman name for Artemis) worship in Paul's time... Syncretism and goddess worship were the issues; gender was not."[110]

Given that such ideas had crept into the church encouraging violence by women against men, the meaning of *authentein* (violent domination, abuse, supporting violence) and Paul's use of that word makes perfect sense.

Catherine and Richard Kroeger researched the cultural background of Ephesus at the time of Paul's writing, and their extensive research supports this conclusion.[111] There is general acceptance among scholars of Kroeger's conclusions.

---

[109] ibid, p. 50
[110] Edwards, *Let My People Go*, p. 40
[111] Richard and Catherine Kroeger. *I Suffer Not a Woman: Rethinking 1 Timothy 2:11-15 in Light of Ancient Evidence* (Grand Rapids: Baker Academic, 1992).

According to the Kroegers, "Paul was addressing a situation in Ephesus where powerful and influential women were coming out of the Artemis cult and entering the church. In doing so, the women were taking up teaching roles without proper training and instruction, being domineering and stubborn, and teaching heresy, while at the same time refusing to accept instruction... Paul was clearly addressing a specific situation ... this text, therefore, cannot be read as a universal injunction for all women in all churches for all time."[112]

Considering the cultural setting into which Paul was writing, and the historical meaning of *authentein*, verse 12 should not be taken as a universal rule against women in leadership. Paul was forbidding women from exercising violent and abusive dominance over men, as was practised by popular female cults at the time. Cultic violence against men was the issue, not gender.

However, we don't need to rely entirely on 'cultural' arguments. There is already such a weight of biblical evidence for women in leadership, along with Paul's own letters fully endorsing women in leadership, that we must discount this passage as a universal ruling banning women from legitimate leadership roles. We will look at the evidence for this later in this chapter.

It is also worth noting that in verse 11 of this passage Paul says: "Let a woman learn quietly with all submissiveness." To our modern ears this sounds like a patronizing putdown. But it's not. All students at that time, male or female, were expected to sit quietly and be submissive to their teachers. Also, women seldom received an education. Romans considered it a waste of time to

---

[112] Peppiatt, *Rediscovering Scripture's Vision for Women*, p. 145.

educate girls, with the result that women were typically illiterate. So this should not be read as a slam on women, but a revolutionary endorsement that women should be educated equally along with men.

1 Timothy 3:1-13

"An overseer must be above reproach, the husband of one wife,"

Along with 1 Timothy 2:12, complementarians rely heavily on 1 Timothy 3:1-13. This chapter contains a long passage outlining the qualifications for leadership in the church, and in many popular English translations it is peppered with male pronouns so that it sounds like it is referring to men.

Except that it isn't. The male pronouns so liberally inserted by some English translations aren't in the original Greek. The Greek text uses gender neutral pronouns 'whoever' and 'anyone'. There isn't a single male pronoun in this entire passage in the Greek text.

The only reference to gender is in the phrase often translated "husband of one wife", which is literally "one woman man".

There are some good modern English translations that translate the Greek text more appropriately for this passage. The CEV, TNIV and The Message are some good modern examples, translating "one woman man" as "faithful in marriage."

Beth Allison Barr says, "We assume 1 Timothy 3:1-13 is referencing men in leadership roles ... But is this because of how our English Bibles translate the text? Whereas the Greek text uses the words *whoever* and *anyone* ... modern English

Bibles have introduced eight to ten male pronouns within the verses. None of those male pronouns in our English Bibles are in the Greek text."[113]

Given the use of gender-neutral pronouns in the Greek text there is no reason to assume this passage refers exclusively to men. The only reference to gender in the passage is, literally, the phrase "one woman man." There is a perfectly good reason why Paul may have added this qualifier, without intending it as a restriction to keep women from leadership.

Polygamy was common at the time, and this was a specifically male issue. Men could have multiple wives, but it was not common for women to have multiple husbands. Paul's intention was likely that polygamists could not be church leaders.

It makes perfect sense, then, to single out men and not women in the context of this restriction. He was restricting men with more than one wife from leadership, not restricting women.

The egalitarian view simply fits better with the Greek text, but there are other problems for complementarians. If this passage means what complementarians claim, then it proves too much: only *married* men can lead.

Following through on the logic complementarians apply to this passage, it does not simply exclude women, it also excludes single men. If we are going to understand the phrase "one woman man", or "husband of one wife", in a restrictive sense – that *only* men can occupy leadership positions – then consistency dictates that it also means only *married* men.

---

[113] Beth Barr, *The Making of Biblical Womanhood*, p.147-48.

Put another way, if the phrase "one woman man" means women are excluded, then so are single men. There is no good reason to apply this restriction to women and not also to single men.

This is obviously a problem. Paul was single, as was Jesus. To get around this, complementarians silently add a qualifier to the text: "if" a man is married, he can only be married to one woman. As a result, divorced men or men in a second marriage are typically excluded from leadership roles in complementarian churches along with women, but not single, never married, men. However, that's not what the text says. Complementarians are applying their hermeneutic inconsistently when they use this phrase to exclude women, but not single men.

Fortunately many modern English Bibles, such as The Message, the CEV and TNIV, are doing a better job of translating this passage more faithfully according to the gender-neutral Greek text.

Regardless, the use of gender specific pronouns shouldn't throw us off. Even though they are not in the Greek, just for arguments sake let's for the moment allow the use of male pronouns in this passage, since they are found in some English Bibles popular with complementarians. Can we really assume that the presence of a gendered pronoun is meant to be taken exclusively? That women are excluded, that *only* men are intended, just because a male pronoun is used?

Of course not, and it isn't difficult to see why. Throughout the New Testament we find many passages using male pronouns for which we know women are included. I'll stick with the ESV for this exercise, since the ESV is popular with complementarians and notorious for liberally inserting male pronouns not in the Greek text.

141

Case in point: In 1 Thessalonians 4:4 we read: "that each one of you know how to control *his* own body in holiness and honor, not in the passion of lust like the Gentiles." A male pronoun is used here. Should we understand this passage in a gender exclusive sense? Are we to understand from this, therefore, that Christian women are excluded from the requirement to control their passions, and are free to indulge their lusts? According to the logic complementarians apply to 1 Timothy 3, the use of a male pronoun here means that Paul intended that it should only apply to men.

In Ephesians 2:15 we find the phrase "one new man" in Christ. Are we to take this in a gender exclusive sense? Because Paul uses "man", is his intention that only men are in view? Are we prepared to exclude women from the body of Christ?

In Ephesians 5:25 we have the well-known phrase "Husbands, love your wives." Does it mean *only* husbands need to love their wives? Are women relieved of the duty to love their husbands, because only husbands are mentioned here? As a married man, I certainly hope not!

I could go on, but I think I've made my point. A survey of the entire New Testament will find passages too numerous to list, in which a gendered pronoun or noun is used but we know is intended for both sexes. Yet complementarians think that it is only as it relates to leadership that male pronouns are intended exclusively.

It is not only masculine pronouns and nouns we find used in the Bible, in which we know both genders are intended. The Bible is also filled with female nouns and pronouns – many of them in reference to God himself – that no one thinks is intended to exclude men. In the parable of the lost coin, God is portrayed in the image of a woman (Luke

15:8-10). In Matthew 25, the church is portrayed as ten young girls, and wisdom is personified as a woman in the Book of Proverbs (Proverbs 1:20-33; 8:1-9:12).

Dr. Peppiatt has compiled a list of feminine images of God used in the Bible: [114]

- God is a nursing mother (Numbers 11:12)
- She is a mother who gave birth to the nation of Israel (Deuteronomy 32:18)
- A woman in labour (Isaiah 42:14)
- A mother who births and protects (Isaiah 46:3-4)
- A mother who does not forget her child (Isaiah 49:14-15)
- A mother who comforts her children (Isaiah 66:12-13)
- A mother who teaches and cares for her young (Hosea 11:1-4)
- Other maternal images can be found in Psalm 131:2; Job 38:8,29; Proverbs 8:22-25; 1 Peter 2:2-3; Acts 17:28.

God is described in terms of a woman's cultural activity:

- A seamstress making clothes (Nehemiah 9:21)
- A midwife assisting with birth (Psalms 22:9-10; 71:6; Isaiah 66:9)
- A woman in authority (Psalm 123:4)
- A woman working leaven into bread (Luke 13:20-21)

---

[114] Peppiatt, *Scripture's Vision for Women*, p.19-21.

God is also described using the imagery of a female bird or animal:

- A female bird protecting her young (Psalms 17:8; 36:7; 57:1; 91:1,4; Isaiah 31:5; Deuteronomy 32:11-12)
- A female eagle (Deuteronomy 32:11-12; Exodus 19:4; Job 39:27-30)
- A hen (Matthew 23:37; Luke 13:34; Ruth 2:12)
- A mother bear (Hosea 13:8)

1 Timothy 3 isn't explicitly stating women can't lead. Complementarians only infer this from the use of masculine pronouns, but the problem with this approach is twofold: the pronouns aren't in the Greek, only inserted by some English translations; and the use of gendered pronouns and nouns don't necessarily mean the other gender is excluded.

The qualifications listed for leadership in this passage are moral qualifications, and therefore apply equally to men and women.

1 Cor. 14:33-40

"The women should keep silent in the churches. For they are not permitted to speak."

One of our favorite television sitcoms is *Kim's Convenience*, centered on a Korean family who own and operate a corner convenience store in Toronto. The family attends a Korean Pentecostal church, and in one episode a parishioner is invited up to the pulpit during Sunday service to choose a verse for reading.

The parishioner makes her way up front and takes her place in the pulpit. The verse she chooses is 1 Corinthians

14:34, and she reads it aloud: "Women should keep silent in the church, for they are not permitted to speak."

The result is hilarious, of course. The church pastor, a woman, wasn't expecting the parishioner to choose that verse and is caught by surprise. Pandemonium breaks out in the church as several young women sitting in the pews stand up and shout their revulsion at the blatant misogyny.

The pastor jumps up from her chair and rushes to the pulpit, and gently steers the guest speaker off to the side. Then she stands in the pulpit and quickly turns the pages of her Bible to a more acceptable passage, 1 Corinthians 13:4, and begins reading "Love is patient and kind…" But it's too late and several women storm out of the church in protest.

Taken at face value, the "plain sense" of the text so often championed by complementarians, their anger is completely understandable. It is a deeply troubling passage on the surface of it.

1 Corinthians 14:34 appears to literally tell women to shut up, in any and all situations. It's not just precluding them from leadership roles, but tells them to remain silent. This would, if taken literally, effectively keep women from practically *any* role in the church, including participation in worship. Could that really have been Paul's intention? Does Paul really mean that women are to remain silent? Is this a rule for all time?

There are three ways this text can be understood, and we will have a look at each approach in turn:

1. As a universal ruling. The words on the page are to be understood literally, at face value without qualification. It is therefore a universal ruling for all time in all churches.
2. Paul was quoting a Roman law to refute it.

3. It is situational to cultural issues of the time. Paul was addressing a specific situation in that church at the time. It's not a universal ruling to be normative for Christian churches.

The difficulty with the literal approach is immediately apparent. First, this does not simply preclude women from leadership, it says they are to remain silent. They are not allowed to speak in public, and if they have any questions, they are to wait to ask their husbands privately at home. Taken literally, it commands them to keep their mouths shut and stay quiet.

Could Paul really have meant this as a general rule for all churches? There are compelling reasons why that's highly unlikely. Such an interpretation is jarringly at odds with many passages in the Jewish Scriptures (what we call the Old Testament) that explicitly endorse women leaders who were very vocal in public settings.

Paul, an expert in Jewish law and scripture, would have known about Deborah, Huldah, Esther, and the passage in Joel (we will cover these shortly). These women all spoke out publicly, were strong leaders, and their biblical stories portray them in the most favorable light possible – as favored by God.

We would also have to believe that Paul had forgotten what he'd just written earlier in the same letter, in which he encouraged women to exercise their spiritual gifts at church, including speaking out in 'tongues' and prophesying (11:5; 12:1-11).

If a literal interpretation of this passage makes no sense, then what are we to make of it? Another approach gaining ground with scholars is that Paul's intention was to argue against Roman law and custom. When Paul writes that "women should keep silent...they are not permitted to speak...even as the law says", he was actually quoting Roman law and custom to *refute* it.

Paul's wording here echoes Roman law and is very close to a popular Roman text of the day. The Roman world considered it shameful for women to speak in public, and Roman law as well as custom directed women to remain silent in public forums, and speak to their husbands privately at home.

Beth Allison Barr notes that "the Roman world viewed women as subordinate to men. The Roman world declared that men should convey information to their wives at home instead of women going out into the public forum. The Roman world told women to be silent in public forums."[115]

Furthermore, there is no biblical law forbidding women to speak, so when Paul writes "as the law says", he could not have had an Old Testament law in mind – since there is none. But there was a Roman law, and Paul's wording comes very close to the wording of a contemporary Roman historian referencing that law.

Titus Livy was a Roman historian who wrote the *History of Rome* in the early 1st century, just a few decades before Paul. Livy's work was very popular throughout the Empire when it was published, and he became a huge celebrity. In his *History*, he records a speech given by a Roman senator supporting laws that direct women to ask their husbands questions at home, rather than speak out publicly.

It was a common rhetorical practise to first quote a 'saying' or belief before refuting it. Livy's *History* was well known in Paul's day. While not an exact quote, Paul's wording in verses 14:33-40 is very close to Livy and matches

---

[115] Barr, *Biblical Womanhood*, p.60.

Roman custom and law of the time. Dr. Beth Allison Barr explains the significance of this:

"Paul was an educated Roman citizen. He would have been familiar with contemporary rhetorical practices that corrected faulty understanding by quoting the faulty understanding and then refuting it. Paul does this in 1 Corinthians 6 and 7 with his quotations of 'all things are lawful for me', 'food is meant for the stomach and stomach for food,' and 'it is well for a man not to touch a woman.' In these instances, Paul is quoting the faulty views of the Gentile world, such as 'all things are lawful for me.' Paul then strongly modifies them. Paul would have been familiar with the contemporary views about women, including Livy's, that women should be silent in public and gain information from their husbands at home."[116]

Many of our English translations obscure the nuances of the Greek, but the RSV does a respectable job of bringing out an inflection that makes all the difference in our understanding of this passage.

> "As in all the churches of the saints, the women should keep silent in the churches. For they are not permitted to speak, but should be subordinate, even as the Law says. If there is anything they desire to know, let them ask their husbands at home. For it is shameful for a woman to speak in church. *What! Did the word of God originate with you*, or are you the only ones it has reached? If anyone thinks that he is a prophet, or spiritual, he should acknowledge that what I am writing to you is a command of the Lord. If anyone does not recognize this, he is not recognized. So, my brethren,

[116] Barr, *Biblical Womanhood*, p.60.

earnestly desire to prophesy, and do not forbid speaking in tongues; but all things should be done decently and in order." (vv.33-40, RSV, emphasis mine).

Paul is calling out their wrong practice ("women should keep silent") to question it ("What!"), and then correct it ("do not forbid…"). Which would mean Paul's intention was to allow women to speak, the exact opposite of how the passage has been understood by complementarians.

We know that it was a common method of arguing in Paul's day to first quote the opposing belief, then refute it. And we already know he does this in the same letter, in chapters 6 and 7. Paul is likely doing the same thing in chapters 11 and 14.

This would explain the jarring change in Paul's tone beginning at verse 36 ("What!"). Paul is first laying out the faulty practise of the Corinthians, who were following Roman custom, and then challenging it, just as he does elsewhere (chapters 6 and 7). He then concludes with correcting the Corinthians: "desire to prophesy, and *do not forbid* speaking in tongues; but all things should be done decently and in order." In other words, don't forbid women from speaking.

Paul's intention was not to enforce Roman gender hierarchy, but to encourage the Corinthians to jettison it and embrace the freedom we have in Christ. He was countering a custom that the Corinthian men were dragging into the church from the Roman world in which they lived. They were forbidding women from speaking in public, according to the customs of the day, and Paul was correcting them.

This interpretation is consistent with Paul's encouragement of the public exercise of spiritual gifts in chapters 11 and 14 of the same letter, which place no

149

restrictions along gender lines. Not to mention Paul's open acknowledgement of female leaders in his other letters.

Even if this interpretation is wrong, then it is much more likely Paul is referring to a specific situation rather than making a universal ruling.[117]

It needs to be pointed out, though, that the literal approach is so problematic that even most complementarian churches allow for a 'cultural' exception of this verse in order to avoid the obvious difficulties with a literal interpretation.

However, this is a case of complementarians wanting to have their cake and eat it too. They'll allow for a cultural understanding of "women should keep silent…they are not permitted to speak" in 1 Corinthians 14:34, but dismiss any cultural understanding of "I do not permit a woman to teach…" in 1 Timothy 2:12. This is inconsistent, to say the least, a red flag for any hermeneutical approach.

There is an overwhelming body of biblical evidence fully supporting women in leadership. Taking this evidence into consideration, these three passages (1 Timothy 2 and 3, 1 Corinthians 14) should not be interpreted as normative rules forbidding women from leadership. Such an interpretation puts Paul in conflict with his own words, and Paul himself did not practice complementarianism – as we will shortly see.

The complementarian view of these passages would require us to believe that Paul is contradicting himself, and that he'd forgotten about Phoebe and other women leaders he mentions in other letters. It also requires us to believe that Paul had forgotten about Deborah, Huldah and Joel 2:28-32 in the Old Testament.

---

[117] Swartley, *Slavery, Sabbath, War & Women*, p. 173-174

Wifely Submission and the 'Household Codes'

Another small group of passages are directed specifically at married men and women, (Ephesians 5:22-33, Colossians 3:18-19, 1 Peter 3:1-7). Collectively, these three passages are commonly known as the 'household codes.' Complementarians believe that the hierarchy of male leadership in church government also extends into the home and marriage. For complementarians, one of the key markers of a Christian marriage is male authority and leadership in the home, 'complemented' by female submission, and these three passages are their go-to prooftexts.

On the surface of it, a plain reading of these passages appears to provide solid support for complementarians. Ephesians 5:22 exhorts "Wives, submit to your own husbands, as to the Lord, for the husband is the head of the wife even as Christ is the head of the church." In Colossians 3:18 we read, "Wives, submit to your husbands," and in 1 Peter 3:1 we again read "Likewise, wives, be subject to your own husbands."

My discussion of wifely submission and the household codes will center mostly on Ephesians 5:22-6:9 for a couple of reasons: the passage in Ephesians discusses all the household roles more thoroughly than the other two passages. Not just wives, but also husbands, children, slaves and masters are covered, whereas 1 Peter addresses only wives and husbands. We'll see why this is important to the discussion shortly. Colossians 3:18-19 is very similar to Ephesians 5, so the conclusions we draw from Ephesians can be safely applied to Colossians without the need to repeat. And 1 Peter also calls upon wives to "be subject" to their husbands, so our discussion of submission will also apply.

The text in Ephesians calling wives to submit to their husbands (v.22-24) is organically part of a long passage addressed to the entire household, addressing husbands (v.25-33), children (6:1-3), fathers (6:4), household servants (6:5-8) and finally masters (6:9).

Wives are to be submissive and respectful to their husbands, and husbands are to love their wives. Children are to obey and honor their parents, while fathers are not to provoke their children needlessly to anger. Slaves are to obey their masters and masters are "to do the same" and treat slaves decently, and are reminded that they also have a master in heaven. We will focus on v.22-24, but the verses concerning wives must be understood within the context of this wider passage to the entire household.

In v.22-24 married women are called upon to submit to their husbands. There really does seem to be a distinction between men and women in their marital roles. Married women appear to be singled out in this requirement to submit, and complementarians see this as proof that God has ordained a hierarchy between men and women within marriage.

For the complementarian understanding of this passage to have any merit, the wifely submission of verse 22 can only work one-way. In their view, because wives are mentioned in v.22, then *only* wives, and not husbands, are required to be submissive to their spouse. It has to be so, otherwise what's the point? If husbands are also to be submissive to their wives, then there is no real hierarchy of male headship.

And this is precisely where the complementarian argument breaks down. Immediately following "wives, submit to your husbands," we read "husbands, love their wives." We need to ask if these exhortations were intended exclusively, to work only the one way. Are we going to argue that because husbands are mentioned in verse 25, that *only* husbands need love their wives? Wives do not need to love their husbands? Are we to infer from this that women are exempt from loving their husbands?

If we interpret v. 22 as applying exclusively to women, because only women are cited, then by the same logic v. 25 should apply only to men because only men are referenced. Women are therefore exempt from loving their husbands. It is hard to imagine that was Paul's intention.

If we admit that wives are also to love their husbands in return, then we should also admit that husbands are to submit to their wives. I see no way around this for the complementarian. If they are going to insist on a wifely submission within a hierarchy – that it works only one way and that only wives are required to submit – then I don't see how they can avoid the same conclusion regarding the requirement to love your spouse: only husbands need to love their wives, and wives need not return that affection.

These verses go together and should be interpreted consistently. To argue that husbands are exempt from submission because only wives are mentioned in v.22, but of course wives are to love their husbands; that v. 22 only works in one direction, but v. 25 works both ways, strikes me as special pleading, not to mention inconsistent. So we must ask ourselves how much hierarchy in marriage we can legitimately infer from this passage. I would argue that the requirement to be submissive doesn't work just one way, any more than the requirement to love.

We also need to consider just how exclusive the use of gender references in any particular passage is intended to be. The use of a gendered noun or pronoun here, as in any passage of the New Testament, isn't necessarily exclusive to that gender. Throughout the New Testament there are passages that make use of gender references that we know are intended for both genders. We looked at a few examples above, but there are too many such passages in the New Testament to list.

So the use of gender references in v. 22-25 does not mean it's intended as a universal rule only for that gender. This is perhaps easier to see in v.25, "husbands, love your wives", because it is easier for us to grasp that both men and women should love their spouses; but I would argue the same applies to "wives, submit to your husbands", and so I don't think we can use this passage to enforce a rigid male dominated hierarchy.

It gets even worse for the complementarian position. Our understanding of any single verse or passage must take into account the rest of scripture, and the household codes are no exception to this hermeneutic rule. They need to be understood within the context of the entire New Testament, the meta-narrative of the gospel, in which Christians, both men and women, are exhorted to love, to be respectful, to be at peace, to treat others as we wish to be treated, to be humble and place others first, to lay down our very lives for each other.

In verse 21, the verse immediately prior to this passage, all men and women in the church are called to mutual submission. Married men are not excluded from this. So while we find in verse 22 a specific call for wives to submit to their husbands, we also find that Christians in general, everywhere, are called to submit to "one another" (v. 21).

Over and against the three passages complementarians focus on for wifely submission, there are, as Peppiatt notes, fifty-nine "one another" passages exhorting all Christians to love one another,[118] to submit to one another, to be humble towards each other, to be forgiving, to live in peace. This also includes married couples.

Verse 25 says: "Husbands, love your wives." And what is love, if it is not also humble and carries with it a submissive attitude. According to the classic passage read at so many weddings, 1 Corinthians 13 tells us that love is patient, love is kind, love is not arrogant or proud, love does not seek its own, but seeks what is best for others, it does not insist on getting its own way. A better definition of a humble and submissive attitude is difficult to find.

The Subversion of Hierarchy

If wives are also to love their husbands, and husbands are also to be submissive, then why would Paul intentionally reference wives and husbands in vv. 22-25?

I don't think Paul's intention in this passage was to underwrite male patriarchy. He certainly didn't need to. It was already well established in Roman society. I think he was doing just the opposite: subverting it and leveling the hierarchical playing field between men and women.

The entire passage from verses 5:21-6:9 is an organic whole addressing the typical Roman household, which often included "slaves" (household servants). Roman society and households were extremely patriarchal, and Paul was referencing the key relationships within the typical Roman home: husbands, wives, children, servants, and masters. It is difficult for the modern reader to pickup on the subtleties of this passage because we are so far removed from that

---

[118] Peppiatt, *Scripture's Vision for Women*, p. 90.

culture, but Paul was not endorsing male hierarchy, he was undermining it.

The subversive element of this text is found in its address to the men, rulers of the Roman household. Paul tells them to love their wives, to treat their slaves decently, and – shockingly – after outlining how servants are to behave, tells the male patriarchs to "do likewise." The men are to behave *like the slaves*.

This would effectively, as the new paradigm takes hold, overturn the oppressive societal structures of slavery and hierarchy. I believe the same "cultural" argument that complementarians (as all Christians) make for "slaves, obey" (Eph.6:5) also applies to "wives, submit," (Eph.5:22) and thus, far from an endorsement of these institutions, when properly read in their historical context, this passage overturns slavery *and* hierarchy.

The shock to the system these words must have conveyed to Roman men of the time is difficult for us to appreciate today. Roman men were at the top of society, slaves at the very bottom. Slaves were barely people, had no status, and were certainly not worth noticing. And here Paul is telling masters, immediately after outlining the duties of slaves, that they are to "do likewise".

Men can no longer simply do whatever they wanted with other people (as Roman law and custom allowed). They were now expected to behave within boundaries of love and decency towards all other people. Men and masters were being brought down a few notches, women and slaves elevated, bringing a clear shift towards full equality across all lines of gender, race and social status as expressed in Galatians 3:28.

Peppiatt summarizes the revolutionary impact of this passage: "For an ancient reader, there would have been no

156

surprise in the instruction to a wife to submit to her husband. This would have been a standard pattern...however, the instruction to the husbands, read aloud for all to hear, would have caused considerable ripples throughout the household because they and those around them would now know that this behavior is also expected of *him*, and here is where we find the Christian revolution."[119]

Roman men had the legal power of life and death over everyone in their household, not just their slaves, but their wives and children. Into this atmosphere of extreme patriarchy Paul calls upon men to love their wives as they love themselves, to cherish them as they cherish their own bodies. He reminds the masters (again usually the same male heads of households) that they have a master in heaven and that God is not partial to them, that God looks upon slave and master the same, a revolutionary idea that would have shocked people at the time.

The Christian Revolution

When Paul tells men that they are to love their wives as Christ loves the church, he is reminding them what love means. It is self-sacrificial. It is not about dominance and control, but self-sacrifice and giving. This love puts others ahead of itself, it regards the welfare of others as more important than its own welfare. It seeks the good of others, not its own good.

Whereas complementarians harp exclusively on a couple of passages to argue for gender-based control, the message of love, self-sacrifice, humility and mutual

---

[119] Peppiatt, *Scripture's Vision for Women*, p.93.

submission is infused throughout the entire New Testament like sugar and cinnamon is baked into sweet rolls.

This is the Christian revolution, which changes society from the inside out and the bottom up. By changing hearts and the way we view our fellow humans. By seeing all people, regardless of gender, race, age, class, net worth or social status, as human beings fully worthy of dignity and respect.

Christ reminds us that God loves the poor and lower classes as much as the wealthy and powerful. This is the heart of the Christian message when we are being true to the words of Christ and the New Testament. *To regard others ahead of ourselves*. How could the institution of slavery or hierarchy, of any system that oppresses and subjugates others, survive in such an atmosphere?

Ephesians 5:22-6:9 isn't a biblical endorsement for a universal, never ending male hierarchy. Rather, it contains within it the seeds that bring it to an end. Despite Paul's specific reference to woman in 5:22 to be submissive, we cannot read into this an endorsement of a gender hierarchy anymore than we should see within 6:5 a biblical support for slavery. It is curious that complementarians will see hierarchy in this passage, but not slavery. They will allow for a cultural understanding of "slaves, obey your masters" but not for "wives, obey your husbands" found in the very same passage.

As I argued in Chapter 4, this passage and passages like it, along with the entire New Testament in general, contain within it the seeds of a new society that would eventually sprout, take root and grow to destroy slavery as an institution. The same thing is happening here for patriarchy. Which is exactly what happened as Christianity grew in influence and spread through the Roman Empire. We must not read into this passage a biblical endorsement of patriarchy anymore than we should read into it an endorsement for slavery.

The Limited Scope of Ephesians 5

Some of my best friends are complementarians, and I have no wish to intrude on the private relationship between a husband and wife. How they wish to arrange their personal relationship and home is entirely their business.

Which brings us to the salient fact of this passage that must not be ignored – its extremely limited scope. The text about submission addresses only married women in relationship to their husbands. It has nothing to say to unmarried women, whether widowed, divorced or never married. It says nothing about church leadership or other roles, and says only that those wives are to be submissive to their own husbands. There is nothing in this passage that can be used to exclude any woman, especially single women, from leadership roles. There is no hint of hierarchy outside the marriage bond.

For arguments sake let's allow, for the moment, the complementarian reading of the household codes. Even taken literally at face value, they can at the very most only be used to regulate the relationship between husband and wife within the private sphere of their home and marriage.

It has nothing to say about women in leadership roles, and certainly cannot be taken to mean women in general are to have submissive attitudes towards men in general. They do not preclude an unmarried woman from leadership.

Paul is clearly limiting his address to married Christians and their personal relationship within their marriage. Married women are certainly not being asked in this passage to adopt a submissive attitude towards any other man but her husband. What complementarians cannot do is infer from these passages a general hierarchy between men and women, nor can it be used to keep women from leadership.

The Biblical Evidence for Women in Leadership

I still remember the ripples of nervous laughter through the congregation that Sunday morning. The pastor was preaching through the Book of Judges, and had just finished reading the story of Deborah.

I could see that the pastor, a firm hierarchicalists, was not happy with the obvious implications of the story. He concluded his sermon with a warning to the men: "You see men, that's what happens when there's no real men around. God couldn't find a real man to lead the nation, so he was forced to use a woman."

Before a monarchy was established in Israel, before King David, there was a 400-year span in early Jewish history referred to as the period of the judges. This period stretched from shortly after the Jews left Egypt and ran up until the first King. During this time Israel was ruled by a succession of Judges. Most of them were men, but one was a woman, named Deborah. You can read her story in Judges chapters 4 and 5.

The intellectual gymnastics of our pastor were impressive, because even from this story of Deborah he was still able to twist it to conform to his complementarian worldview. Except the text doesn't allow for that. The biblical narrative of Deborah is extremely positive. She's portrayed as a very successful and effective leader.

Deborah ruled over the nation, including male military commanders, with all the authority of any of her male counterparts. This is, as they say, the exception that proves the rule. There's no restriction on women. In fact, a comparison of her story with the stories of her male counterparts in the same book shows that she was in many respects a more able leader than some of the other Judges – notably Samson, who as a national leader was a miserable failure.

The Prophetess Huldah. (2 Chronicles 34:22-28). Huldah was a prophetess who instructed the King – a male sovereign. Huldah had words of warning to the King that would not be particularly welcome. She was a woman who bravely spoke truth to power.

Queen Esther. When a plot to exterminate all the Jews in the Empire is revealed, Queen Esther moves boldly to save her people and avoid a holocaust. Esther was a heroic female leader of her nation. The stories of Deborah, Huldah and Esther alone completely pulls the rug out from underneath complementarians and everything they try to tell us the Bible says. These women taught and led not just men, but kings and other top national leaders. So much for the complementarian view of "I do not permit a woman to teach or have authority over a man" in 1 Timothy 2:12.

Your daughters shall prophesy. Joel 2:28-32: "And it shall come to pass afterwards that I will pour out my spirit on all flesh, your sons and your daughters shall prophesy[120] ... Even on the male and female servants in those days I will pour out my spirit."

The Book of Joel is in the Old Testament. Here Joel is declaring that women are to be preachers and teachers in full equality with men, when the Spirit of God would be poured out on 'all flesh'. And just so any patriarchal minded man doesn't miss the point of 'all flesh', Joel spells it out for them:

---

[120] i.e., preach and teach with authority.

it includes "sons and daughters." The daughters will prophesy, which includes public preaching and teaching.

The technical formulation of the phrase "your sons and daughters shall prophesy" makes no distinction between gender or gender-based roles, and levels the playing field. The full inclusion of women is in view with this passage. Sons and daughters, men and women, are portrayed in the same roles.

The significance of this passage for the spiritual life of the church should not be underestimated. Acts chapter 2 records the birth of the Christian church, the first public preaching and teaching by the followers of Christ, proclaiming for the first time the resurrection of Jesus Christ from the dead.

In his first public sermon on the day the church was born, Peter quoted this passage from Joel and specifically applied it to the birth of the Christian church. The Old and New Testaments clearly support women in public preaching and leadership.

Gal 3:28. This verse has been called the high-water mark of the New Testament, a magnificent declaration of freedom and equality for men and woman of all races: "There is neither Jew nor Greek, there is neither slave nor free, there is neither male nor female, for you are all one in Christ." (See also Col. 3:11).

Since Greek (pagan gentiles) and Jews were the major racial barrier at the time, this should be understood as a radical statement of full racial equality. Slaves and free people were the major class barrier at the time in Roman society, so this is a huge statement on the complete removal of class distinction. This verse is declaring full equality across the three major divisions between people: race, gender and social class. We cannot just apply this statement of equality to race and class, but not gender.

Col. 4:15. "Give my greetings to...Nympha, and the church in her house." When Paul refers to the church in Nympha's house, he is not commending her as just a "hostess with the mostess", like someone who has just opened up her home to others. Having a church in your home typically meant you were a leader, and it would be very difficult to assume Paul expected her to "remain silent" or be subordinate in her own home.

The Apostle Junia. In Romans 16:7, Paul refers to a woman named Junia as notable or outstanding among the apostles. There has been some modern debate over the gender identity of 'Junia', and some English bibles translate Junia as Junias (a man), but for the first several centuries of church history Junia was understood to be a woman apostle.

The early church fathers all recognized Junia as a woman. Chrysostom, who was not in favour of women in leadership, wrote that Junia was a woman, and extolled her as "outstanding among the apostles – just think what a wonderful song of praise that is!"[121]

All early church commentators recognized her as a woman.[122] It's not until the Middle Ages we find some commentators – for the most part following Luther's lead, who did not believe it was possible for a woman to be an apostle – switching Junia (female) to Junias (male).

But for the first ten centuries Junia was recognized as a woman.

---

[121] John Chrysostom, *Homilies on the Epistle of Paul to the Corinthians* (Edinburgh: T&T Clark, 1889).

[122] Origen, 185-253 A.D.; Jerome 340-419; Hatto, 924-961; Theophylact, 1050-1108; Peter Abelard, 1079-1142.

The history of how Junia has been translated over the centuries is fascinating, and serves as an excellent example of how some men have tried to obscure or erase the roles of women in the Bible. In some cases even Greek New Testaments were intentionally edited to change Junia to Junias!

Modern scholarship on the subject is conclusive. New Testament scholar Eldon Jay Epp compiled tables of all the Greek New Testaments from Erasmus down to the 20th century. His research demonstrates that the Greek name *Junia* was almost always translated in its female form up until the 20th century. Then, translations suddenly switched over to the male form of the name, Junias.[123]

"Why?" asks historian Beth Barr, and then goes on to answer: "Epp makes it painfully, maddeningly clear that a major factor in twentieth century treatments of Romans 16:7 was the assumption that a woman could not have been an apostle. *Junia* became *Junias* because modern Christians assumed that only a man could be an apostle." [124] The early church Fathers and translators made no such assumption. The mistranslation of Junia to Junias has been corrected in recent years, and scholars now accept that Junia in 16:7 is a woman.

Some complementarians, forced to concede that Junia was a woman, switched their strategy to claim that she was only "well known *to* the apostles," not "outstanding *among* the apostles." However, the entire time Junia was believed to be a man there was no doubt that "he" was an apostle – and not just an apostle, but a prominent apostle. As Peppiatt notes, "while translators believed Junia to be a man, there

---

[123] Eldon Jay Epp, *Junia: The First Woman Apostle*, p. 60-65.
[124] Barr, *The Making of Biblical Womanhood*, p. 66-67.

was no such ambiguity"[125] about Junia's status as an outstanding apostle.

A careful examination of the Greek words involved show that 16:7 is more accurately translated as "prominent or outstanding among the apostles," and not simply "well known to the apostles."[126]

Despite some modern attempts to obscure the fact and erase Junia the woman from history, there is no serious doubt among scholars that the apostle Junia was a woman, and prominent among the apostles. For a detailed study, please see the following references.[127]

Phoebe. Ro. 16:1-2. "I commend to you our sister Phoebe, a deacon of the church." The Greek word here translated 'deacon', (or in some English translations 'servant') is the same word used elsewhere for male deacons, a church leadership role.

In v.2 Phoebe is also referred to as a 'patron'. The Greek word is *prostatis*, and means 'ruler over many people', including no doubt many men. Paul is perfectly comfortable commending this female leader to his readers.

While the meaning of some Greek words, such as *authentein* used in I Timothy 2, might be debatable, the Greek word used here is not. It means deacon and is translated everywhere else as deacon. It is only some complementarian leaning translations (ESV, NIV, KJV) that chose to translate it as 'servant' here, when referring to a

---

[125] Peppiatt, *Rediscovering Scripture's Vision for Women*, p. 122.
[126] Bob and Helga Edwards, *Equality Workbook* (2016), p. 40-41.
[127] Eldon Jay Epp, *Junia: The First Woman Apostle* (Augsburg Fortress, 2005); Rena Pederson, *The Lost Apostle: Searching for the Truth About Junia* (Jossey-Bass, 2006); Scott McKnight, *Junia is Not Alone: Breaking the Silence About Women in the Bible and the Church Today* (Patheos, 2011);

woman's position. Along with complementarian translations of 1 Timothy 3 which insert male pronouns that don't exist in the Greek, this is one of the more striking examples of how biased English translations have misled people concerning the role of women in leadership.

Phoebe was a deacon. Therefore we know that the passage in 1 Timothy 3 could not have been intended to restrict the role of deacon, and likely elders, to men only.

Prisca. In Romans 16:3-4, Paul refers to "Prisca and Aquila", fellow workers in Christ. (This couple and their work are also described in Acts 18:1-4, 26).

Nowhere is it suggested that Prisca is inferior to or under the authority of Aquila in ministry. She shares the same title; she is recognized as sharing equally in the ministry work as well as the risks ("*they both* risked their necks for my life," says Paul). There is nothing suggesting a subordinate role for Prisca as one of the church leaders.

Euodia and Syntyche. Phil. 4:1-3: Referring to two women, Euodia and Syntyche, Paul says: "Yes, I ask you to help these women who labored side by side with me in the gospel together with Clement and the rest of my fellow workers, whose names are in the book of life." It is clear that these women were considered equals.

Note the striking language Paul used: he says that they labored *side by side with* me, *together with* other men *and the rest of my fellow* workers. These women worked *next* to Paul *along with* other men. There is nothing subordinate in this language.

Paul speaks of these women in equal terms along with himself and the other men he worked with. He wasn't just saying these women were nice and served him food and drink while the men did the important work. I don't think we can take this passage for anything else other than straightforward evidence that women worked at Paul's side as fellow leaders.

1 Corinthians 11:5. This verse sits within a challenging passage discussing head coverings for women as well as men. Paul says that women who prophesy publicly with their heads uncovered dishonor their husbands. Hairstyles for women in first century Corinth were significant. They indicated whether a woman was single, married, a temple prostitute or a follower of one of the pagan mystery cults. Paul is not making a universal rule, but discussing cultural propriety.

The message here for the church at large is that we should dress ourselves appropriately for our culture when in public. All societies have their cultural baggage, but we shouldn't let this discussion around women's hairstyles distract us from the crucial point: Paul isn't saying women can't speak out in public, only that they should do so in a culturally appropriate manner. Verse 5 carries a very implicit endorsement of women ministering publicly. The issue here is cultural relevance and decorum, not gender.

1 Cor 12:1-14: Both men and women, "brothers and sisters", are addressed at the beginning of this lengthy passage discussing the public exercise of spiritual gifts for the common good. We are all baptized by one Spirit into one Body, and we all drink from the same Spirit. There are no gender distinctions.[128]

Acts 21:8-9. Phillip, one of the earliest leaders of the church, had four daughters who were all prophets. We know from Paul's letters that prophesying involved public speaking, the authoritative teaching and instruction to the

---

[128] See Lucy Peppiatt, *Women and Worship at Corinth*, for a thorough treatment of these passages about women.

entire assembled congregation. This would include men as well as women. (1 Corinthians 14:4,30,31). Prophecy was didactic, and there is nothing to suggest in 1 Corinthians 12-14 that any of the gifts, prophecy included, were gender specific.

Many women leaders are mentioned in the New Testament. Phoebe is the only 1st century deacon for whom we have a name. In Romans chapter 16 we are given a long list of names, and more women than men are identified by their ministry. "Whether as missionary 'co-workers' (Priscilla, Euodia, Syntyche), leaders of house churches (Priscilla, Nympha, Phoebe), fellow apostles before Paul (Junia and possibly Phoebe), or those who 'labored hard in the Lord' (Mary, Tryphaena, Tryphosa, Persis), these women are never portrayed in subordinate positions to Paul or to other men."[129]

Jesus and Women

Jesus was a moral and social revolutionary, and his position on women was extremely progressive. Roman and Jewish society at the time had an overwhelmingly negative attitude towards women.

In some circles, women couldn't even leave the house without a male escort. Women were typically illiterate, not being allowed to read, write or study the scripture. Education was considered wasted on women, whose primary role was to get married and raise children (boys, preferably).

---

[129] Swartley, *Slavery, Sabbath, War & Women*, p. 177

In this setting, it is significant that Jesus had women disciples[130] who made up a large contingent of his followers, something that was offensive to the culture at large.

It is also significant, therefore, that the early church writers of the gospels made no attempt to disguise this fact.

In Luke 8:3 prominent women who followed Christ are named. The gospels record that large numbers of women were among his disciples and 'ministered' to him.[131] The Greek word for 'ministering' is *diakonoun*, the same basic word for 'deacon' used of men in a church leadership role. Complementarian leaning English Bibles, such as the ESV and NIV, translate this word 'servant' when it is describing women, and 'deacon' when describing male leaders.

"Most significantly, the prominence of women in the story of Jesus' resurrection – this central event of the gospel narrative... is a strong statement about the role of women: Jesus disclosed himself first to women and entrusted them with the responsibility of telling the apostles."[132]

In a society where women were not even allowed to testify in courts of law because they were not considered reliable, Jesus chose women, not men, to be his first witnesses. This is hugely significant and obviously intentional on Christ's part.

It's also significant that the authors of the gospels recorded this fact, because it was not something that would assist the early church with its message to the world or help

---

[130] By 'disciple', I am not of course restricting the term to 'the 12'. In the Gospels, the term was also applied to many people who followed Jesus beyond the well-known 12, including women.
[131] Mark 15:40-42
[132] Swartley, *Slavery, Sabbath, War & Women*, p. 162

with its credibility. In fact, it would only hinder its credibility in the eyes of the larger culture.

Leonard Swidler dryly notes: "The effort of Jesus to centrally connect these two points (his resurrection and the role of women) is so obvious that it is an overwhelming tribute to man's intellectual myopia not to have discerned it effectively in two thousand years."[133] Women were prominent in all four resurrection accounts. They were the first preachers of the gospel, the first to tell the disciples of the resurrection. These women taught and instructed the apostles; as some have pointed out, they were "preachers to the preachers".

Christ's treatment and attitude towards women was remarkable. In a world that considered women suitable for little more than their sexual function, he said: "Do not look upon a woman to lust after her." (Mat.5:27-28). In other words, women are not to be viewed as sex objects, but as persons.

The stories of the sinful woman (Luke 7:36-50) and the woman taken in adultery (John 8:1-11) also confirm that Jesus did not regard women as inferior or as sex objects, but as persons with full equality.

In John 4 we have a long and detailed story of Christ's interaction with a Samaritan woman who he met at a well. Jesus whole encounter with this woman broke social taboos of all kinds between race and gender. Christ's interaction with her, while appearing harmless to us today, was hugely offensive according to cultural convention of the governing male-female interactions.

---

[133] Leonard Swidler, "Jesus Was a Feminist", p. 181. Quoted in Swartley, *Slavery, Sabbath, War & Women*, p. 162

In the Gospel of Luke, chapter 15, Jesus tells the parable of the lost coin. It is notable that in this story, Jesus portrays God in the image of a woman.

The story of Mary and Martha in Luke 10:38-41 is a fascinating study. Jesus visits the home of Mary and Martha, two sisters who followed Christ, along with his disciples. One evening the disciples and a large crowd gathered in their home. A houseful of men sat down to listen to Jesus teach, and Mary sat down with them, leaving Martha to do all the serving. Martha grew frustrated that all the work of preparing and serving food had been left to her, and that her sister Mary wasn't "lifting a finger" to help with the kitchen duties.

Martha went to Jesus to complain and asked him to tell Mary to help her in the kitchen. Martha was of course following the social conventions of her time and was not asking anything that would be considered unconventional. In fact, Mary sitting down with the men to learn with them was unconventional, and she likely earned a few sideways glances from the men for her impertinence. Remember, in this society women were not educated with men, and were usually denied education altogether.

But Jesus responded to Martha that Mary "had chosen the better thing and it would not be taken from her." He overturned custom, and reaffirmed Mary's right to sit with the men and learn alongside them. In fact, he asserted that Mary had chosen the *better thing*. Here we have Jesus affirming that it is better for women to sit and be educated along with men, rather than participate in traditional gender-based duties.

Jesus did not support the traditional view that a woman's primary place was in the kitchen. Instead he affirmed Mary's place equally alongside men in intellectual and cerebral activities; and through Mary, all women. This presents a radically different view of women and women's roles.

In Luke 11:27-28 a woman in the crowd called out to Jesus: "Blessed is the womb that bore you, and the breasts that nursed you." Jesus responds with: "Blessed rather are those who hear the word of God and obey it."

Again, Jesus does not reaffirm the traditional role for women. Instead, he said they would be more blessed in hearing and keeping the word of God. He affirmed their spiritual and intellectual identities as people, and the implicit equality with men in this statement is obvious and must not be brushed aside. "Women are called to the work of the kingdom rather than motherhood as the first priority in their lives",[134] thus overturning traditional gender roles and the primary sexual function of women.

In his book *Biblical Affirmations of Women*, Leonard Swidler compiled an exhaustive collection of passages from the Gospels supporting an incredibly positive view of women. He covers in great detail these passages that I have briefly surveyed above. I like the way he sums it up: "From this evidence it should be clear that Jesus vigorously promoted the dignity and equality of women in the midst of a very male dominated society...Can his followers attempt to be anything else?"[135]

The Hermeneutics of Liberation

I'm going to borrow a page from the abolitionists' playbook. Here's why: many of the arguments used by abolitionists to refute slavery can also be applied to the issue

---

[134] Swartley, *Slavery, Sabbath, War & Women*, p. 163
[135] Leonard Swidler, *Jesus Was a Feminist*, p. 183

of hierarchy and the subjugation of women. And that should certainly arouse our suspicions.

Quakers in Philadelphia were early abolitionists, and one of their arguments was based on the words of Christ: "I tell you the truth, when you did it to one of the least of these my brothers and sisters, you were doing it to me!" (Mat. 25:40, NLT).

Quakers used this passage to argue that how we treat other people, including the lowliest of society, is how we treat Christ. When we enslave the Black man, they pointed out, we enslave Christ. It's not much of a stretch at all to apply this argument to patriarchy and women. When we subjugate women, we subjugate Christ.

Abolitionists also based arguments on the *imago Dei*. All humans are made in the image of God. How can anyone in the image of God be enslaved? We might well ask the same question of the subjugation of women in a male hierarchy. How can women, made in the image of God as fully as men, be subjugated? How can they be told that they cannot lead or teach, if they are gifted to do so? The subjugation of women in a hierarchy is a violation of their *imago Dei*.

In a similar vein, abolitionists argued that slavery violates the priesthood of all believers. I'd say the same for hierarchy. Through Christ, all believers come into a direct relationship with God. We no longer need a priest or someone else to approach God for us, or to act as God's spokesperson for us. Through Christ we all come into direct personal contact with the Divine.

As Peter declares, believers are now part of a spiritual temple of "holy priests", a "royal priesthood" (1 Peter 2:5,9). Readers at the time would have understood exactly what Peter was getting at. They were all very familiar with Old

Testament regulations that required priests to approach God as intermediaries for them.

Under the Old Testament system people could not go to God themselves, a priest had to do that for them. But now in Christ, Peter was saying, they were all priests who could draw near to God directly. They no longer needed others to do that for them.

The significance of this must not be underestimated. It is really one of the key revolutionary concepts of the Christian gospel. This is something that complementarians and egalitarians agree on, and is a basic theme of the New Testament.

Throughout the New Testament, again and again, we find this emphasis: that in Christ we have a new and living way into the presence of God. The need for an intermediary between us and God has been swept away by the cross of Christ – His life, death and resurrection. We all, from the least to the greatest, have the privilege of approaching God directly through Christ, and seeking his will and guidance for our lives.

Christians do not contend this. Yet a complementarian reading of scripture is ultimately inconsistent with it. A hierarchy requiring women to submit to men, to follow and obey men, in which women are kept from leadership on the basis of their sex, effectively places the male in a priestly role for women. As such it reduces women to a secondary spiritual status. Intrinsic within this is an implicit assumption that men will know better, at least in spiritual matters and church governance. As Dr. Barr asks: "How can we apply a hermeneutic of liberation to the slavery debate to blacks, but not to women?"

We can know modern hierarchicalists are wrong for the same reasons we know advocates of slavery in the 19th century were wrong about the Bible. Their interpretation of the Bible does not line up with the rest of scripture and the freedom we *all* have in Christ. While appearing to be faithful to the words on the page, the so-called plain reading, of a small handful of isolated verses, it takes them to a place that is inconsistent with the rest of the New Testament. They will argue for a contextual understanding of the slavery texts, but deny the same for the gender texts. This is an inconsistent application of their hermeneutic, and consistency is a key to correct interpretation.

This isn't simple caving into political correctness, although the PC crowd isn't always wrong, and they aren't wrong about equality. Throughout most of human history, in almost every society, patriarchy was politically correct. It was the acceptable norm.

The Roman Empire was extremely patriarchal and the early churches radical position on equality for women and slaves was offensive to Roman culture.

It was a craven capitulation by the church in later centuries to the surrounding culture that brought male hierarchy into the church. Historically, it is male headship that's PC, not equality. It's only recently in the West that equality has become associated with political correctness.

"Come now, let us reason together"[136]

The biblical evidence endorsing women in leadership roles is overwhelming and incontrovertible. Over and against that, we have a limited handful of passages used by complementarians to keep women out of leadership.

---

[136] Isaiah 1:18

There are a few other passages that sometimes come into the conversation, notably 1 Corinthians 11:1-16 and Titus 2:5. Like Ephesians 5:22, the passage in Titus speaks only of wives submitting to their husbands and has no bearing on church leadership. Our conclusions from Ephesians will also apply to Titus.

1 Corinthians 11, with its extensive discussion on head coverings and hair, screams out for a cultural understanding. And again, while there is discussion of women submitting to husbands within their marriage relationship, nothing in this passage can be used to preclude women from church leadership and has nothing to say to unmarried women.

What's striking here is the lack of passages that could even remotely be used by complementarians to bolster their position. Only two of them have any possible bearing on gender regarding authority and leadership in the Church. If male headship was as important to the Divine economy as complementarians seem to think, then we have to wonder why God did not include more passages on the subject.

Christianity teaches the full equality of men and women, going right back to the creation story in Genesis 1 and 2, in which men and women are created equal and given the same duties in the garden. We have a solid foundation for the full equality of all races and genders in the doctrine of creation. This is the basis for the historical Church teaching of *imago Dei* that *all humans* carry.

Gender based hierarchy was a pagan concept. It existed in the world in virtually every pagan civilization prior to the coming of Christ. As far back as recorded history allows us to look, gender-based hierarchy was there – and almost always male.

The Gospel of Jesus Christ subverts this, as it does slavery and all forms of private and institutional oppression.

Isn't it time that we fully embrace the freedom that Christ is trying to bring us through His gospel, rather than embracing an oppressive, rigid gender hierarchy that the Church originally adopted from pagan cultures?

For those interested in exploring the Christian message, and have been perhaps put-off by the unfortunate stand some churches take on women in leadership, I would encourage you to look into the central tenets of the faith: the historical life, death and resurrection of Jesus Christ.

Through his resurrection, humanity is restored to a relationship with God. Through Christ you can be forgiven of your sins and come into a relationship with God who loves you. If you believe that full equality for women means that women should be allowed leadership roles just like men, then by all means hold on to that. There are many good churches out there that also believe that, and they have solid biblical support for it.

It is not necessary to accept gender roles to be a good Christian. In fact, I believe the best expression of the faith of Christ will only be found in Christian communities that fully accept women on equal grounds with men in the exercise of their gifts and calling. Many churches are also completely egalitarian, completely open to women in top leadership roles. Christianity worldwide is over 60% female and has been a haven for women from the days of the Roman Empire.

The debate is shifting, and the egalitarians have the weight of historical and biblical scholarship on their side, even if complementarians seem not to be paying attention to that. The day will soon arrive when the issue of equality for women will be no more a debatable subject than racism and slavery. It can't arrive soon enough.

I believe the egalitarian view simply fits better within the overall meta-narrative of Scripture, and therefore must be the correct view. As Peppiatt says:

"I frame this with Paul's theology of what it means to be 'in Christ' as a male and female, baptized into one faith, and one church, filled with the same Spirit who pours out gifts as he will regardless of race, sex, age, and status. For this reason I believe the onus is on the hierarchicalists to explain why and how they understand the impact of the Christian gospel on families, communities, churches, and societies to give rise to the exclusion, subordination, and silencing of women. There is no precedence for this in Scripture."[137]

Exactly. There is no precedence in Scripture for the subordination of women. The freedom we have in Christ isn't just for white men. The complementarian view of so-called 'biblical womanhood' is no more biblical than slavery.

---

[137] Peppiatt, *Scripture's Vision for Women*, p.141-2.

Further Reading

Barr, Beth Allison, Dr. *The Making of Biblical Womanhood: How the Subjugation of Women Became Gospel Truth* (2021).

Bessey, Sarah. *Jesus Feminist: An Invitation to Revisit the Bible's View of Women* (2013).

Edwards, Bob. *Let My People Go* (2013).

Edwards, Bob & Helga. *Equality Workbook: Freedom in Christ from the Oppression of Patriarchy* (2016).

Jenkins, Phillip. *The Next Christendom* (2011).

Peppiatt, Lucy. *Rediscovering Scripture's Vision for Women* (2019).

_____. *Women and Worship at Corinth: Paul's Rhetorical Arguments in 1 Corinthians* (2015).

Swidler, Leonard. *Jesus Was a Feminist* (2007).

_____. *Biblical Affirmations of Women* (1979).

Webb, William. *Slaves, Women & Homosexuals* (2001).

6

Isn't the Old Testament Archaic?

If everything in the Bible is not 100% relevant to us in the 21st century, can it still be the Word of God?

THE ORIGINAL *STAR TREK* series that ran from 1966 to 1969 was radical for its time, both ethically and morally. The cultural backdrop of the late 60's was dominated by a hugely unpopular and bloody war, racial tensions and civil unrest. The civil rights movement was at its peak and race riots were setting American cities on fire.

Some US states had laws forbidding inter-racial marriages, and there were still racist laws that allowed Blacks to be banned from lunch counters, restaurants, clubs and public washrooms. Sexism was alive and well, and it was particularly difficult for women to enter most careers outside of nursing and homemaking, let alone rise to senior management in almost any organization.

Against this background *Star Trek* introduced a senior *female* bridge officer, and not just a woman, but a *Black* woman! Uhura remained a leading character throughout the entire series. The simple fact that there were *any* female crewmembers was ahead of its time. Yet the Enterprise was packed with women officers and crew of all races, a very progressive statement in itself for 1966.

As hard as it is to believe now, in the 1960's inter-racial dating and marriage was still hugely controversial. Many college and university campuses banned inter-racial dating.

Against this racially charged atmosphere, a *Star Trek* episode portrayed the first ever Black-White kiss on television.[138] NBC execs were so worried about the backlash from viewers in the South that they tried to have the scene edited out before the episode aired.

Star Trek episodes often carried anti-war and anti-racist themes, portraying the stupidity of racism and the senselessness of war and violence. Many anti-war themed episodes sought to show that we had to find a better way.

I'm old enough to remember what the social atmosphere was like in the late 60's and 70's, and so it's easy for me to appreciate how amazingly progressive and bold the writers, actors and producers of *Star Trek* were really being for their day.

But when my kids watch it with me, they don't get it. And in a way, I'm thankful for that. Because the things that were huge issues when I was their age are no longer considered controversial. It doesn't even occur to them that it could be a problem.

An inter-racial kiss? No one thinks anything of it and romance between races is common fare in movies and television. And rightfully so. A Black female officer? Of course, why not?

Back in the day these things in *Star Trek* were so ahead of its time that it was risky to portray them on TV, yet millennials watching re-runs today can easily miss those cues. In fact, they may be offended at the subtle sexism still evident in the original series.

---

[138] Season 3, Episode 10, "Plato's Stepchildren"

The Old Testament (OT) is like that. For its day, 3400 years ago in the 2nd millennium B.C., the OT was ahead of its time, but it's easy for modern readers to miss that because we are no longer familiar with the cultural climate of the original writers, and simply dismiss it as archaic.

In the first chapter we looked at how the Bible, especially the words of Christ and the New Testament, is ethically advanced by modern standards, and in many crucial ways ahead of us when it comes to a just and fair vision for society.

In this chapter we'll look at the Old Testament and the archaic passages found in it – those parts of the Bible that aren't so advanced – and show why the presence of archaic passages should not be taken as evidence that the Bible can't be the Word of God. In fact, such passages were there for good reason, even if they no longer apply to us in the 21st century.

In a nutshell (spoiler alert), they presented a giant leap forward ethically for people at the time, meant to get an iron age tribe moving in the right direction, socially and morally speaking. Those laws appear outdated to us only because we have the privilege of being further along on the moral journey.

What You Didn't Know About the Ancient Near East Could Hurt You

A favorite pastime of militant atheists is to dig up a weird verse from the Old Testament and hold it up for ridicule, using it as evidence that the Bible can't be the word of God.

But as we will see, that only works by 'parking' on a few isolated passages and ignoring the rest of the Bible. You can say anything about anyone, or any book, if you lift its words out of context.

So what do we do with these archaic passages of the Old Testament? Do we take them as evidence that the Bible can't be the inspired word of God? Do we just chuck it and walk away?

The Bible is a collection of 66 books written over a span of some 15 centuries, containing a rich heritage of aesthetically beautiful literature in a wide range of literary forms: allegorical, historical narrative, apocalyptic, wisdom literature, poetry, prophetic literature, legal statutes, case law, and didactic (instructional) letters.

The first 5 books of the Bible (Genesis, Exodus, Leviticus, Numbers, Deuteronomy) are collectively known as the Pentateuch. They are also referred to as the Law, or the *Law of Moses*, because the majority of content in these books is the 'Law' given to Israel by Moses.

Authorship of these books has traditionally been credited to Moses. It is beyond the scope of this book to dive into a full scholarly discussion of authorship, but the prevailing general consensus among biblical scholars is that the Pentateuch, as it has come down to us, had several authors and was edited into its final form much later in Jewish history, shortly after the Babylonian captivity.

However, these later editors were almost certainly working on documents originally written by Moses, and possibly others, during the 40 years the Hebrews lived in the desert before Joshua led them across the Jordan River into Canaan.

The OT begins with the Pentateuch, followed by 17 books of history, poetry, songs, wisdom literature, allegory and even some romantic literature.

At the end of the Old Testament is another group of 17 books collectively referred to as the *Prophets*, written by several different prophets living hundreds of years after Moses, from around 700 B.C. to 400 B.C.

Readers today may be inclined to think that the content of the prophetic books will be prophesy – predictions of the future – because of what the term 'prophet' has come to mean today.

But that's not the case with the Jewish prophets. The main role of the Old Testament prophet was to remind the people of Israel of the Law and bring them back to faithful obedience to it. It was not to predict future headline news.

However, not the laws we may think. They were entirely unconcerned with religious rules, ceremonial practices or civil legal codes. Never once do they criticize the Israelites for failing to stone an adulterer or execute a homosexual.

Instead, they berate the nation, especially the rulers and wealthy upper classes, for their religious hypocrisy and failure to help the needy.

The prophets were relentless in denouncing the ruling class for their dutiful observance of religious ritual and temple (church) worship, *while at the same time they neglected the plight of the poor and robbed their hired workers of fair wages!*

This was the main thing that got them into trouble with the prophets, and according to the prophets the main thing getting them into trouble with God, and the reason God was getting ready to judge the nation.

For instance, the prophets Isaiah and Amos thundered that God expected the nation to act justly towards all people, *especially the poor and vulnerable*.

Isaiah said that God hated their outward shows of religion, because "in the day of your fast [religious ritual observances] you *do as you please* and *oppress all your workers*." He called on them to "take away the yoke (of oppression)," and reminded them that instead of observing ceremonial temple worship, God wanted them to free people from economic and legal oppression:

> "This is the fast I choose: loose the bonds of wickedness, undo the straps of the yoke, to let the oppressed go free and to break every yoke", "share your bread with the hungry, bring the homeless poor into your house, to cover the naked." (Isaiah 58).

In other words, instead of fasting and performing other religious rituals, take steps to alleviate human suffering. According to the prophets, true religion is practised by how you treat other people, not in singing, dancing and making donations to your church.

At no time do any of the prophets bring up any archaic Mosaic law, of the sort that modern people would find offensive today (for good reason), such as laws in Leviticus to stone adulterers and execute homosexuals.

The salient point to be noted here is the movement in the biblical narrative *away* from archaic legal codes written in the early days of Jewish history, towards something better.

By the time we reach the prophets, at the end of the Old Testament hundreds of years after Moses, the archaic punitive laws have completely dropped from the biblical narrative, replaced by reminders of what true religion consists of: compassionate care towards the poor and needy and removing the yoke of oppression.[139]

This theme is picked up by Jesus Christ and carried through in the Gospels, in which Jesus explicitly overturns Mosaic legal codes requiring law breakers to be executed, replacing them with the greater "law of love."

Not once do you ever see Jesus saying anything to the crowds like, "Hey, I've notice you haven't been very vigilant about rounding up adulterers, fornicators, drunks, homosexuals and other sinful people for the punishment they deserve. There haven't been nearly enough adulterers and homosexuals stoned lately. Come on, get with it. Have you forgotten what it says in Leviticus?"

Instead, Jesus abolished the repressive legal codes in the Old Testament, replacing it with a new command: "A new command I give to you, that you love one another... By this all people will know you are my disciples." (John 13:34-35).

Jesus illustrated this when he stopped a crowd of Pharisees and Scribes, two groups known for their zealous adherence to the Law of Moses, from stoning a woman caught in adultery.

The significance of this is that the Pharisees intended to do only what the Old Testament law commanded. Jesus stopped them, effectively abolishing that legal code and all the archaic, punitive laws in the OT.

We'll have a closer look at how Jesus did this a little later in this chapter. For now, we just want to make note of the ethical movement in the Bible from the OT to Jesus and the Gospels.

---

[139] For a fuller and deeper look into this fascinating topic, please read *The Prophets* by Jewish scholar Abraham Heschel.

However, much of the legal code in the OT, including many of the laws we find so archaic and backwards today, were still ahead of its time in Moses' day.

A big part of the challenge for the modern reader is that we are far removed from the cultural and historical context of the Ancient Near East (ANE), so it's hard for us to fully appreciate what's happening within the message of the Old Testament. We're separated by 3400 years of time, and are light years away, figuratively speaking, from that cultural milieu.

Life in the ANE was crude, harsh and brutal beyond imagination in comparison to the 21st century. They didn't have the same sets of ideas around social justice, fair play, equality and human rights that we take for granted today.

For instance, in that world, child sacrifice, bestiality (sex with animals) and incest were culturally normal. So Moses actually had to tell them things that you generally wouldn't have to tell people now. Things like: "don't sacrifice your children to the gods", "don't have sex with close relatives", "don't have sex with animals," and "slaves are people, not property. You can't just kill and maim them."

Child sacrifice was routine and common place. Slavery was considered natural – just part of the natural order of things. The lower classes were considered inferior by nature and suitable only as slaves. They did not have the same aversion to slavery and human sacrifice that we have today. Our concept of 'human rights' which we take for granted was not even a category of thought for them.

When we read the laws laid down by Moses in Exodus and Leviticus and compare them to the surrounding cultures of Moses' day, we see that the Old Testament laws were a substantial improvement for their time. They weren't archaic for the original audience – they were shockingly liberal.

In *Is God a Moral Monster?* Paul Copan examines the laws of the Old Testament, plots them against the background of the ANE at the time Moses wrote them, and shows how they were a big step forwards morally and ethically for the day.

> "How then did God address the patriarchal structures, primogeniture (rights of the first born), polygamy, warfare, servitude/slavery, and a number of other fallen [inferior, backwards] social arrangements...He met Israel partway. As Jesus stated in Matthew 19:8, 'Because of the hardness of your hearts Moses permitted you to divorce your wives; but from the beginning it has not been this way.' We could apply this passage to many problematic structures within the ancient Near Eastern context: 'Because of the hardness of your heart Moses permitted servitude and patriarchy and warfare and the like, but from the beginning it has not been this way.' They were not the ideal and universal."[140]

Bill Webb termed this as 'redemptive movement'.[141] The idea is straightforward enough. In the Bible, God is portrayed as meeting people where they are, socially and

---

[140] Copan, *Is God a Moral Monster?* p. 60
[141] William Webb, *Slaves, Women & Homosexuals* (2001). Dr. Webb was my professor in seminary, and I'm grateful for his insights on how to handle ethical issues raised by some difficult Old Testament passages.

ethically, and taking them in incremental steps in the right direction.

The Imperfect Gives Way to the Perfect

A major theme of the New Testament (NT) is that the Gospel of Jesus Christ – including His message of love, mercy and forgiveness – is *better* than the Old Testament regulations which emphasize obedience to the letter of the law, and judgement for breaking it.[142]

This is woven throughout the NT. Ephesians 2:13-16 describes how Christ has abolished the OT laws and ordinances, making a better way of reconciliation for us with God.

An entire book in the NT, Hebrews, is devoted to the theme that "Jesus deserves far more glory than Moses" (3:3). The book of Hebrews is one long sustained argument that the New Testament under Jesus Christ is "far better" than the old laws under Moses:

7:22, "This makes Jesus the guarantor of a *better* covenant."

8:6, "But now Jesus, our High Priest, has been given a ministry that is *far superior* to the old priesthood, for he is the one who mediates for us a *far better* covenant with God, based on *better* promises." (NLT)

The writer of Hebrews uses the OT itself to make the case. In Heb. 8:1-12, Jeremiah 31:31-34 is quoted at length, starting with: "The days are coming, says the LORD, when I will make a new covenant with the people of Israel."

This passage in Hebrews points out that the Old Testament laws were less than perfect, concluding with: "In

---

[142] See Mat. 19:8; Romans 7:6; 8:2; Heb. 1:1-14; 3:3; 7:22; 8:1-13.

speaking of a new covenant, he makes the first one obsolete. And what is becoming obsolete and growing old is ready to vanish away." (8:13).

In other words, the OT wasn't perfect and was meant to be replaced. Even the Old Testament admits this, as the book of Hebrews points out.[143]

So we needn't get too hung up on those OT passages we find difficult to accept and agonize over questions about why they are there. Jesus abolished them and the Bible itself says that they've been made obsolete. The biblical story has moved away from the archaic elements of the OT and into the good news of the Gospel.

However, the OT laws were a necessary starting point considering where people were socially at the time. As Paul Copan summarizes:

> "...these laws [in the Old Testament] weren't the permanent, divine ideal for all persons everywhere. God informed his people that a new, [better and] enduring covenant would be necessary (Jer.31:31; Ezek. 36). By the Old Testament's own admission, the Mosaic law was inferior and future looking."[144]

Can Archaic Laws Still be the Word of God?

Of course this raises the question: why have the less-then-ideal passages at all? Even if the laws in Exodus and Leviticus were an improvement over the times, many of them are still crude and backwards compared to what we know today. If the Bible is the Word of God, and God is

---

[143] See also Ezekiel 36.
[144] Copan, *Is God a Moral Monster?* p.59

supposed to be perfect and all-knowing, why are those archaic passages there? Why not just go right for the ideal and lay it all out?

Short answer: because God knows people can't change that fast.

Slightly longer answer: the ideals are found in the Bible. So keep reading. Don't stop at Leviticus.

God doesn't change, but people and society need to, and God accommodates Himself to us. He is also smart enough to realize, something his critics seem to overlook, is that moral improvement can't be made all at once. You have to meet people where they are and start from there, and then take them in manageable steps in the right direction – morally speaking.

Trying to force people to change faster than they are capable of is not a compassionate way to treat them. And on a more pragmatic level, it simply doesn't work.

For arguments sake, lets just assume that we are at the apex of social evolution, with our superior approach to equal rights, improved civil rights (at least in comparison to the 14th century B.C.), rejection of slavery, and so on. God, being all-knowing, would presumably have expected these ancient nomads to be more like us.

Not to put too fine a point on it, I think it goes without saying that getting a society of ancient nomads to make the leap into a 21st century system of ethics and social values is impossible.

It can't be done, anymore than, say, you could force our 21st century society to suddenly implement *en masse* the value systems of a superior future society like that of, say, *Star Trek*: eliminate poverty, eliminate the use of money; eliminate hunger and homelessness; make universal education and healthcare available to everyone regardless of social status.

Even if you could get everyone to agree that such goals were desirable ideals to work towards, (and many today would argue the point), it has to be worked towards gradually. It can't be done all at once.

God isn't a tyrant, despite Dawkins' assertions to the contrary. God's approach is very compassionate. Those archaic bits are there precisely because God is omniscient and compassionate. He was meeting the original audience where they were, culturally, spiritually and ethically, and moving them forwards, in steps they could handle.

Incremental Steps in the Right Direction

Critics often disparage the Bible for its perceived antiquated passages. If God really inspired the Bible, as the argument goes, He would have known better than to decree such laws.

But giving up on the Bible because of a few outdated passages at the beginning of the OT is like stopping halfway through a book and not reading through to the last chapter to see how it concludes.

A quick survey of the Bible from beginning to end on some of the more troublesome passages will illustrate what is meant by incremental steps from an iron age society towards the moral ideal: stoning, slavery, women and retaliation.

Jesus' New Approach to the Old Testament

In Exodus there are commands that adulterers and other certain lawbreakers are to be put to death by stoning.

1,500 years later Jesus Christ abolished them and radically reinterprets the entire Old Testament legal code.

A woman caught in adultery is dragged out in front of the crowd to be stoned according to the Law of Moses. Jesus stopped them and said: "Let him who is without sin among you be the first to throw a stone at her." (John 8:1-11, ESV).

The men who wanted to execute the woman all dropped their stones and walked away, leaving Jesus alone with the woman. He said to her, "I don't condemn you, go and from now on sin no more."

That's it. Having released her from capital punishment, he didn't give her a reduced sentence. No fines, reduced jail time, or community service. No lingering conviction. He just released her.

The significance of this is far reaching. Christ didn't limit his injunction to the particular sin at hand. He didn't say to the men holding the rocks, "Let him who is without the *sin of adultery* be the first to cast a stone." He simply said, "let him who is without sin be the first..."

Any sin.

Since Christ's eligibility requirement for throwing rocks was to be free of sin – any sin – this will also apply across the entire Mosaic code, not just the law for adultery. No one is without sin, so no stone can be cast at anyone for anything.

Therefore the principle Christ established in this passage overturns all the Mosaic laws that required punishment for breaking a law – any law – not just adultery.

If the charge against the woman happened to be theft, the same criteria would apply: let him who is without sin be the first to cast a rock.

If a man is caught with another man: well, let him who is without sin be the first to cast a rock.

So Christ not only overturned the archaic Old Testament code to stone adulterers, he also effectively overturned all the Old Testament codes requiring punishment for any offense.

No one is without sin, so no stone can be thrown for any sin.

While this may be viewed as a 'get out of jail free' card, Jesus wasn't handing the woman a license to keep on sinning. He also told her: "go, and sin no more."

Christ took this even further, beyond the punitive laws in the Old Testament, to how we are to view and interpret the *entire* Old Testament.

During the course of an extended conversation with Jesus, an expert in the Law of Moses asked him which of all the commandments was the greatest (Mat. 22:34-40). Quoting Deut. 6:5, Jesus answered: "You shall love the Lord your God with all your heart and with all your soul and with all your mind."

But Jesus didn't stop there. Without being asked, he went on to include Lev.19:18, "And the second is like it: You shall love your neighbor as yourself. On these two commandments depend all the Law and the Prophets."[145]

Jesus packed a lot into this short message. The entire Old Testament *depends* – is summed up – in these two commands. Another way to think of that is these two commandments are to take precedence in how we interpret and understand the entire Old Testament.

---

[145] The Law and the Prophets is how Jews at that time referred to their Scripture, what we call the Old Testament in our Bibles today.

Therefore any conclusions we might draw from any particular verse *must not conflict* with these two overriding rules. The entire Old Testament is to be interpreted through the lens of Deut. 6:5 (love God) and Lev. 19:18 (love your neighbor as yourself).

Even our love for God fits within the "law" to love our neighbor. As already discussed in chapter 1, and touched on as well in chapter 4, we cannot love God without loving people: "he who does not love his brother cannot love God" (1 John 4:20-21).

In other words, we are to view the entire Old Testament in a new way, through the lens of love for people, compassion for others, and re-interpret the Scripture along those lines.

As Jesus said in Mat.7:12, treating others as we want to be treated, was "the *essence* of the Law".

On this basis Christ showed us we aren't to follow the archaic passages in the Old Testament, such as stoning. He abolished them. No longer are we to view religious faithfulness to the Bible as legalistic adherence to archaic legal code, but that: "The entire law is fulfilled in a single decree: 'Love your neighbor as yourself.'" (Galatians 5:14).

This is a clear example of the ethical movement in Scripture from the Old Testament to the New, from archaic to progressive.

Second, servitude/slavery. We tackled the slavery texts in detail in chapter 4, so I will be brief with this illustration.

The very earliest parts of the Old Testament contain legislation on the treatment of servants and slaves. Sometimes this word is translated as *slave* in English language Bibles, which can cause confusion. As discussed in chapter 4, translating the word as servant would more accurately reflect the original meaning.

The laws in Exodus are a significant improvement over what was common in ancient societies at the time. The Mosaic laws stipulated that you could not mistreat a servant. If you mistreated your servant, they were to be set free. If you injured or maimed your servant, they went free.

All servants were to be set free after a period of six years service and given enough money when they left so they could get a new start on life.

Runaway servants and slaves were not to be returned to their masters, but sheltered, protected and given refuge.

The slave trade was severely condemned. Kidnapping was forbidden. Kidnappers, as well as and anyone caught with a stolen person in their possession, were to be put to death and the slave freed.

These Jewish laws established the concept of "human rights". That human beings were not property, but people with rights, and were more important than money or the financial gain of their masters.

I don't imagine many of us will have difficulty with such concepts today, but for 1400 BC they were shockingly liberal and light-years ahead of the cultural norms of the time.

In the ancient world, slaves were property, fully owned by their masters who could do with them what they wished – like any other piece of property. The slave owner's rights over their slaves were absolute.[146] Babylonian Law said that runaway slaves were to be returned to their masters, and stipulated the death penalty for anyone assisting or hiding a fugitive slave.[147]

---

[146] Peter Garnsey, *Ideas of Slavery from Aristotle to Augustine* (Cambridge University Press, 1996), p. 1.
[147] The Laws of Hammurabi, codes #15 to 20.

Paul Copan summarizes: "Are these Exodus laws perfect, universal ones for all people? No, but in this and other aspects, we continually come across improved legislation for Israelite society in contrast to surrounding ancient Near Eastern cultures. As Jewish scholar Nahum Sarna observes... 'This law – the protection of slaves from maltreatment by their masters – is found nowhere else in the entire existing corpus of ancient Near Eastern legislation.'"[148]

As we move forward through the Bible from Exodus into the New Testament, we see further progression to the ideal, in which all people, men and women of all races, are fully equal and to be released from all forms of oppression, discussed in some detail in chapters 1 and 4.

Third, the treatment and standing of women. A survey of passages discussing women will also illustrate the ethical movement from the less-than-ideal of the Old Testament to the ideal we find in the New. I'll also be brief here because this topic is covered in detail in Chapter 5.

In Exodus we find passages discussing the roles of women that are certainly less than ideal from our vantage point. However, they were a big improvement for its day.

Later in the Old Testament, women are allowed to inherit from their fathers just like sons – another step in the right direction. Then a few hundred years after Moses, a woman is the top political leader of the entire nation.

The story of Deborah can be read in the Book of Judges, chapters 4 and 5. Not only is she a very successful national leader, but she's also described as being more effective as a

---

[148] Paul Copan, *Is God a Moral Monster*, p. 136. Sarna quote taken from *Exodus* (Philadelphia: Jewish Publication Society, 1991) page 124, by Nahum M. Sarna.

leader than some of the male judges in the same book – especially Samson.

A few hundred years after Deborah, in the Book of Joel, women are invited into priestly roles just like men.

Finally, the New Testament puts the final nail in the coffin for misogyny and racism. Galatians 3:28 says that in Christ, there is no longer any male or female, slaves or free, Jew or Gentile. In other words, we are all equal.[149]

Fourth, retaliation. In Matthew 5:38-42, Jesus said (quoting an Old Testament law): "You've heard it said, 'an eye for an eye, a tooth for a tooth'. But I say unto you, do not resist the one who is evil. If someone slaps you on the cheek, turn to him the other also. If anyone sues you for your tunic, let him have your cloak as well…Give to the one who begs of you, and do not refuse the one who would borrow."

"An eye for an eye" is found in several places in the Old Testament.[150] This OT law was not an endorsement for revenge, but intended to place limits on punishment to fit the crime. In an ancient world in which punishment and acts of revenge often far exceeded the original crime,[151] this law, while not perfect, was an improvement and served to temper punishment to be proportional.

In the New Testament we see further improvement. This ethical progression from the OT "an eye for an eye" is reflected throughout the New Testament. In 1 Peter 3:9 we find: "do not trade insult for insult, evil for evil, but on the contrary bless." And in Romans 12:17-21: "Repay no one evil

---

[149] For those familiar with the New Testament, you may be thinking of a couple of troublesome passages that would appear to contradict Gal.3:28. I cover that in detail in Chapter 5.
[150] Lev.24:20; Ex.21:24; Deut.19:21.
[151] For example, see the Babylonian Code of Hammurabi.

for evil...do not be overcome by evil, but overcome evil with good."

The entire chapter of Matthew 5 is a series of formulaic expressions: *"You've heard it said ..., but I say unto you..."* in which Jesus quotes an OT law and then improves on it with his interpretation emphasizing the greater compassion and concern for other people by which we are to behave. In doing so he laid down the interpretative principles we are to follow.

This is illustrated throughout the gospels. On one sabbath day Jesus and the disciples were walking through a field of wheat. When the disciples start to pick wheat and eat it, some scribes (experts in the OT law) complain that they are breaking the sabbath. Christ responded with "Leave them alone. The sabbath was made for man, not man for the sabbath."

On another sabbath day, Jesus healed a blind man. When some religious leaders complained that he should not be healing on the sabbath, Jesus pointed out that "who of you if he has a donkey that falls into a ditch on the sabbath would not pull him out. How much more should this man be healed on the sabbath."

Putting Our Thinking Caps On

From these stories we see that Jesus was not a biblical literalist, but advocated a thoughtful interpretation of God's word that placed a greater emphasis on mercy and compassion.

On several occasions he ripped into the Jewish experts of the Old Testament for their literal, static interpretation of the law while ignoring "the weightier matters of the law: justice and mercy and faithfulness" (Mat. 23:23).

There are several instances where Christ Himself used reasoning to show how we are to properly interpret the Scripture. One of my favorites is from Luke 13:10-17.

On one Sabbath day Jesus was teaching in a synagogue. There was a disabled woman present who He healed. This offended the ruler of the synagogue, who said that there are six days for work, and the woman should have returned on any other day to be healed, not on the Sabbath.[152]

Jesus didn't quote scripture back at them, but called them hypocrites and blasted them with a solid bit of logic, pointing out that they all untie their ox or donkey from the barn and lead it away for watering on the Sabbath. How much more, Jesus said, should this crippled woman be healed on the Sabbath.

There are other situations where Jesus used reasoning to re-interpret the Law along the lines of love, mercy and compassion. Take for instance the case of the woman caught in the act of adultery discussed earlier.

When the pharisees dragged the unfortunate woman out into the public square, Jesus said to them: "Let the man without sin throw the first stone." Then he started writing in the dust of the ground.

What he wrote isn't recorded, but interpreters have long suspected that he was listing the sins of the men present who wanted to stone the woman. We don't really know, but I think it's a good guess. All the men walked away and left the woman alone with Jesus.

Point taken. On the surface, in one sense Jesus dismissed the commandment to stone adulterers. But something much deeper and profound was happening. He

---

[152] The 4th Commandment stipulates that people are to rest from all work on the Sabbath. Exodus 20:1-17.

was setting aside legal codes so that a much more important 'law' could be fulfilled: the 'law' of mercy, love and forgiveness.

The overriding theme in the NT is that everything in Scripture is to be interpreted through the lens of love. Historically Christians have understood that the Bible need not always be interpreted literally. Clement in the first century taught this, and said that some passages are allegories. Augustine said the same.

The Catholic church has always held that scripture was not necessarily literal and was subject to interpretation. The Protestant reformers rejected literalism, and the need to interpret the Bible was one of the key principles of the Reformation.

Critics delight in disparaging the Bible by selecting certain passages and holding them up for ridicule. But that only works by 'parking' on a few isolated passages and insisting on a static, literal interpretation which ignores Jesus and the rest of the Bible. In their antagonism towards the Bible, they are only interested in trashing it, and as a result often fail to properly understand it.

Conclusion

As we read through the entire Bible from the days of Moses to the time of Christ, we see a clear movement from the iron age ethics of Moses' day to the modern ethics we're more familiar with today, as taught by Christ.

The presence of a few outdated passages should not be taken as evidence that the Bible isn't the word of God. The Bible is an old book, originally written for an ancient audience thousands of years ago. So of course there are going to be some passages that, for us, are no longer relevant. Why should that surprise us?

Not everything in the Bible is going to be about us. But that doesn't mean it's not the word of God. What should surprise us is that a two-thousand-year-old book *not only remains* extremely relevant today but *is ahead of us ethically!* As discussed in Chapter One, the New Testament presents us with a social ethic vastly superior to our own culture.

Further Reading

Cahill, Thomas. *The Gift of the Jews* (1999).
Copan, Paul. *Is God a Moral Monster?* (2011).
Fee, Gordon. *How to Read the Bible for All Its Worth* (2014).
Heschel, Abraham. *The Prophets* (1955).
Pritchard, J.B., ed., *Ancient Near Eastern Texts Relating to the Old Testament* (2nd ed., Princeton, 1950).
Webb, William. *Slaves, Women & Homosexuals* (2001).

7

Is God a Genocidal Monster?

"…they even burn their babies in the fire to their gods."[153]

THE BIBLE PORTRAYS GOD as a God of love, mercy and compassion who is very patient with our failings. My job as a theologian would be a lot easier if that's all I had to talk about. You can talk all day about a God of love without ruffling any feathers. But the Bible also talks about a God who will judge, and that doesn't always go down so well.

There's no way around it. God did order the destruction of Canaan – and according to the Bible he had good moral reasons. Just as the Nazi's burned Jews in fiery ovens, the Canaanites burned babies in the fire to their gods. That's not an exaggeration, nor a description of just some weird peripheral cult in Canaan at the time. Burning babies had become a normalized part of their regular, mainstream life. Just as it had in many ancient nations, human sacrifice was normal and expected.

Let me repeat that. It was part of their mainstream life. One of the main Canaanite deities was called Molech. The idol of this god was a large statue built of iron, with a fire pot in its belly and long outstretched arms. The priest of Molech would build a fire in the idol's belly, heating up the entire iron god. When the arms got red hot, worshippers would place live babies into its outstretched arms.

---

[153] The Book of Deuteronomy, 12:31.

Whenever a new city or village was founded, babies would be buried alive under the foundations of the walls as a sacrifice to the gods. Temple sex and bestiality were also normal. Sex was seen as a magical act, initiated to excite the gods, who would respond by pouring their semen out upon the earth to fertilize it.

Then there was Anath, the Canaanite goddess of sex. She was pleasant enough. Here is a description of Anath given by an archeologist:

> "The blood was so deep that she waded in it up to her knees – nay, up to her neck. Under her feet were human heads, above her human hands flew like locusts. In her sensuous delight she decorated herself with suspended heads while she attached hands to her girdle. Her joy at the butchery is described in even more sadistic language: 'Her liver swelled with laughter, her heart was full of joy, the liver of Anath was full of exaltation.' Afterwards Anath 'was satisfied' and washed her hands in human gore before proceeding to other occupations."[154]

These are what the pagan gods were like, and their human worshippers gave them the form of worship the gods demanded. In speaking of the Canaanites, Deuteronomy tells us that: "every abominable thing that the Lord hates they have done for their gods, for they even burn their sons and their daughters in the fire to their gods."[155]

---

[154] William Albright, *Archeology and the Religion of Israel* (Baltimore: John Hopkins Press, 1968), p. 77. Quoted in Paul Copan, *Is God a Moral Monster?* p. 159.
[155] Deut. 12:31

It was for this evil God said he was driving the Canaanites out.[156] Later in Deuteronomy God warns Israel not to be like the Canaanites, who "burn their sons and daughter" in the fire as an offering. "For because of these abominations the Lord your God is driving them out before you."[157]

Militant atheists accuse God of being a genocidal maniac, but this is not an accurate characterization. Perhaps they simply aren't reading far enough into the Book to understand what's going on. A more accurate characterization would be that this nation had sunk to such depraved levels that God's actions were justifiable.

Think Nazi Germany.

Nazi's burned Jews in ovens. What would it say of us if we had been ambivalent in the face of such horror? Were we wrong in our fight to bring the Nazi reign of terror to an end? The Bible documents that the Canaanites imposed similar horrors on their own children, and the historical and archeological evidence supports it. Why are we offended that God should judge such atrocities?

It would be a very dysfunctional God indeed who didn't judge. As Paul Moser puts it: "It would be a strange, defective God who didn't pose a serious cosmic authority problem for humans. Part of the status of being God, after all, is that God has a unique authority, or lordship, over humans. Since we humans aren't God, the true God would have authority over us and would seek to correct our profoundly selfish ways."[158]

---

[156] Deut. 9:4

[157] Deut. 18:10-13

[158] Paul Moser, philosopher. Quoted in Paul Copan, *Moral Monster*, p. 193.

Many people in the West today are fine with a God of love, if they deign to believe in Him at all, but have great difficulty accepting a God who judges. But it might help to stop and consider that this hasn't always been the case. Many people and cultures through history had no problem with a God who judges. That was expected of any self-respecting deity.[159] What they had a problem with were those very aspects of the Christian message Westerners find so appealing. Love, mercy and forgiveness.

The central message of the Christian gospel is that God will forgive us of our sin and evil-doing if we repent. This made no sense to Romans. To Roman thinking that would only encourage bad behavior. The Vikings, Saxons and Angles all eventually converted, but it took a long time, and one of the major stumbling blocks for these warrior cultures was the Christian message of love and mercy. Such virtues made a man weak. They were fine for women, but men of action had no use for them.

It is worth pointing out that it was for these 'weak' characteristics of the Christian religion that Hitler hated and despised Christianity. He considered Christian morality dangerous sentiments that weakened the race, because the weak and infirm were preserved and allowed to dilute the gene pool. There is no evolutionary survival value in allowing weak members of the species to survive. Nietzsche, the founding father of modern atheism, also despised Christianity for the same reason. It is no coincidence that during the Nazi Holocaust, it was not just Jews who were

---

[159] One of the most interesting stories of the Bible records how the Prophet Jonah was angry with God for *NOT* judging the nation of Assyria.

exterminated, but they also killed gypsies, invalids, and anyone considered weak and of a lower nature.[160]

Throughout the Bible we are told that God will judge various nations, and the reasons given for judgement are very informative: their treatment of the poor, the vulnerable and the innocent. Hundreds of biblical verses tell us that God evaluates societies by their treatment of the poor, and we are warned that He will judge accordingly.

Read through the Minor Prophets. This is a collection of short books at the end of the Old Testament. God judges Egypt because "they have shed innocent blood." (Joel 3:19). God promises to judge Israel "because they sell the righteous for silver, and the needy for a pair of sandals," (Amos 2:6). They are judged for "trampling on the heads of the poor", driving them down into the dust, and refusing to assist the afflicted (Amos 2:7). The wealthy (referred to as "cows") are those "who oppress the poor, who crush the needy" (Amos 4:1). Amos goes on to warn the wealthy of Israel: "Therefore because you trample on the poor and exact taxes from him," they will be judged (Amos 5:11). They will be judged because they "afflict the righteous" and "take bribes" and "turn aside the needy" (v.12).

God says that He despises their technically correct religious observances because they oppress the poor. Rather, he would prefer that they "let justice roll down like the waters, and righteousness like an ever-flowing stream." (Amos 5:21-24). Because they oppress and tax the poor, all their religious observance were meaningless to God. In the face of the social injustice and oppression of the poor as

---

[160] It is estimated that the Nazi's killed 200,000 disabled people, including the deaf and the blind, because they were considered useless burdens on society.

described by Amos and many other prophets, it would take a lobotomized God *not* to judge.

Militant atheists like Richard Dawkins and Sam Harris charge God with genocide. Genocide is their preferred term because it is much more emotionally charged and evocative then simply saying God judged the Canaanites for their extreme wickedness. Genocide carries overtones of racial hatred and prejudice, of undeserved massacre.

But God's judgement on Canaan wasn't genocide. It wasn't racially motivated. The Canaanites weren't an innocent group of nice people who just happened to be at the wrong place at the wrong time and got in Israel's way. God had morally justifiable reasons for judging them.

It's interesting that the call to destroy Canaan is also found in the same book of the Bible in which we find some of the highest and greatest calls to moral and social justice in all of literature. The calls to social justice in this book, frankly, are at least as great if not greater than the standards of our own western culture. There shall be no poor among you. Love your neighbor as yourself. Love the stranger and foreigner in your midst as yourself. Provide for the poor. Do not oppress the weak or take advantage of people's infirmities. Release all debtors of all debt every seven years. Don't be greedy.

The writer of Deuteronomy was not embarrassed to place the judgement of Canaan along side these texts. Could it be that's because Moses and the ancient Israelites saw no contradiction between the two concepts? They understood that the judgement of God flows out of his righteousness and that nations will be judged for their wicked treatment and oppression of the poor.

While difficult for our western minds to accept, God had good moral reasons for judging the Canaanite nation. We want a Santa Claus god who does what we want, gives us goodies, and never questions us or – horror of horrors – has the impertinence to judge us for wrong behavior. Since that is not the picture of God in the Bible, many refuse to believe.

But our dislike for an aspect of the Divine Nature presented in the Bible is not proof against His existence, and just might, instead, have more to say about us then we realize. As Paul Copan puts it: "Maybe the ideal 'God' in the Westerner's mind is just too nice. We've lost sight of good and just while focusing on nice, tame and manageable."[161]

I will conclude with the following thought from Miroslav Volf, a Yale Theologian who lived through the Yugoslavian civil war and saw first-hand the atrocities and horrors committed during that war.

"One could object that it is not worthy of God to wield the sword. Is God not love, long suffering and all powerful love? A counter question could go something like this: Is it not a bit too arrogant to presume that our contemporary sensibilities about what is compatible with God's love are so much healthier than those..." of other people through history? "...one could further argue that in a world of violence it would not be worthy of God not to wield the sword; if God were not angry at injustice and deception and did not make the final end to violence God would not be worthy of our worship."[162]

The Bible presents a God who is both love and anger, mercy and judgement. Many in the West would assume these are incompatible, but they aren't. Both aspects of the Divine Nature are necessary and necessarily go together. In fact, if God didn't get angry at injustice and take action, he

---

[161] Copan, *Is God a Moral Monster?* p. 192

[162] Miroslav Volf, *Exclusion & Embrace*, p. 303.

would hardly be a God of love. Indifference and ambivalence in the face of injustice and cruelty is not love. (1 Peter 2:21,23; Romans 12:18-21.)

In Christianity we find the spiritual resources to respond to violence with peace, and not continue the cycle of violence. What gives us the strength to *not* pick up the sword is understanding that God is also angry at injustice, a deeper and much more settled anger than the fickle human emotion we are capable of, with the sure knowledge that He will act. This is the promise of Revelation, in which God says he will judge the entire world for its wickedness and social injustice. This is the warning to us found in the Prophets and in Christ's own words. This is what we've seen in history. This is what we see in God's judgement on the Canaanites.

Further Reading

Copan, Paul. *Is God a Moral Monster?* (2011).
Lennox, John. *Gunning for God: Why the New Atheists Are Missing the Target* (2011).
Volf, Miroslav. *Exclusion & Embrace* (1996).

8

Is Faith Delusional?
(And Other Questions)

WHEN ATTACKING CHRISTIANS, Dawkins & Co. like to fill the pages of their books with a lot of small-caliber cheap shots, such as: faith is blind, prayer doesn't work, prayer is for lazy people, religion poisons everything and is generally bad for you, religious people are intolerant, religion is responsible for most of the wars in history, Hitler was a Christian, and so on.

The major themes of the God debate along the lines of science, evolution, morality, and social relevance are treated in separate chapters. In this chapter we'll look at many of the smaller pot shots often taken at believers.

Most of these small-caliber rounds are easily deflected by any well-read believer with a decent education. Atheists, however, are not always totally off the mark. Some criticisms of 'religion' are very fair. There have been brutalities, murders and crimes of all sorts committed by 'believers', sometimes even in the name of Christ.

Some religions are big business. Some churches, especially those that have bought into the 'Prosperity Gospel', are little more than money making rackets. The leaders of such churches often own mansions, yachts and airplanes worth millions of dollars.

Mainstream Christians are as alarmed as anyone at these lies and excesses in the name of Christ. The leaders of such churches do more harm than good and are an embarrassment to the community of faith. And Christians have often been the first to say so.

Some religious leaders are charlatans taking advantage of people's sincere faith, and it is the responsibility of Christians to make sure their giving is not going towards funding the lavish lifestyle of a charlatan.

However, it is not accurate or fair to paint all Christians with the same brush. As I said in chapter 4 regarding Christian support of slavery in the past, it bears repeating here: *Just because some Christians have been untrue to the Gospel doesn't make the Gospel untrue.*

Unfortunately, there are bad people in any large group, whether secular or religious in nature, and Christianity is not exempt from this. People being what they are, if you get enough of them together in any group, for any good or benign purpose, you are going to get some bad apples.

Faith is Delusional

According to Dawkins & Co., faith is delusional because it's not based on evidence. It is therefore a blind leap in the dark. They generally get it wrong on two major counts. First, they insist on their own narrow definition of faith, and they discount or ignore how Christians typically define faith.

It is a very self-serving approach. Naturally, atheists would prefer to think of faith as blind – it helps support their whole 'faith is delusional' mantra. But I find it odd that atheists, as persons who claim not to have faith, are so adamant in telling believers what faith should mean to them.

For instance, in his book Sig Sawyer references an online dictionary[163] that lists several definitions for the term 'faith'. The very first one is: Confidence or trust in a person or thing. But this meaning doesn't suit Sawyer's purpose, and he dismisses it. The 2nd, 3rd and 5th are more to his liking – and prefers option 2 the most: belief that is not based on proof.[164]

Naturally this is the meaning of faith preferred by atheists, but it is not what Christians usually mean by it.

Like many words in a language, the term 'faith' can carry a lot of different meanings. Sometimes the word is used in the sense of 'blind faith': believing in something without evidence, like the recent trend in some scientific circles to believe in various multiverse theories.

Sometimes it simply means belief in a system of thought, or a code of ethics, or a set of doctrines. It can mean all these things at different times. For the Christian, faith typically means confidence and trust in God. None of this precludes the use of evidence to support faith in God, nor does this require an absence of evidence. Many Christians have become believers *because* of the evidence.

When debating Christians, atheists should pay attention to how believers use the term. Because, frankly, when we are talking about our faith, it is our understanding of the term that applies. This brings us to the passage Sawyer quotes in Hebrews 11: "Faith is the assurance of things hoped for, the conviction of things not seen." (ESV)

There is of course a mystical element to faith, and Christianity has a rich mystical tradition. By its very nature, faith in God means we are believing in Someone who we can't see. As a believer, I have confidence in God, but let's be

---

[163] www.dictionary.com
[164] Sawyer, *Christianity Disproved*, page 142.

clear, He's not sitting on the couch next to me as I write this. I've never seen Him. Hebrews 11:1 is defining faith as an assurance and conviction of things not yet seen. Because we are confident in God, we trust that he will bring about his promises in the future, even if they are not yet here. Thus, biblical faith is grounded in a confident trust in the character of God. It is not a blind leap in the dark.

That's what the writer of Hebrews is talking about. John Lennox supplies a good definition of faith as understood by Christians.

"Faith is not a leap in the dark; it's the exact opposite. It's a commitment based on evidence... It is irrational to reduce all faith to blind faith and then subject it to ridicule. That provides a very anti-intellectual and convenient way of avoiding intelligent discussion."

Sawyer is repeating the same mistake made by Dawkins. Insisting on a definition of faith – a self-serving one that is an easy target – and knocking it down in order to claim some sort of victory over Christianity. But that whole approach lacks credibility.

It needs to be said that millions of Christians around the world from all walks of life claim to have had personal and powerful experiences of God's presence and Divine interventions in their life, as well as powerful answers to prayer, all of which has had a positive impact on their personal lives.

None of which can be empirically proved, of course, but I fail to understand why militant atheists feel the need to attack it. Not that their attacks are any real threat, I just don't understand why they bother. How is ridiculing the personal experience of believers any kind of rational argument against Christianity? Faith has helped many people turn their lives around in positive ways. Please explain to me how this is a bad thing?

Religion Still Poisons Everything – Even if it Does Make People Feel Better

Atheists typically assert that religious faith is generally a bad thing; some sort of neurosis or wish fulfillment – a crutch needed by weak people. This echoes the common assumption in mental health circles during the first half of the twentieth century that religion was some form of neurosis and would soon be replaced by the therapists' couch.[165]

Things have proven to be otherwise. Clinical studies from non faith-based research institutes have shown that religion is in fact good for people, and by extension society.

> "Yet the last quarter of the twentieth century has not been kind to the psychoanalytical vision. Most significant has been the exposure of Freud's views of religion (not to mention a host of other matters) as entirely fallacious. Ironically enough, scientific research in psychology over the past twenty-five years has demonstrated that, far from being a neurosis or source of neuroses as Freud and his disciples claimed, religious belief is one of the most consistent correlates of overall mental health and happiness. Study after study has shown a powerful relationship between religious belief and practice, on one hand, and healthy behaviors with regard to such problems as suicide, alcohol and drug abuse, divorce, depression, even, perhaps surprisingly, levels of sexual satisfaction in marriage, on the other.

---

[165] Freud, *Future of an Illusion*

In short, the empirical data run exactly contrary to the supposedly 'scientific' consensus..."[166]

David B. Larson, former National Institutes of Health psychiatrist, catalogued many of these studies. He had this to say regarding the summary of findings:

"If a new health treatment were discovered that helped to reduce the rate of teenage suicide, prevent drug and alcohol abuse, improve treatment for depression, reduce recovery time from surgery, lower divorce rates and enhance a sense of well-being, one would think that every physician in the country would be scrambling to try it. Yet, what if the critics denounced this treatment as harmful, despite research findings that showed it to be effective more than 80 percent of the time? Which would you be more ready to believe – the assertions of the critics based on their opinions or the results of the clinical trials based upon research?"[167]

The health treatment Larson is referring to is religious faith. A summary of the various studies can be found in David B. Larson and Susan S. Larson, *The Forgotten Factor in Physical and Mental Health: What Does the Research Show?* Rockville, MD: National Institute for Healthcare Research, 1994.

Contrary to the assertions made by Dawkins and others, repeated by Sawyer, religion is good for people and

[166] Patrick Glynn, *God: The Evidence*, pp. 60-61
[167] David B. Larson, "Have Faith: Religion Can Heal Mental Ills," *Insight on the News*, March 6, 1995, p. 18.

good for society. Many studies have born this out, but the findings are often ignored or overlooked. How can this be so?

Patrick Glynn hits the nail on the head: "To have overlooked such a powerful source of mental well-being – indeed, to have mistaken it for a form of mental *disorder* – cannot be counted a minor oversight in a discipline that nominated itself as the 'science' of mental health. It shows to what degree the term 'science' has been abused by the thinkers of modernity to mask what amounts to little more than a prior prejudice against the idea of God. In truth, there was nothing scientific about Freud's theory of religion."[168]

Guenter Lewy, prominent secular researcher, set out to prove that America doesn't need religion. Many people have argued that religion is foundational to morality and social stability, and Lewy intended to prove them wrong. In his own words, his book would be "a defense of secular humanism and ethical relativism."[169]

But as he examined the evidence, he changed his mind completely and ended up writing a book arguing that religion, particularly Christianity, correlates with lower rates of crime, drug abuse, teen pregnancy, and family breakdown.

Lewy, persuaded by the sheer weight of the evidence, instead wrote *Why America Needs Religion.* He concluded: "Contrary to the expectations of the Enlightenment, freeing individuals from the shackles of traditional religion does not result in their moral uplift…. No society has yet been successful in teaching morality without religion."[170]

---

[168] Patrick Glynn, *God: The Evidence*, p. 62

[169] Guenter Lewy, *Why America Needs Religion* (Grand Rapids, Michigan: Eerdmans, 1996).

[170] Lewy, *Why America Needs Religion*, p. 132-133

An article in The Boston Globe had this to say: "Even non-Christian researchers are beginning to acknowledge the correlations. Herbert Benson of Harvard, who claims no religious faith is famous for his catchy saying that we are all wired for god. Our bodies simply function better, he says, when we believe in god."[171]

While atheists like to argue that Christianity is bad for people and society, the evidence proves otherwise. A much better argument can be made that militant atheism is bad for society. One only has to look into North Korea and the atheist regimes of Eastern Europe prior to the collapse of the U.S.S.R.

Prayer is for Lazy People

"Prayer will forever be the recourse of the inactive," Sawyer announces in his book. People who pray are lazy, according to Sawyer, because they use prayer as an excuse to not do anything. [Sawyer:157].

Once again, we see an atheist expressing their idea of religion without reference to the facts. He may imagine this, but Christianity certainly doesn't teach it.

Christian doctrine does not teach passivity, or that prayer replaces social action. Quite the opposite: Christian doctrine teaches that active service must accompany prayer and faith. In fact, the New Testament explicitly warns us against the type of faith that would pay lip-service to belief in God that is not backed up by practical social action. As Christians often say: *you have to walk the talk.*

---

[171] See the interview with Benson by John Koch in *The Boston Globe Magazine*, November 9, 1997, at www.bostonglobe.com/globe/magazine/11-16/interview/. Cited in Pearcey, *Total Truth*, p. 60.

Saint James, the brother of Christ, said that we are not to just pray, but act: "But be doers of the word, and not hearers only." James 1:22

"Religion that is pure and undefiled before God and the Father is this: to visit orphans and widows in their affliction," James 1:27. At the time James wrote, the most vulnerable members of society were orphaned children and widows. In other words, true religion is demonstrated by taking care of the weak and vulnerable in our society.

James 2:14-17 says: "What good is it, my brothers, if someone says he has faith but does not have works? Can faith save him? If a brother or a sister is poorly clothed and lacking in daily food, and one of you says to them, 'Go in peace, be warmed and filled,' without giving them the things needed for the body, what good is that? So faith, by itself, if it does not have works, is dead."

James also made the point that merely believing in God isn't enough. "You believe in God, do you? So what? Even the demons believe, and shudder."

Saint John, one of the twelve apostles, had this to say: "but if anyone has the world's goods and sees his brother in need, yet closes his heart against him, how does God's love abide in him?... Let us not love in word or talk but in deed and in truth." (1 John 3:17).

Martin Luther King Jr. was a believer, a Baptist minister and a man of prayer. I don't think anyone needs to be reminded of how hard he worked for civil rights and the ultimate price he paid. His example is an inspiration for us all.

William Wilberforce was the British leader of the abolition movement. For decades he laboured for the abolition of slavery in the British Empire in the early 1800's. He was also a devout Christian and man of prayer.

I could also mention Florence Nightingale, the British nurse who founded the Red Cross. She worked harder than most of us work at our daily jobs. A believer and a person who prayed. I could go on, but I think you get the drift.

There are currently tens of thousands of faith-based organizations around the world with the goal of assisting the poor:

> "Instead of decreasing, religion is taking an increasingly central role in African political and developmental life (Deneulin and Bano, 2009; Haar and Ellis, 2006). Religious organisations do development for their ethos; notions of social justice, charity and service are critical to the work of religious groups, but also (and most of all) because of the lack of action and capability of the state. In Africa, and elsewhere, religious organisations have often had to pick up the slack precipitated by these failures of development and shortcomings of the state due to their inherent ability to connect to local contexts, communities and their beliefs. According to a World Bank report, 50 per cent of health and education services in Sub-Saharan Africa in 2000 were provided by faith-based organisations (World Bank, 2008). The evangelical development agency World Vision had an effective aid budget of $1.25 billion in 2002 (World Vision International, 2003). The World Bank noted that in Benin the Church represents "the most prominent and effective protection network" (Kliksberg, 2003). In Southern Africa the Church is equally prominent, in Malawi in the 1970s it was claimed that the annual budget of the *Christian Service Committee of the Churches of Malawi,* a key ecumenical organisation, was 1.5 times

the size of the state's entire development budget (World Faiths Development Dialogue, 2003). Until very recently in South Africa, the Catholic Church was providing more anti-retroviral treatment for people suffering from HIV than the state. In agriculture, too, the Church plays an important role not only in terms of agricultural extension but also in terms of influencing policy." [172]

"In many African countries facing severe shortages and poor distribution of health workers, faith-based organizations (FBOs) provide between 30%-70% of health care services. Moreover, FBO facilities often serve remote and rural areas where governments have the greatest difficulty in attracting and retaining health workers. Yet FBO health workers frequently remain under-recognized for their contributions and uncounted in national statistics." [173]

What About Other Religions? Isn't It Arrogant to Think Yours is the Right One?

"What is it that makes some people believe they have the absolute answer, and everyone else is wrong?" Sawyer asks.[174] Good question. However, the same scalpel can be applied to atheism. What makes atheists think they are right, and by default everyone else wrong? For that matter, what makes any of us think we are right about anything we

---

[172] https://www.e-ir.info/2011/09/27/religion-and-faith-based-organisations-in-africa-the-forgotten-actors/. Accessed Nov.18, 2019
[173] https://www.capacityplus.org/faith-based-organizations.html. Accessed Nov. 18, 2019
[174] Sawyer, *Disproved*, p.189.

believe? We can't direct this question at one group, religious or otherwise, without including atheists.

We are once again treated to the argument against God from the number of religions. No book written by a militant atheist would be complete without it. Some have estimated there are around three thousand religions in the world, including all the small tribal religions. For the sake of argument or rebuttal, it doesn't much matter if there are two or twenty-thousand. So, as the logic goes, given there are so many religions, how do you know yours is the correct one? Good question, but we also need to include all belief systems in the equation. The question can cut both ways and atheism is not exempt from this critique.

How do we come to think any particular religion or non-religious view is correct? The same way anyone comes to a position: by looking at the options and weighing the evidence. Isn't that what we all do? By reading, studying, doing the research, and talking to other people we know and trust and thinking deeply on the subject. That's not being arrogant, that's just what we all do as we try to decide what we believe.

I am a Christian because I believe there really is a God who cares how we live and treat each other. I believe faith is therefore a rational response to the existence of God. Atheists claim that faith is irrational only because they are making an *a priori* assumption that there is no God. But that is an assumption based on their worldview.

I am not an atheist because I don't believe it provides a sufficient rational basis for many things I know to be true – like *objective* moral standards.[175] The feeling that napalming babies is morally evil isn't just an illusion of my genes

---

[175] See Chapter 12 in this volume.

developed out of evolutionary processes. I am a Christian because I think it corresponds to reality better than any other system of thought, especially atheism. I believe that the existence of God is much more probable than His non-existence, making faith more reasonable, and therefore more rational, than atheism.

Religion is Responsible for Most of the Wars

Of course, no rant against Christianity would be complete without an oblique reference to all the wars religion is apparently responsible for. Usually they can't name any of them, other than the crusades,[176] but they just 'know' there's a bunch of them, and they'll repeat that assertion with all the moral certitude that only the uninformed are capable of mustering.

So how many wars in all of history can be properly blamed on 'religion'?

About 7%, actually.

Yes. I checked. Fortunately, I didn't have to count them all myself, someone else has already done that.[177] The *Encyclopedia of Wars* has catalogued all the wars in history over the past 5,000 years – totalling 1763. Only 123 were religious wars (7%). If you remove the 66 wars of Islam, that cuts it down to 3% and change. Another scholarly source, *The*

---

[176] Even those who bring up the Crusades usually know very little about them, how many there were and when they were fought, or what the body count was. There were very few and the body count was low, comparatively speaking.
[177] *The Encyclopedia of Wars*, 3-Volume Set, by Charles Phillips and Alan Axelrod

223

Encyclopedia of War by Gordon Martel,[178] confirms this, setting the count at 6% for religious wars.

What about secular wars? "...it actually gets worse for the atheists' claim. A strong case can be made that atheism, not religion, and certainly not Christianity, is responsible for a far greater degree of bloodshed. R.J. Rummel's work in his books, *Lethal Politics* and *Death by Government* places the secular body count at more than 100 million in the 20th century alone. Millions have died at the hands of atheist regimes like Mao Zedong, Joseph Stalin, Adolph Hitler, Vladimir Lenin, and others."[179]

Sawyer repeats what has become a mantra in our culture: "...there would be less bloodshed in the world...without religion." [Sawyer:164]. Despite the frequency of this assertion, the evidence shows that the opposite is true. There would be a whole lot less bloodshed in the world without atheism. Christianity accounts for just 3% of all the wars in all of history. Atheism is responsible for *much* more, the direct result of atheist states seeking to stamp out religion and establish their secular ideology. A 2014 report from the Institute for Economics and Peace further confirms this.[180]

More People in Prison are Religious, Therefore Atheism is Better and Must Be True

Citing an internet article that shows only a very small percentage of the prison population are atheists, and the

---

[178] *The Encyclopedia of War* edited by Gordon Martel.

[179] Brett Kunkle, http://www.str.org/articles/debunking-the-religious-wars-myth#.VzjJmTUrK00

[180] https://www.visionofhumanity.org/#/page/news/1085

majority are religious, Sawyer makes the argument that this is a real problem for believers. More prison inmates are religious, very few are atheists, therefore atheists are better.

I won't quibble with the stats – that is not my area of expertise. I did do an internet search of other articles trying to corroborate the article Sawyer uses. Without quibbling over the exact percentage, (the research I found varied) it does seem that over 50% of prison inmates are religious.

More than half the world population is religious, so it shouldn't be surprising that this is reflected roughly in the prison population. But that is rather beside the point. The problem is Sawyer's deeply flawed logic and the deductions he makes from these prison population stats.

Jews, as a people group, are *under-represented* in prison as a percentage of the overall population. Very few Jews, statistically, end up in jail. Does that make Jews better than the rest of us? If he can make that argument for atheists, then it must apply to all groups.

There are also more African-Americans in prison than Caucasians;[181] there are more men than woman. Using Sawyer's logic, what should we make of that? I think we need to be very careful indeed.

How would Sawyer apply his 'prison population' logic to church attendance? Women have a much higher representation in Christianity than men. Since militant atheists deride faith in God as delusional, wouldn't that make women more prone to delusion than men?

More than 60% Christians worldwide are women, and not predominantly white. Dark skinned people outnumber white skinned people dramatically around the world. In fact, given the numbers, the face of the Christian church

---

[181] U.S. Bureau of Justice Statistics, 2018

worldwide is best represented by a young, dark-skinned female. What deductions would they care to make about young women of colour using the same logic he applies to prison populations?

God is a Poor Designer

Atheists will often make an argument against the existence of God based on apparently bad design in nature. They will present examples of what they consider to be poor design, and from that argue that there cannot be a designer.

To use Sawyer's words: "If our creation was made by an all-knowing perfect designer then it would be without error..."[182]

Intelligent design theory (ID) argues that we can all intuitively distinguish the difference between the results of random forces in nature and the results of intelligent action.

> "An illustration that design theorists often use is Mount Rushmore. If you were driving through the mountains of South Dakota, and suddenly came upon the faces of four famous presidents carved into the rock, you would not think for a moment that they were the product of wind and rain erosion. You would instantly recognize the handiwork of an artist."[183]

Recognizing the imposition of order by an intelligent agent does not require that the results of this order also be 'perfect', at least as far as how we might define perfection.

---

[182] "Christian Viewpoints" in Christianity Disproved.
[183] Nancy Pearcey. *Total Truth*, p. 181.

I've already quoted this passage from Nancy Pearcey at length in Chapter 2, but I will repeat some of it here:

> "...design theory is the claim that design can be empirically detected ... this is something we do all the time. Walking along the beach we may admire the lovely pattern of ripples running across the sand, but we know it is merely the product of the wind and the waves. If, however, we come across a sandcastle with walls and turrets and a moat, do we assume it too was created by the wind and waves? Of course not ... But we intuitively recognize that those starting materials have a different kind of order imposed upon them. Design theory merely formalizes this ordinary intuition – just as all of science is largely formalized common sense."[184]

The sandcastle and Mount Rushmore do not simply *appear* to be designed. They *are* designed. Yet the sandcastle doesn't have to be perfect to recognize that it's the result of an intelligent agency. However, we often hear the claim from atheists that if a perfect designer is responsible for creation, then all of creation should therefore be absolutely perfect.

This is the 'if I were God game' atheists like to play. *If I were God, I would do such-and-such in such-and-such way. Since it has not been done that way, there can't be a Creator.*

> "The bad-design versus good-design discussion is often framed by an engineer's perspective, not an artist's or a mystic's... Why do we assume that God created the universe to be a watch, in which a self-winding

mechanism makes it 'better'? Maybe the universe is like a piano, or a novel with the author as a character, or a garden for other beings with whom God wants to interact."[185]

"For instance, in the Blind Watchmaker, Richard Dawkins ignores the larger demands of vision in his critique of the mammalian eye, zeroing in on the eye's so-called backward wiring...His analysis collapses under two mistakes. First, geneticist Michael Denton has clearly demonstrated that the backward wiring actually confers a distinct advantage by dramatically increasing the flow of oxygen to the eye. Dawkins the reductionist misses this because he analyzes organs in isolation when it suits his purpose. Then there is Dawkins obsession with neatness, his assumption that any proper Creator would idolize tidiness overall."[186]

Why assume that a Creator would approach design like an engineer with OCD, obsessed with neatness and utility? What if he is more like a whimsical artist? Aardvarks and platypuses come to mind. Creatures like Panda's and Koala bears speak to me of God's whimsicalness. God doesn't have to be concerned with efficiency and utilitarianism. He is allowed to have fun and be inefficient.

Then there is the question of optimal design in sub-components. There are many reasons why we should not expect to see perfection, from our limited viewpoint, in nature.

[185] William Dembski, (Ed.). *Evidence for God: 50 Arguments*, p. 117
[186] Dembski, (Ed.). *Evidence*, p. 118

First, component re-use. Engineers design systems with components that are meant to be re-used in other systems. This often means the sub-components will have parts that aren't needed for every system they are used in. Adaptive systems are inherently wasteful.

Second, God usually makes use of secondary agents to accomplish his work. These secondary agents often include physical laws. He does not need to make each atom as an act of special creation.[187] We are rarely in a position to fully understand all of the design objectives and constraints. Just because we can't see a purpose doesn't mean there isn't one.

> "It seems to me we should not make the mistake of assuming that God's perfect will for us is biological perfection, any more than we should assume that God's perfect will for us is the absence of suffering. It is those occasions when things aren't perfect that we often learn the most, and when our closeness to God, which is a higher goal than our own happiness, is most likely to come about. And so perhaps God in a merciful way speaks to us through our imperfections, and we shouldn't neglect the significance of that. The underlying assumption that we should all be genetically perfect doesn't necessarily make sense to me."[188]

Christian belief does not require perfection in nature. While Christian theology maintains that God is perfect, and the original creation was good and without error, Christian

---

[187] William Dembski, (Ed.). *Evidence for God: 50 Arguments for God*, p. 110.
[188] ibid., p. 110

theology also talks about humanities fall into sin and corruption. Nature was corrupted as well in the Fall. This corruption includes sickness, disease and death. So what we see around us isn't God's perfect, original intention, but a corruption of what God originally created.

The Devil in Fish-Net Stockings

According to Sawyer, "the devil made me do it" or "someone led me into temptation" [Sawyer:140] is used by religious people to excuse bad behavior. This is an assertion he makes without giving any evidence and is really nothing more than mud slinging on his part.

Christianity does acknowledge a spiritual world and the existence of various temptations, but never does it allow Christians off the hook because of it. One of the clearest themes in the New Testament is that people are responsible for their own thoughts and actions and will ultimately answer to God for them.

Christianity does not endorse victimology. Never are Christians in the New Testament presented as helpless victims of the spirit world. Nothing in the New Testament lets people off the hook with an argument like "the devil made me do it" or "that woman led me into temptation."

The New Testament is very clear on this: people are responsible for their own actions, and cannot blame the devil, or others, or how a woman was dressed, as an excuse for immoral or evil behavior or thoughts.

In Matthew chapter 5, Christ warned men: "Do not look upon a woman with lust." It is very telling that Christ said nothing about how she is dressed. No exemption is provided for provocative clothing, or if the women's skirt was a bit too short, or the neckline a bit too low. The responsibility for

230

moral behavior, and for treating women as persons, is placed squarely on the man's shoulders.

Regarding Sawyer's assertion that Christians can blame the devil for their bad behavior – *the devil made me do it* – maybe it should be asked if the shoe doesn't fit better on the other foot: "My DNA made me do it."

As Dawkins and militant atheists are fond of reminding us, DNA neither knows nor cares, and we just dance to its music. We can't help ourselves. We're just wired that way by our DNA.

9

Did Jesus Rise from the Dead?

CHRISTIANITY IS FOUNDED on the historical resurrection of Jesus Christ. If Jesus did not rise from the dead, then he was at best a religious leader with some inspiring words, but nothing else we might say about him would matter very much. We might appreciate his message of love, but we'd be free to take it or leave it as we wish.

However, if Jesus did rise from the dead, then God has broken in on human history with Divine power and authority, and a 'take-it-or-leave-it' attitude is no longer an option. It also means, gloriously, as Timothy Keller puts it, that "we don't have to be afraid of anything... If Jesus rose from the dead, it changes everything."[189]

I believe the tomb was empty on the third day. There is good reason to believe He did in fact rise from the dead, just as Christians have been claiming for two-thousand years. In this chapter we'll explore the historical evidence for this.

Since most of the material for this chapter will come from the New Testament, a word about its reliability is in order. The New Testament is a collection of letters written in the first century, not long after the crucifixion in AD 30. Most of the letters were written by several of the disciples who

---

[189] Timothy Keller, The Reason for God, p.210.

lived and walked with Christ, and St. Paul who encountered the risen Christ on the road to Damascus.

The Reliability of the New Testament Documents

We no longer have the original letters, but we do have a vast quantity of manuscript copies (MSS) ranging in age from the early second century to the fourth and fifth century. One of the first problems we can see from this is the introduction of errors. It is virtually impossible for someone to copy a large document by hand without making some mistakes. If the New Testament is the result of centuries of copying by hand, how can we have any real confidence in the reliability of the New Testament that has come down to us?

The Number of New Testament Manuscripts

Up until the invention of the printing press in the 15th century all books and letters had to be hand copied by scribes. Scribes were skilled professionals who specialized in making copies, and were very careful with their trade. As a result, the number of errors were not so great as we might imagine today. Never-the-less, there were errors introduced into the New Testament copies.

Fortunately, these errors need not be a cause for concern for several reasons: we have a large number of original MSS, the MSS were copied reasonably soon after the original letters, and no two MSS contain the same mistakes.

There are 5,664 partial or complete manuscripts of the New Testament in the original Greek. In addition to that, there are over 9,000 early translations into Latin, Syriac, Coptic, Arabic and other languages.

The earliest partial MSS is the John Rylands Fragment, dated AD 130, with 5 verses from the Gospel of John, attesting to the early origins of that gospel. The earliest surviving copy of the entire New Testament is from 325-350 AD. There are several, but the two most important are the *Codex Vaticanus* and *Codex Sinaiticus. Sinaiticus* is "regarded as one of the most important witnesses to the text of the New Testament, because of its antiquity, accuracy, and lack of omissions."[190]

Applying the science of Textual Criticism[191] to the vast number of New Testament manuscripts, scholars are able to determine that only 2 percent of the New Testament text is in doubt. Furthermore, of the 2 percent that is in doubt, the errors are insignificant and do not impact any important Christian doctrine.

Oxford mathematician John Lennox summarizes the results of Textual Criticism as applied to the New Testament:

> "...no two manuscripts contain exactly the same mistake. Therefore, by comparing all these manuscripts with each other, it is possible to reconstruct the original text to a point where expert opinion holds that less than 2 percent of that text is uncertain, with a large part of that 2 percent involving small linguistic features that make no difference to the general meaning. Moreover, since no New Testament doctrine depends solely on one verse or one passage, no New Testament

---

[190] John Lennox, *Gunning for God*, p. 193.
[191] Textual Criticism is the science of determining the original words of a text as close as possible by analyzing copies and their variants.

doctrine is put in doubt by these minor uncertainties."[192]

Of the significance of the large numbers of MSS in our possession, New Testament scholar F.F. Bruce has this to say:

"Fortunately...the great number of MSS increases proportionately the means of correcting such errors, so that the margin of doubt left in the process of recovering the exact original wording is not so large as might be feared; it is in truth remarkably small. The variant readings about which any doubt remains among textual critics of the New Testament affect no material question of the historical fact or of the Christian faith and practice."[193]

By way of comparison, there are only 9 or 10 original MSS of Caesar's *Gallic Wars* (written between 58 and 50 BC) that are any good, and the earliest was copied 900 years after the original. The famous Roman historian Livy (59 BC to 17 AD) wrote *The History of Rome* in 142 books. Only 35 of those books survive in just 20 MSS, and the oldest is from the 4th century AD.

Flavius Josephus wrote *The Jewish War* in the first century. He participated in the siege and destruction of Jerusalem in AD 70. Most of what we know of that historical event and the Jewish rebellion against Imperial Rome comes from Josephus. There are only 9 MSS from the 10th and 11th

---

[192] John Lennox, *Gunning for God*, p. 194
[193] F.F. Bruce, *The New Testament Documents: Are They Reliable?* pp. 14-15

century, 1 Latin MSS from the 4th century, and a few Russian versions. Altogether, less than 15 MSS.

Homer's *Iliad*, c. 800 BC, survived in 643 MSS dating from the 2 and 3rd centuries AD. A gap of 1000 years from the original book. Tacitus, a Roman historian, wrote *The Annals of Imperial Rome*. The first 6 books survive in only one MSS, copied in AD 850. Books 11 to 16 are in one other single MSS from the 11th century, a time gap of 700 years.

The point here is that scholars treat these as authentic representations of the originals. In comparison, the MSS evidence for the New Testament is overwhelming. With its thousands of MSS, copied relatively soon after the original documents, it is the best attested document from the ancient world.

Sir Frederic Kenyon, Director of the British Museum, wrote: "The number of manuscripts of the New Testament, of early translations from it, and of quotations from it in the oldest writers of the Church is so large that it is practically certain that the true reading of every doubtful passage is preserved in some one or other of these ancient authorities. This can be said of no other ancient book in the world."[194]

Dating the New Testament Writings

It is beyond dispute that all the letters of the New Testament were written and in wide circulation by AD 100 at the latest, with most of the letters circulating much earlier. According to F.F. Bruce, "The New Testament was complete, or substantially complete, by AD 100, the majority of the writings being in existence twenty to forty years before this...

---

[194] Frederic Kenyon, *Our Bible and the Ancient Manuscripts*, 4th ed., Harper New York, 1958, p.55.

A majority of modern scholars fix the dates of the four Gospels as follows: Matthew, c. 85-90; Mark, c. 65; Luke, c. 80-85; John, c. 90-100." [195]

The earliest New Testament letter is 1 Corinthians, written AD 55, a mere 22 to 25 years after the crucifixion. Contemporaries of Christ, including Peter and many of his original twelve Apostles were still alive. All of the Pauline epistles can be dated between AD 55 and AD 65.

According to F.F. Bruce: "the situation is encouraging from a historian's point of view, for the first three Gospels were written at a time when many were alive who could remember the things that Jesus said and did, and some at least would still be alive when the fourth Gospel was written." [196]

About the middle of the 19th century and into the 20th, it was fashionable for a while in some circles of so-called "higher criticism" to assert that the New Testament wasn't written until very late, well into the 2nd century, but no serious scholar believes this. As FF Bruce says, "This conclusion [of late dating the NT] was the result not so much of historical evidence as of philosophical presuppositions ... but the amount of such evidence available in our own day is so much greater and more conclusive that a first century date for most of the New Testament writings cannot be reasonably denied, no matter what our philosophical presuppositions may be." [197]

Probably one of the most interesting testimonies to the extreme early date of the New Testament, evidence that is irrefutable, are letters written by early church leaders

---

[195] F.F. Bruce, *The New Testament Documents*, p. 6-7
[196] Ibid p.7
[197] Ibid p.10

collectively known as the Apostolic Fathers. Some of them were disciples of St. John. We know historically who these men were and when they lived. Writing chiefly from AD 90 to AD 160, their letters contain vast numbers of quotations from and allusions to almost all the books of the New Testament.

For example, we have the *Epistle of Barnabas*, written AD 100; the *Didache*, dated AD 100. Then there is the *Letter to the Corinthians* by Clement, written AD 96, which quotes from most of the New Testament books. There are letters from Ignatius, AD 115, and Polycarp, AD 120, which contain numerous quotations from various New Testament letters. This means that the New Testament letters were already in existence, were well known and in wide circulation by AD 100.

All together, there are 38,289 quotations of the New Testament by the Apostolic Fathers and other early church leaders between the second and fourth century. If we lost all of the New Testament MSS we could still reconstruct the entire New Testament from these quotations, with the exception of eleven verses.

We know that the New Testament in our possession is very reliable.[198] The science of textual criticism and the number and quality of ancient manuscripts assure us that the New Testament in our possession today is, for all practical purposes, what was originally written. It doesn't of course prove that it's true, but it proves that what we have is an accurate copy of the original NT letters. So we have a solid basis from which we can discuss the evidence for the resurrection and what the original witnesses had to say.

---

[198] For a more in-depth discussion on this, please see my recommended reading list at the end of this chapter.

I will conclude this discussion on the reliability of the New Testament with this quote from Sir Frederic Kenyon, Director of the British Museum and leading authority on ancient manuscripts:

"The interval then between the dates of the original composition and the earliest extant evidence becomes so small as to be in fact negligible, and the last foundation for any doubt that the Scriptures have come down to us substantially as they were written has now been removed. Both the authenticity and the general integrity of the books of the New Testament may be regarded as finally established."[199]

Facts That Only Fit the Empty Tomb

The Christian faith was born on Easter. On that first Easter morning a group of women made their way to the tomb where Jesus had been buried after his execution. They carried with them spices and oils so that they could complete the anointing of his body – a common burial custom of the time. All four gospels record what happens next. When they arrived at the tomb, instead of finding the dead body of Christ they met the risen Lord. These women were the first people in history to claim that Christ had risen from the dead.

That's the Christian story, but others have had different explanations for the empty tomb. The Jewish religious authorities, the same group of men who'd ordered the crucifixion, also believed that the tomb was empty, although

---

[199] Sir Frederic Kenyon, *The Bible and Archeology* (1940), pp. 288-289. Quote taken from F.F. Bruce, *The New Testament Document*, p. 15.

they claimed that Christ's disciples had stolen the body at night while the guards slept.

Did the disciples of Jesus steal the body, as the authorities claimed? There are several reasons why this explanation isn't credible. At least two armed Roman soldiers guarded the tomb. We'd have to believe that the disciples were able to roll away a huge stone, enter the tomb and get away with the body, all without waking the sleeping guards.

It's a flimsy story, but if the tomb was empty what else could the authorities say? The simple fact that the authorities published such a weak story is in itself very telling; they could hardly claim that they took the body themselves, and admitting that the body simply disappeared of its own accord or really did get up and walk away clearly wouldn't be acceptable. The only other possible explanation is that the disciples stole it.

We can be confident the disciples didn't steal the body for several reasons. If they had stolen the body, then the disciples would have known the resurrection story was a hoax – a hoax they maintained for decades, were persecuted for, eventually tortured and executed for,[200] and each one of them took the secret of the hoax to the grave with them.

To accept this explanation for the empty tomb, we'd have to believe that all of the disciples died for something they knew was a lie, and that not one of them ever cracked and confessed under threat of torture and execution.

We could perhaps imagine one or two people, for some unknown reason, choosing to die for a hoax; but it is not reasonable to think that all eleven[201] would die a painful

---

[200] With the exception of St. John, who died in exile.
[201] Counting the 10 original apostles and St. Paul. Judas hung himself, and St. John died in old age of natural causes in exile.

death for a lie, maintaining it to the very end. And not just the eleven Apostles, but the dozens of women who were a part of that original group, the first to see the risen Christ, and many other disciples as well, suffered for their testimony.

Furthermore, the disciples had no reason to steal the body and make up such a story in the first place, because no one was expecting a resurrection. The Jews believed in an eventual resurrection, but only at the end of history when everyone would be resurrected together, when God restored the promised Messianic Kingdom to the nation of Israel. They did not believe in individual resurrections before the final judgement.

If you told a 1st century Jew that a deceased person had been resurrected, they would have dismissed it as ridiculous because the promised Kingdom of God had not arrived. Such a hoax would not have worked with 1st century Jews.

Neither did pagans want or believe in a resurrection. The pagans didn't think a physical resurrection of the body was even a good thing. In pagan belief, the whole point of dying was to escape your mortal body and enter the afterlife as a free spirit, released from the weakness and constraints of your physical body. To the pagan mind, a physical resurrection – returning back to your body – wasn't a good thing. If no one was expecting a resurrection, including the followers of Jesus, why come up with a story that would only seem ridiculous to anyone who heard it?

No one would have believed them for a moment if the tomb wasn't really empty. If the tomb wasn't empty, it would have been very easy for the Jewish and Roman authorities to produce the body, thus killing off the false rumours. It would have been all too easy for anyone hearing the story to make

241

the few minutes walk out of town and check the tomb for themselves.

A couple of other explanations for the empty tomb should be briefly mentioned before moving on, although neither of them are taken seriously any longer. One such theory was that Jesus didn't really die on the cross. After being taken down from the cross and placed in the tomb, he later resuscitated and walked out. This has been commonly known as the swooning theory. As the theory goes, people later saw Jesus walking around and assumed that he'd risen from the dead.

However, we can be certain that Christ died on the cross. Crucifixion was a very common method used by Romans to execute criminals, and they were very good at it. The Roman soldiers who carried out the crucifixion of Christ would have known what death looked like; furthermore, they would have ensured that the execution had been completed, because Roman soldiers suffered severe penalties for failing to carry out an execution successfully. The gospels record that the soldiers even pierced Christ's side with a spear to ensure he was dead.

The swooning theory also requires us to believe that Christ, severely injured and weakened after being beaten and crucified, rolled back the heavy stone blocking the door to the tomb[202], and then surprised and overcame several armed soldiers.

Another possibility needs to be mentioned: the disciples simply went to the wrong tomb. When they didn't

---

[202] The round stones that were rolled in front of tomb weighed several hundreds of pounds and required more than one man to move.

find Christ's body as expected they assumed he'd arisen, and that's how the story got started.

This scenario is the least likely of all. Jesus was buried in the tomb of a wealthy man, Joseph of Arimathea. He was a well known, highly placed leader in the Sanhedrin. Everyone in Jerusalem knew who Joseph was and where his tomb was located. The authorities placed guards at the entrance to this tomb. Large crowds of people saw where the body of Christ was placed after he was taken from the cross. The gospels recording these facts where in circulation while many of the people living in Jerusalem at the time were still alive. It's not possible that the women and all the other disciples had gone to the wrong tomb.

The Resurrection Appearances

Hundreds of people claimed to have seen the risen Christ in the days and weeks following the crucifixion. Several women who went to the tomb that first Easter morning were the first. Later, he appeared to many other disciples at different times.

The apostle Paul wrote that Christ had appeared to Peter and the "Twelve", and *"to more than five hundred brothers and sisters at the same time, most of whom are still alive,"* as well as to James, all the other apostles, and last of all to himself (1 Corinthians 15:3-8).

There are only a few possible explanations:

1. The resurrection story was a fabrication.
2. The witnesses were sincere, but wrong. It was some sort of hallucination or wish fulfillment.

3. The original 'witnesses' and first Christians never claimed that Christ had risen. The resurrection story is just a myth or legend that developed later.
4. Christ rose from the dead and appeared to his followers.

One logical possibility is that the witnesses claiming to see Christ were lying. However, as a theory this has serious problems. It requires us to accept that hundreds of people got together, and for some unknown reason all agreed to tell this lie. Hundreds of people took the lie to the grave with them. Dozens of them endured torture and death for a story they knew to be a lie. St. Paul and all of the disciples, except John, were executed. For the reasons already discussed above regarding the empty tomb, this simply isn't a credible theory to entertain.

There are other reasons that this theory is problematic. There are numerous details provided in the gospel stories that are too counter-intuitive to be fabrications.

All four gospel writers record that the first people who found the tomb empty and saw the resurrected Christ were women. Some of the details differ between the four accounts, but that is because there were different groups of women coming and going between the city and the tomb that morning.

In first century Judah, women had very little social standing. In fact, women were considered so unreliable as witnesses that their testimony wasn't allowed in court. Even the disciples dismissed the women's story at first as idle talk. None of them believed the women until they saw the risen Christ themselves.

Also, in the Gospels the male leaders are made to look pretty foolish, timid and afraid. All of them ran away and went into hiding when Christ was arrested, afraid for their own lives. Peter was even too frightened of a lowly servant girl to admit to being one of Christ's followers, and denied Christ three times.

You wouldn't do that if you were going to invent a lie to support a new religious movement. In the first century, involving women as the first eyewitnesses would only damage the credibility of the new movement, and you wouldn't portray the male leaders as frightened cowards who betrayed the person they were now claiming to be the risen Messiah.

Furthermore, these first Jewish believers were claiming that a man – who everyone in Jerusalem had just a few days previously seen walking around town – was in fact God, that God had come to earth as a man, and they were now worshipping this crucified man as God. To the fiercely monotheistic Jews who firmly believed that God was a spirit, such a thing was anathema and extremely offensive. No Jew would make up such a story.

Furthermore, if the first followers of Christ were telling invented stories, then they had a serious marketing problem. They were making up a story no one would want.

No one expected a resurrection, no one wanted it, and no Jew could accept a man as God. So if the early Christians were making it up, they were making up stories for a new religion that no Jew would ever want to join.

If you are going to make up stories to encourage others to join your group, you would make up stories that would be believable, something that would make your movement attractive and desirable so that others would want to join. You don't tell lies that turn people away; you tell lies to attract people.

However, everything the first Christians said and did was very unattractive to Jews. So if the early Christians were making it up, they were making up a story that no one in Jerusalem would want or accept.

Another reason the disciples weren't lying: they had no reason to. There had been several other messianic movements. Jews were expecting the Messiah promised by the prophets of the Old Testament. This Messiah was to be a political and military leader who would lead a rebellion against Rome and free Israel. So from time to time some charismatic leader would get it into his head that he was the man for the job, and gather a few followers.

The leaders of such messianic movements were almost always hunted down and executed because Imperial Rome had no tolerance for any challenge to their authority. When that happened, the followers simply moved on, and either dispersed or found a new leader. They didn't concoct ridiculous stories that no one would ever believe.

As Keller notes: "There were dozens of other messianic pretenders whose lives and careers ended the same way Jesus' did. Why would the disciples of Jesus have come to the conclusion that this crucifixion had not been a defeat but a triumph – unless they had seen him risen from the dead?"[203]

Then there is the strongest reason they weren't lying, as already discussed – many of them died for it. But what if they weren't intentionally lying, but sincerely believed the story? This brings us to the next possibility: that the witnesses were sincere – but wrong. They genuinely believed that they had seen the risen Christ, but were mistaken. It was really just some form of wish fulfillment or hallucination.

---

[203] Keller, *The Reason for God*, p. 217.

Wish fulfillment requires that they were expecting a resurrection in the first place, but there was no pre-existing expectation of a risen Messiah. We can discount the resurrection sightings as 'wish fulfillment' for many of the same reasons we can discount it as an elaborate hoax. No one wanted or expected a resurrection.

The followers of Christ were all stunned and demoralized when Jesus was executed, and were not expecting him to return from the dead. As we touched upon above, the resurrection of an individual wasn't in their theology. It was a very un-Jewish thing to think.

There is another point to consider: many of the witnesses saw Christ at the same time, in small groups and in some instances, large groups. On one occasion five hundred people reported seeing the risen Christ at the same time. Paul reported this in 1 Corinthians, a public letter written just 20-25 years after the event, while many of the witnesses were still alive.[204] The invitation to his readers to go talk to them is clearly implied.

In this letter Paul lists many of the witnesses, and records that Christ "appeared to more than five hundred of the brothers and sisters at the same time, most of whom are still living, although some have fallen asleep." In other words, check it out. Go and talk to the witnesses. This was easily done during the pax Romana, when travel around the Roman Empire was relatively safe.

While it is possible for individuals to experience hallucinations, people don't see the same thing and mass hallucinations don't happen.[205] "In contrast, 100 per cent of

[204] 1 Corinthians 15:3-8, written 50-55 AD.
[205] Andre Aleman and Frank Laroi, Hallucination: *The Science of Idiosyncratic Perception* (Washington, DC: APA, 2008).

the disciples experienced what they believed were visual appearances of Jesus. That's a far greater percentage than can be supported by hallucination research completed during the past century."[206]

This brings us to a final alternative. That the resurrection story was a legend that grew in the church over time. According to this theory, the early Christians did not in fact believe Christ had risen from the dead. The church was initially a religious movement that sprang up around the teachings of an inspirational spiritual leader whom they admired as a prophet, but they knew he was just a man who had died and never did believe he had risen.

As an alternative to the resurrection, this is perhaps the easiest theory for modern skeptics to accept. It also has the added benefit of dispensing with the problems attending the other alternatives. If the resurrection was not something the first Christians claimed, then it gets around the problems of having to explain why, if they were propagating an elaborate hoax, they all died for it, or were suffering from some sort of mass delusion.

The 'legend' theory, while superficially appearing to be plausible, is even less credible than the other alternatives because there can be no serious doubt that the first Christians were spreading the message of the resurrection immediately following Christ's death – within days.

Three of the four gospels were written down and in circulation while many people living in Jerusalem at the time were still alive. Luke travelled to Judah and interviewed Mary, the mother of Jesus, as well as many of the people who lived through the events. Paul's letters were written and in

---

[206] Justin Brierley, *Unbelievable? Why after ten years of talking with atheists, I'm still a Christian* (2017), p. 138.

circulation just 20-40 years after the death of Christ, while many contemporary witnesses were still living.

The letter of 1 Corinthians is the earliest book of the New Testament, written and in circulation by 55 A.D. We already talked about 1 Corinthians 15:3-8 above. In this passage Paul is saying that he is simply passing on to them what's been told from the beginning. Paul's letter to the Corinthians was a public document, meant to be read aloud to the congregation. You can't put something like that in a public document if it isn't true. It's too easy to check. If this letter had been a later invention, it would have been immediately recognized as fraudulent.

It's not possible that the resurrection sightings were just stories or legends invented by the Church in later centuries. The New Testament letters were already in circulation too soon after the gospel events, while many contemporaries were still alive. Myths and legends take generations to develop, as stories are passed down and the original events fade into the mists of time. You can't invent a legend close to the original events, especially not when contemporaries of the events are still living.

The first Jewish believers and witnesses to the resurrection were telling people in and around Jerusalem within days of the crucifixion that Jesus had risen from the dead, within a few minutes walk to the tomb where he had been buried.

The crucifixion had been a very well-known event: the public execution of a famous heretic, deceiver, agitator, charlatan, prophet, or promised Messiah – depending on your point of view. Headline news of the day with hundreds of local witnesses. Everyone in Jerusalem knew who Jesus was, and everyone knew he was dead and where he'd been buried.

Yet within a few short weeks, thousands believed he'd been resurrected and joined the new Jewish sect. Had the tomb not been empty, it would have been a simple matter for someone to produce Christ's body.

It is very telling that the enemies of this new sect, the Roman authorities and Jewish religious leaders, never did produce the body. The Jewish leaders had every reason to, and would have been highly motivated to do just that. They detested Jesus as a heretic and troublemaker, and despised his followers.

Had the tomb not been empty, the body could have been easily produced, quickly snuffing out this minor Jewish sect. Had the tomb not been empty, the population of Jerusalem would have laughed at anyone telling stories of a resurrection, dismissing it outright.

The Birth of the Church

Within a few weeks of Christ's crucifixion, the church sprang to life and grew rapidly, expanding to embrace pagans and gentiles of all races, with an entirely new worldview and set of beliefs which had no precedent.

If we discount the resurrection, then historians are faced with a serious problem explaining the existence of the Christian church. Every other attempt to account for the birth of the church ultimately fails. No other explanation fits the facts we have of 1st century Jewish culture.

Jews did not believe in an individual resurrection – only a general resurrection of the dead at the end of history. Stories of an individual returning to life would not have convinced anyone and simply didn't fit within the Jewish worldview.

Under normal circumstances it takes decades of discussion for new worldviews to develop. The sudden appearance of the church, with thousands of people suddenly believing what no Jew or pagan could ever believe, requires an explanation. In the words of Timothy Keller:

"After the death of Jesus the entire Christian community suddenly adopted a set of beliefs that were brand-new and until that point had been unthinkable. [E]very one of these beliefs was unique in the world up to that time, but in every other instance that we know of, such a massive shift in thinking at the worldview level only happens to a group of people over a period of time. However, the Christian view of resurrection, absolutely unprecedented in history, sprang up full-blown immediately after the death of Jesus. There was no process or development. His followers said that their beliefs did not come from debating and discussing. They were just telling others what they had seen themselves. No one has come up with a plausible alternative to this claim."[207]

I will conclude with this summary from N.T. Wright. There can be no water-tight, absolute proof in the mathematical sense, of course. But history is not like that, as N.T. Wright explains:

"What we are after is high probability; and this is to be attained by examining all the possibilities, all the suggestions, and asking how well they explain the phenomena. It is always possible that in discussing the

[207] Keller, *The Reason for God*, p.217-218.

resurrection someone will come up with the skeptical critic's dream: an explanation which provides a sufficient condition for the rise of early Christian faith but which … causes no fluttering of the critical dovecotes. It is worthy of note that, despite the somewhat desperate attempts of many scholars over the last two hundred years … no such explanation has been found. The early Christians did not invent the empty tomb and the 'meetings' or 'sightings' of the risen Jesus in order to explain a faith they already had. They developed that faith because of the occurrence, and convergence, of these two phenomena. Nobody was expecting this kind of thing; no kind of conversion experience would have generated such ideas; nobody would have invented it, no matter how guilty (or how forgiven) they felt, no matter how many hours they pored over the scriptures. To suggest otherwise is to stop doing history and to enter into a fantasy world of our own… In terms of the kind of proof which historians normally accept, the case we have presented, that the tomb-plus-appearances combination is what generated early Christian belief, is as watertight as one is likely to find."[208]

If you don't discount out of hand the possibility that God did perform a resurrection miracle, then the resurrection of Jesus Christ is the best explanation that fits all the evidence. There simply is no better explanation for the empty tomb, the sightings of the witnesses and the explosive appearance of the Christian faith.

---

[208] N.T. Wright, *The Resurrection of the Son of God*, p.706-707.

Further Reading

Brierley, Justin. Chapter 6 "Facts that only fit the resurrection", in *Unbelievable? Why after ten years of talking with atheists, I'm still a Christian* (2017).

Bruce, F.F. *The New Testament Documents: Are They Reliable?* (6th ed. 1981).

Keller, Timothy. Chapter 13 "The Reality of the Resurrection", in *The Reason for God* (2008).

Lennox, John. Chapter 8 "Did Jesus Rise from the Dead?", in *Gunning for God: Why the New Atheists are Missing the Target* (Lion Hudson Press, 2011).

Wright, N.T. *The Resurrection of the Son of God* (Fortress Press, 2003).

10

Is There Evidence for God?

"It would be very difficult to explain why the universe should have begun in just this way, except as the act of a God who intended to create beings like us."[209]

GOD, BY HIS VERY NATURE, is not a good subject for scientific scrutiny. He is, by the very essence of being God, something beyond nature, outside of the universe – supernatural – and therefore not subject to the tools available to science. The result is that God can never be subject to scientific investigation because science can only investigate the natural world. Any questions and investigations into the existence of God, therefore, will be metaphysical in nature.

Christians hold that the universe is something made by God. It is not God, nor is God something inside it. He is transcendent. We cannot study the universe and expect to 'see' God anymore than we could go to the Empire State building and expect to find its architect living in the basement, or embedded in its walls, or operating the elevator for us.

But, like any designed artifact, it is reasonable to expect to study it and find evidence that it is a designed thing. If the universe really is the creation of God, it would be reasonable

---

[209] Francis Collins, *The Language of God*, p.75

to find some clues; fingerprints, as it were, of God left on his creation. Clues that the universe is an intentionally designed artifact and not the result of an accident. That's what this chapter is about.

In a previous chapter we talked about the compatibility of faith and reason and showed how God and science are very compatible. In this chapter we will take this line of thought farther and talk about the positive scientific evidence for God.

We often hear things like: "there's no evidence for God" or "you can't prove God." What atheists typically mean by the word 'proof' is some kind of water-tight, absolute empirical evidence that removes all question and settles the debate, of the sort we now have that the earth is round and orbits the sun. And that normal racoons have four legs, not six. That sort of thing. The sort of thing that no rational person could debate once they've had their morning coffee.

Atheists often bring this kind of empirical thinking into the debate about God: if you can't prove His existence beyond reasonable doubt, in the same way we can prove the earth orbits the sun, then faith is irrational and we're under no obligation to believe in God.

This approach to 'proof' has its roots in the extreme rationalism that arose in the late 1800's. It was a school of thought that basically said: only what can be empirically proven is true and people should only believe what can be empirically proved. This is the foundational faith of naturalism.

Naturalism as a philosophy holds that only the physical, material universe is real and true, and that there is nothing beyond or outside of nature. It also means, according to naturalism, that everything we are is physical. We are material objects and there is nothing about us that is non-material. There is no soul or spirit or non-material mind. We are our bodies and nothing more, and there is nothing about us that cannot eventually, as our knowledge grows, be explained in material, physical terms.

Science as a tool is only calibrated to investigate natural phenomena. That's fine as far as it goes, but people who believe in philosophical naturalism also believe that only what science is capable of measuring, seeing and investigating could be true.

The problem with this approach is that, as Alvin Plantinga put it, they are like a drunk looking for his lost keys at night under the streetlight, and only looking for them within the pool of light provided by the streetlight. When asked why he doesn't look beyond the light, the drunk responds that the keys can't possibly be outside the pool of light because he'd never be able to see them in the dark.

That's not a slam on science – it's pointing out the fallacy of philosophical naturalism: nothing can be real beyond the capacity of science to investigate. If we are not able to 'see' it scientifically, then it's not real.

Atheists who insist on that approach to the existence of God are about 75 years behind on their philosophy, because philosophers and scientists have long recognized the fatal flaw in the logic: you can't empirically prove that only what is empirically proven is true. It is therefore a self-defeating argument and cannot be true.

Scientists have themselves never acted like that, anyway. Scientists, like all of us, will often take a position on something before all the evidence is in. Scientists accept theories based on the *weight* of evidence even if it isn't absolutely proven. No one thinks it is irrational to do so. This happens all the time with scientific theories, as it also does with most things in life we hold true.

The irony is that nothing really worth believing can be proven empirically.

> *"For nothing worth proving can be proven,*
> *Nor yet disproven: wherefore be thou wise,*
> *Cleave ever to the sunnier side of doubt."*[210]

So what does this all mean? Does it mean there is no point in looking at the evidence? Does it mean that we're off the hook? We don't need to make a decision because we can't know for sure?

That would be a tragic response because the question of whether or not there is a God is the single most important question facing us. Everything else hangs from that. The question is much too big to ignore.

It might be more helpful to think of the scientific facts that will be presented in this chapter not as air-tight 'proof' – few things are like that – but as clues. Clues to the existence of God. You may find some clues very persuasive, and others not so much, but taken together all the clues take on a weight of 'evidence' that is very persuasive. Theists believe the weight of evidence is so overwhelming that taken together points to a conclusion that is extremely hard to avoid: there is a God.

Many scientists, after looking at the evidence, have concluded that the universe is a cosmic 'fix'. That someone monkeyed with the properties of the universe from the very beginning so that the universe would be capable of supporting life. As Sir Fred Hoyle said: "A common sense interpretation of the facts suggests that a super-intellect monkeyed with the laws of physics."

---

[210] Alfred Tennyson, *Ancient Sage*

What follows over the next few pages is a listing of some of the scientific evidence for God we find in the universe. There are hundreds of excellent books and papers written by scientists that talk about these things. The works I used to pull this information together is referenced at the end of this chapter.

Scientists have for a long time noticed the extremely large number of cosmological coincidences in the universe that are necessary for any sort of life to be possible. This is often referred to as the 'fine-tuning' of the universe. It means that the characteristics of the universe are precisely what is necessary for life, and that if any one of those characteristics were just slightly different, life wouldn't be possible. Not just different, but impossible.

None of this is a "God of the gaps" kind of argument.[211] It is the exact opposite of "God of the gaps." It is looking squarely at what we already know. As Francis Collins said about the evidence: "There are good reasons to believe in God, including the existence of mathematical principles and order in creation. They are positive reasons, based on knowledge, rather than default assumptions based on a temporary lack of knowledge."

Robin Collins provides a good definition of 'fine tuning': "[It is] generally referring to the extraordinary balancing of

---

[211] 'God of the Gaps' is a term applied to an erroneous approach some Christians took in the past to try to 'prove' God by pointing out phenomena for which there was no known scientific explanation at the time, claiming that God must be the explanation since science couldn't account for it. The problem with this approach will be immediately obvious: as science advances, these 'gaps' in knowledge get filled in. 'God of the Gaps' arguments have been a complete failure and have been rightly criticized for trying to 'stuff God' into our gaps of knowledge.

the fundamental laws and parameters of physics and the initial conditions of the universe." This fine-tuning strongly suggests that our universe was not an accident, but very intentional.

One of the most complete books on the subject is the classic by Barrow and Tipler, "The Anthropic Cosmological Principle", published in 1988. It goes into tremendous scientific and mathematical detail and is filled with mathematical formulas behind all the cosmological forces. Reading the book is a university course in itself. If you like math and scientific detail, this book is for you. More recently, astronomer Martin Rees wrote *Just Six Numbers*, an excellent book discussing the finely tuned properties of the cosmos. It's a very comprehensive review of the scientific facts of 'fine-tuning.'

So here are some fun facts to keep in mind next time you hear someone at a party say: "There's no evidence for God." I'll start with the following summary of Rees' book, provided by Allister McGrath, which I have taken from *A Fine-Tuned Universe*.[212]

1. The ratio of the electromagnetic force to the force of gravity. This measures the strength of the electrical forces that hold atoms together, divided by the force of gravity between them. If this were slightly smaller than its observed value, 'only a short-lived miniature universe could exist: no creatures could grow larger than insects, and there would be no time for biological evolution.'

2. The strong nuclear force, which defines how firmly atomic nuclei bind together. This force "controls

---

[212] Alister McGrath, *A Fine Tuned Universe*, p. 119-120.

the power from the Sun and, more sensitively, how stars transmute hydrogen into all the atoms of the periodic table." The value of this constant is 0.007. If it were 0.006 or 0.008, we could not exist.

3. The amount of matter in the universe, referred to by the cosmic number 'Omega'. Thus, omega tells us the relative importance of gravity and expansion energy in the universe. 'If this ratio were too high relative to a particular 'critical' value, the universe would have collapsed long ago; had it been too low, no galaxies or stars would have formed. The initial expansion speed seems to have been finely tuned.'

4. Cosmic repulsion. In 1998, cosmologists became aware of the importance of cosmic antigravity in controlling the expansion of the universe, and in particular its increasing importance as our universe becomes ever darker and emptier. Fortunately for us...[it] is very small. Otherwise its effect would have stopped galaxies and stars from forming.

5. The ratio of the gravitational binding force to rest-mass energy, Q, is of fundamental importance in determining the texture of the universe. If Q were even smaller, the universe would be inert and structureless; if Q were much larger, it would be a violent place, in which no stars or solar systems could survive, dominated by vast black holes.

6. The number of spatial dimensions, D, which is three. String theory argues that, of the 10 or 11 original dimensions of the universe at the beginning, all but three were compacted. Time of course is to be treated as a fourth dimension. Life couldn't exist if D were two or four.

The Four Fundamental Forces

There are four "fundamental forces" of the universe: gravity, electromagnetism, the strong and weak nuclear force. Every one of these forces must have just the right strength if there is to be any possibility of life. If any one of these had been a slightly different strength, life would not be possible. Either we'd have no atoms, or we'd have atoms but no stars or planets.

Gravity: The force of gravity is precisely what we need it to be. Brandon Carter said: "If the force of gravity were even slightly stronger, all stars would be blue giants; if even slightly weaker, all would be red dwarfs."[213] A change in one part in 10^{100} would have prevented a life permitting universe. By way of comparison, the total number of molecules in the universe is 10^{80}.

Think of a ruler the length of the universe. The gravitational setting has to be within an inch. If any higher – stars would burn too rapidly. The life of stars would be too short. If any smaller – stars would be too small and cool and nuclear fusion would not ignite. There would be no production of heavier elements.

The electromagnetic force: This force is responsible for practically all the phenomena one encounters in daily life above the nuclear scale, with the exception of gravity. Roughly speaking, all the forces involved in interactions between atoms can be explained by the electromagnetic force acting on the electrically charged atomic nuclei and electrons inside and around the atoms. If the value was slightly higher or lower, there would not be chemical

---

[213] Brandon Carter, "Large Number of Coincidences and the Anthropic Principle in Cosmology."

bonding. If it was stronger, no element heavier than hydrogen would form. If too weak, protons would combine too easily and you could never have stable stars. There would be no stars, or only very short-lived stars, in the universe.

The strong nuclear force: This force defines how firmly atomic nuclei bind together. It controls the power from the Sun, and how stars transmute hydrogen into all the atoms of the periodic table. If any different, we would not exist. It binds protons and neutrons (nucleons) together to form the nucleus of an atom. If this was any weaker, multi-proton nuclei could not hold together and hydrogen would be the only element in the universe. If stronger, all of the primordial hydrogen would have synthesized into helium early in the universe's history: no hydrogen, and there would be no stars.

The weak nuclear force: This force controls the fusion process that powers the sun. The weak nuclear force is just right for the slow, steady burn rate of hydrogen in stars. If it had been slightly stronger or weaker, than we could not have stable, burning stars. It is responsible for the radioactive decay of subatomic particles and initiates the process known as hydrogen fusion in stars.

This allows for a slow and steady burn rate in stars. Without it, stars would go off like bombs. A change in one part in 10 to the 100th power would have prevented a life permitting universe. If stronger: too much hydrogen converted to helium at the Big Bang. If weaker: too little helium produced by the Big Bang.

Not only are these forces fine-tuned in themselves, but their relationship to each other must also be very precise for life to be possible. For instance, there is a perfectly precise balance between gravity (G) and electromagnetism (E).

The G force holds the star together, and the E force allows the star to burn and radiate energy. Outside this range all stars would either be blue dwarfs or red giants. If it had been off by 1 part in 10 to the 40th, life supporting suns would not be possible.

More Fine-Tuning Fun Facts

The Existence of Elements necessary for life.

The carbon atom should by all rights not exist or be very rare. In order to form, it must have a very precise level of resonance. The steps required inside a star to create carbon are so improbable that there should not be any carbon in any great amount. Without these steps, the universe would be almost entirely hydrogen and helium. The resonance level of carbon is precise – and perfect – for the creation of not only carbon, but all the other heavier elements, (oxygen, nitrogen). Fred Hoyle said his atheism was greatly shaken when he realized the odds of this happening by chance.

If the electric charge of the electron had been any different, either stars would have been unable to burn hydrogen, or they would have not exploded and the heavier elements needed for life would never have been available. Meaning there would be no production of heavier elements necessary for planets and life.

The Ratio of Proton to Electron Mass.

The ratio between the mass of a proton and the mass of an electron is exactly what it needs to be. If it was any different there would be insufficient chemical bonding for complex molecules, making life impossible.

The proton is 1836 times heavier than the electron. There is no natural reason. It just is. If it were any different, required molecules would not form and there would be no chemistry for life. Stephen Hawking said this ratio is one of the fundamental numbers in nature, and: "The remarkable fact is that the values of these numbers seem to have been very finely adjusted to make possible the development of life."

Protein Formation.

Fred Hoyle and Chandra Wickremasinghe calculated the odds that all the proteins needed for life would form in one place by chance at 1 in $10^{40,000}$. (For comparison, there are only 10^{80} subatomic particles in the universe.)

Even if the entire universe consisted of organic soup this is still an outrageously small probability. Because the facts cannot be explained by random chance, Hoyle and others subscribe to 'panspermia' theory. Others conclude life must have arrived by spaceship. The fact that so many respected top scientists have had to resort to wild SF speculations illustrates just how weak a naturalistic explanation is.

Balance Between the Universe's expansion and collapse.

The balance between gravity and the rate of expansion turns out to be just right: enough gravity so that matter could form into stars and planets, but enough expansion so that the universe did not collapse back on itself very early in cosmic history. The difference is 1 %. The density of the universe had to be within a very critical parameter – 1% of what's needed to cause it to collapse.

The amount of matter in the universe (Omega) happens to be just right to maintain a stable rate of expansion. It was at a critical value a split second after the big bang. If too high, the universe would have collapsed long ago. If too low, no galaxies, stars, planets could form.

The critical density of the universe is 10 to the -29th gram per cubic centimeter on average across the universe. (That's how we know the total number of particles in the universe is 10^{80th}.)

Cosmic Background Radiation.

The ripples in the cosmic background radiation are the right size that allows for the formation of structure. These ripples are also evidence of the Big Bang. It is the radiation left over from it. But it is also evidence of a just right kind of Big Bang. If the ripples had been any larger, than the formation of structures would have been too dense and big, dominated by black holes. Too small, and you would not find galaxies. The expansion would have been too rapid to allow for galaxies and solar systems to form.

Cosmic Repulsion.

This describes the cosmic anti-gravity in controlling the expansion of the universe. The value is very small, otherwise it would have stopped galaxies and stars from forming.

The speed of light.

It turns out that the speed of light has to be what it is. If it was any different, stars would be either too bright or not bright enough for life.

The Cosmological Constant.

This drives the acceleration of the universe's expansion. It is fine tuned to 1 in 10^{120}.

Too low: inadequate inflation in the early universe, and the universe re-collapses.

Too high: expansion rate too fast for star formation.

Astrophysicist Hugh Ross compiled a list of 35 evidences for fine-tuning in the universe, along with 122 characteristics of our galaxy and solar system fine tuned for life. It's an interesting list. He calculates that the probability that all these would occur by accident is 1 in 10^{160}.[214]

We often hear that there is nothing special about the Earth or our place in the vast cosmos – and by extension, atheists claim there is nothing special about us.[215] Atheists need it to be so, because their viewpoint rests on life being common. Life is like a soup mix – just add water and the right ingredients, and life will appear.

According to this principle, there is nothing unusual about us. Our planet is just a small unassuming rock revolving around an average star in a galactic backwater. A lone speck in the great cosmic darkness.

But the evidence is to the contrary. Turns out we are special. Just as there are dozens of 'fine-tuned' characteristics of the universe, there are hundreds of 'fine-tuned' parameters of our planet as well as its location in our galaxy and in our solar system. The size of the Earth, its rotation, tilt, distance from the sun, the mass of the sun, the relative size of the moon, the size and location of the other planets, all conspire to provide a stable life-supporting environment. The very same things that make life possible also make it strangely well suited for observing and analyzing the universe.[216]

---

[214] Hugh Ross, *Why I Am a Christian*, p.138-141

[215] This is known as The Copernicus Principle or the Principle of Mediocrity. The irony is Copernicus, the great astronomer who this principle is named after, was a Christian and didn't see it that way at all.

[216] Astronomer G. Gonzalez, *The Privileged Planet*.

The Language of DNA: More Fun Party Facts

Francis Collins is one of America's top medical experts who led the project that mapped the entire human genome for the first time. He refers to DNA as a "vast instruction book" containing "the parts list for human biology."[217]

The DNA in our cells can be likened to blue-prints or instruction manuals, and the cell itself is like a factory which uses the instructions within DNA to build miniature 'machines' out of proteins. Scientist Michael Denton says that the cell is a "veritable microminiaturized factory containing thousands of exquisitely designed pieces of intricate molecular machinery"[218]

These molecular factories, so small that hundreds of them could fit within the dot in this 'i', are vastly "more complicated than machines built by man and absolutely without parallel in the non-living world."[219]

Bruce Alberts, President of the National Academy of Science of the USA says this of these amazing microscopic factories: "The entire cell can be viewed as a factory that contains an elaborate network of interlocking assembly lines, each of which is composed of a set of large protein machines...why do we call the large protein assembly lines that underlie cell function, protein machines? Precisely because, like machines invented by humans to deal efficiently with the world, these protein assemblies contain highly co-ordinated moving parts."[220]

---

[217] Collins, *The Language of God*, p. 111
[218] Michael Denton, *Evolution: A Theory in Crisis*, p. 250. Quoted in Lennox, *God's Undertaker*, p. 122-123
[219] Op cit, p. 250
[220] Cell 92, 1998, p. 291. See Bill Bryson, *A Short History of Nearly Everything*, 2004, Chapter 24.

The cell, therefore, is a miniature factory of assembly lines producing molecular machines: "Molecular machines like the flagellum are made from proteins, which are in turn made out of what are often called the basic building blocks of life – the amino acids."[221]

DNA is an information bearing molecule at the heart of every cell. It is a very long molecule holding four chemicals representing codes or letters. The arrangements of these letters make 'words' just like language, and words strung together make sentences making up an entire instruction book. A gene is a long string of these letters carrying information for a protein so that a gene can be interpreted as a set of instructions. Like a program for making a protein. A complete set of genes is referred to as a genome – the complete instruction manual for building an organism. The human genome is over 3.5 billion letters long and would fill a whole library. The entire length of the DNA tightly coiled inside a cell is 2 meters. Since there are 10 trillion cells in a human body the entire length of DNA is a mind boggling 20 trillion metres.[222]

As one scientist describes it: "Like a computer hard disc, DNA contains the database of information and the program to produce a specified product. Every one of the 10 to 100 trillion cells in the human body contains a database larger than the Encyclopedia Britannica."[223] So DNA is a complex language akin to a computer program. Scientists use the analogy of letters and words because the vital feature that characterizes proteins is that the amino acids which comprise them must be in exactly the right places in the

---

[221] Lennox, God's *Undertaker*, p. 126
[222] ibid, p. 137
[223] ibid, p. 136

chain.[224] It is the order of the letters that's the key thing, just like a language. Each amino acid letter must be in the right place in the long chain.[225]

Interestingly, there is *no evidence* of evolution among cells. Michael Denton says:

"Molecular biology has also shown us that the basic design of the cell system is essentially the same in all living systems on earth from bacteria to mammals. In all organisms the roles of DNA, mRNA and protein are identical. The meaning of the genetic code is virtually identical in all cells. The size, structure and component design of the protein synthetic machinery is practically the same in all cells. In terms of their basic biochemical design, therefore, no living system can be thought of as primitive or ancestral with respect to any other system, nor is there the slightest empirical hint of an evolutionary sequence among all the incredibly diverse cells on earth."[226]

Nobel Prize-winner Jacques Monod agrees: "We have no idea what the structure of a primitive cell might have been. The simplest living system known to us, the bacterial cell...in its overall chemical plan is the same as that of all other living beings. It employs the same genetic code and the same mechanism of translation as do, for example, human cells. Thus the simplest cells available to us for study have

---

[224] ibid, p. 128-129
[225] If we had a pool that had all the right amino acids floating around, the chance of getting 100 rightly ordered is 1/20 to the 100th power.
[226] Michael Denton, *Evolution: A Theory in Crisis*, p. 250, from Lennox, *Undertaker*, p. 122-123

nothing 'primitive' about them...no vestiges of truly primitive structures are discernable."[227]

This is *not* evidence of unguided common descent, as some like to argue. It is more properly seen as common design – of an Engineer re-using common components across different systems.

The point of describing all this? Meaningful language – information – doesn't happen by chance. You will not get a working computer program or even a single coherent sentence by putting letters in a bag and shaking them up. It has been calculated that the odds against producing the proteins need for life by chance is 1 in $10^{40,000}$.[228]

From the molecular factories hidden within the cells of our bodies, to the enormous structures of the universe billions of light years across, we see evidence of design. It looks very much like someone went to great lengths to build a universe for us, gave us a place to live on Earth, and took great care to design our bodies. In all this we see empirical evidence of intentionality.

The Big Bang Theory

Francis Collins is a distinguished research scientist who headed up the Human Genome Project which successfully mapped the entire human genome. His popular book, *The Language of God*, describes how DNA is precisely like a language. Language is always the result of intelligence and cannot happen by accident. Collins, like many Christians, believe God used some form of evolution as part of the process to bring about life.

---

[227] Jacques Monod, *Chance and Necessity*, 1972, p. 134
[228] Lennox, *God's Undertaker*, p. 129

Collins summarizes the Big Bang in *The Language of God*: "We have this very solid conclusion that the universe had an origin, the Big Bang. Fifteen billion years ago, the universe began with an unimaginably bright flash of energy from an infinitesimally small point. That implies that before that, there was nothing. I can't imagine how nature, in this case the universe, could have created itself. And the very fact that the universe had a beginning implies that someone was able to begin it. And it seems to me that had to be outside of nature."

The fascinating thing about the Big Bang is that it was an exquisitely calibrated explosion – unnaturally so. The Big Bang started with high potential for order (known as low entropy) which makes no sense naturally. Like any explosion, it should have been highly disordered (high entropy).[229]

The rate of expansion of the universe after the initial explosion was precisely balanced. If the rate was slower by 1 in a million, the universe would have re-collapsed when it was only 30,000 years old. If the rate of expansion had been just a little higher, it would be moving too rapidly to allow gravity to gather matter into clumps that formed into stars and galaxies. We would have had a universe devoid of stars, planets and galaxies.

The origin of the universe is well understood, and there are many surprising coincidences. Collins asks us to consider the following observations:

"In the early moments of the universe following the Big Bang, matter and anti-matter were created in almost equivalent amounts. At one millisecond of time,

---

[229] Entropy is a measure of the amount of disordered energy in a system, i.e. unavailable for work.

the universe cooled enough for quarks and antiquarks to 'condense out.' Any quark encountering an antiquark, which would have happened quickly in this high density, resulted in the complete annihilation of both and the release of a photon of energy. But the symmetry between matter and antimatter was not quite precise; for about every billion pair of quarks and antiquarks, there was an extra quark. It is that tiny fraction of the initial potential of the entire universe that makes up the mass of the universe as we now know it.

"Why did this asymmetry exist? It would seem more natural for there to be no asymmetry. But if there had been complete symmetry...the universe would have quickly devolved into pure radiation, [with no matter] and people, planets, stars, and galaxies would never have come into existence.

"The way in which the universe expanded after the Big Bang depended critically on how much total mass and energy the universe had, and also on the strength of the gravitational constant. The incredible degree of fine-tuning of these physical constants has been a subject of wonder for many experts... If the rate of expansion one second after the Big Bang had been smaller by even one part in 100 thousand million million, the universe would have re-collapsed before it ever reached its present size.

"On the other hand, if the rate of expansion had been greater by even one part in a million, stars and planets would not have been able to form...The existence of a universe as we know it rests upon a knife edge of improbability.

"The same remarkable circumstance applies to the formation of heavier elements. If the strong nuclear force that holds together protons and neutrons had been even slightly weaker, then only hydrogen could have formed in the universe. If, on the other hand, the strong nuclear force had been slightly stronger, all hydrogen would have been converted to helium instead of the 25% that occurred early in the Big Bang, and thus the fusion furnaces of stars and their ability to generate heavier elements would never have been born.

"Adding to this remarkable observation, the nuclear force appears to be tuned just sufficiently for carbon to form, which is critical for life... Had that force been just slightly more attractive, all carbon would have been converted into oxygen." [230]

As Collins relates, the initial explosion was incredibly precise. The number of quarks remaining from the fusion of quarks and antiquarks in the first moment of the Big bang was just the right amount to form the precise amount of total mass necessary in the universe. This total mass had to be balanced precisely with the strength of gravity and the strength of the initial explosive force of the Big Bang so that the universe would expand at the correct rate. All these parameters (the amount of matter, the strength of gravity, the rate of expansion) had to be precisely calibrated, not just on their own but with each other so that the rate of expansion would be right. Not enough, and the universe re-collapses. Too much, and it expands too fast for gravity to allow for matter to form into stars and planets.

---

[230] Collins, *The Language of God*, p.71-74

Collins concludes that: "The Big Bang cries out for a divine explanation. It forces the conclusion that nature had a defined beginning. I cannot see how nature could have created itself. Only a supernatural force outside of space and time could have done that."[231]

The chances of all this happening by accident are not unlike a fully functional Empire State Building, with working plumbing, lights and elevators, coalescing out of the dust of a nuclear detonation.

There is little or no debate on the Big Bang. It is one of the most 'proved' theories in science and is entirely compatible with Genesis 1:1. It is scientific proof that the universe had a beginning, exactly what the Bible had been claiming for thousands of years.

But up until the 20th century, atheists, as well as pagans before them, believed the universe was eternal. The discovery of the Big Bang was extremely unsettling to many scientists who were inclined towards atheism, precisely because the religious implications were so obvious. For years Fred Hoyle, like many scientists, resisted it until the weight of evidence became overwhelming. It was Hoyle who coined the term 'Big Bang', which he originally meant as a term of derision because he thought the idea was ridiculous.

Many people, scientists included, see it as clear evidence of the creation event that got the whole thing started. The Bible is very clear that God made the universe and everything in it. It doesn't say *when*, nor does it go into detail on *how* He did it, or *how long* He took, or what processes might have been involved with his creative

---

[231] Collins, *The Language of God*, p. 67.

work.[232] What we have here is the sudden appearance, out of nothing, of the universe appearing instantaneously. To many people this looks like an act of creation. It is false logic to claim that the Big Bang is in conflict with Christianity. It harmonizes very nicely, in fact.

It's perhaps apropos to quote the younger version of Sheldon, the character from the popular TV show *The Big Bang Theory:* Young Sheldon, wanting to encourage his mother in her faith in God, tells her that gravity is precisely as strong as it needs to be, and that if the ratio of the electromagnetic force to the strong nuclear force wasn't 1%, life wouldn't exist. "What are the odds that would happen all by itself?... the precision of the universe at least makes it logical to conclude there's a creator."[233]

What Do Scientists Say About These Facts?

Paul Davies: The odds against the initial conditions of the universe being suitable for later star formation is one followed by a thousand billion billion zeroes. He concludes: "It seems as though somebody has fine-tuned nature's numbers to make the Universe...The impression of design is overwhelming."

NASA Astronomer John O'Keefe: "These circumstances indicate that the universe was created for man to live in."

Sir Fredrick Hoyle famously compared these odds against the spontaneous formation of life with the chance of

---

[232] Notwithstanding a literal interpretation of Genesis 1 that takes the view that God created the universe and the world in a literal 6 day span, six thousand years ago. This is covered in Chapter 3, "Science and Christianity".

[233] Young Sheldon, Season 2, Episode 3.

a tornado sweeping through a junkyard and producing a Boeing 747 jet aircraft.[234]

Hoyle also said: "A common sense interpretation of the facts suggests that a super intelligence has monkeyed with physics, as well as with chemistry and biology, and that there are no blind forces worth speaking about in nature. The number one calculates from the facts seem to me so overwhelming as to put this conclusion almost beyond question."

Richard Morris: "How is it that common elements such as carbon, nitrogen, oxygen happen to have just the kind of atomic properties that they needed to combine to make the molecules upon which life depends? It is almost as though the universe had been consciously designed…"

Freeman Dyson: "the more I examine the universe and study the details of its architecture, the more evidence I find that the universe in some sense must have known we were coming."[235]

Robert Jastrow: "Astronomical evidence leads to a biblical view of origins."

Stephen Hawking: "The odds against a universe like ours emerging out of something like the Big Bang are enormous. I think there are clearly religious implications."

Arno Penzias: "The best data we have are exactly what I would have predicted, had I nothing to go on but the five books of Moses, the Psalms, the Bible as a whole."[236]

---

[234] *The Intelligent Universe*, London, by Michael Joseph, 1983. Quoted in Lennox, *God's Undertaker*, p. 129
[235] Dyson, *Disturbing Universe*, 1979, p. 250.
[236] "Clues to the Universe's Origin Expected", *New York Times*, March 12, 1978. Quoted in Collins, *The Language of God*, p. 76.

Francis Collins: "When you look from the perspective of a scientist at the universe, it looks as if the universe knew we were coming. There are 15 constants - the gravitational constant, the strong and weak nuclear forces, etc. - that have precise values. If any one of those constants was off by even one part in a million, or in some cases, by one part in a million million, the universe could not have actually come to the point where we see it. Matter would not have been able to coalesce, there would have been no galaxies, stars, planets or people."[237]

Referring to the workings of DNA within our cells, Lennox notes that: "The existence of these exquisitely constituted molecular machines is powerful evidence for many scientists of a designing intelligence."[238]

Astronomer G. Gonzalez, one of the authors of "The Privileged Planet", has this to say: "[A]s we stand gazing at the heavens beyond our little oasis [Earth], we gaze not into a meaningless abyss but into a wonderous arena commensurate with our capacity for discovery. Perhaps we have also been staring past a cosmic signal far more significant than any mere sequence of numbers, a signal revealing a universe so skillfully crafted for life and discovery that it seems to whisper of an extra-terrestrial intelligence immeasurably more vast, more ancient, and more magnificent than anything we've been willing to expect or imagine."[239]

Astrophysicist Hugh Ross has said that: "Astronomers who do not draw theistic or deistic conclusions are becoming rare, and even the few dissenters hint that the tide is against

---

[237] Francis Collins, quoted in *The Reason for God*, p.134
[238] John Lennox, *God's Undertaker*, p. 122
[239] Gonzalez & Richards, *The Privileged Plant*, p. 335

them. Geoffrey Burbidge, of the University of California at San Diego, complains that his fellow astronomers are rushing off to join 'The First Church of Christ of the Big Bang.'"[240]

Common Objections

Objections commonly raised against a theistic interpretation of the scientific evidence are: 1) We just got lucky. 2) Where did God come from? 3) The multiverse. 4) There is some as yet unknown unifying principle. 5) The other life-forms objection. 6) The Weak Anthropic Principle.[241]

Dumb Luck Theory.

While we can't logically rule out luck, we need to look at probabilities. The likelihood is so fantastically remote, no sane person would bet on it. To illustrate the amount of luck we're talking about many have used the following analogy: Picture the entire universe filled with coins. Now mark one with an 'x'. Stick your hand in at random, stir around, and pick one at random, blindfolded. What are the chances of pulling the one out with the 'x'? Is it rational to bet against such improbable odds? You'd be crazy to bet the rent money on it.

The gravitational force alone is enough to illustrate the irrationality of assuming we 'just got lucky.' If the force of gravity had been stronger or weaker by one part in 10^{40} then stable, life sustaining stars like our Sun would not be possible.

---

[240] *The Creator and the Cosmos*
[241] Good summaries of the atheistic response to the evidence can be found in *The Language of God*, p.75, by Francis Collins, and *The Reason for the Hope Within*, p.55-65, by Robin Collins.

To illustrate this number, it would be like stretching a measuring tape the length of the entire known universe, and the setting for the force of gravity had to be within one inch.

Gravity is just one of many such finely-tuned properties within the universe. We don't assume such improbable odds in real life. Rational people simply don't live that way. Alvin Plantinga makes the following analogy: You're playing poker with a group of friends, and the same person keeps getting a straight flush. Fifty hands later, he is still getting straight flushes and the mountain of cash on the table in front of him is growing higher. What would you conclude? That he's just exceptionally lucky? You'd be crazy to assume he's not cheating. When you confront him with his cheating, he says: "No, you don't understand. I'm just very lucky, you see. Out of all the billions of universes in the multiverse, in which every possible combination of events gets played out, ours just happens to be the one universe in which I happen to win 50 straight flushes in a row." As Alvin Plantinga says, "Such an argument is not likely to play out very well in Dodge." Gunfire is sure to ensue.

To illustrate the luck argument, atheists talk about an infinite number of monkeys banging away on an infinite number of keyboards. Given enough time they could, by chance, type up King Lear.

This line of argument has been discredited. One of the major problems with this is that the math doesn't work. Working out the mathematical probability of monkeys managing to get *King Lear* by accident, you get a number that far exceeds the life of the universe. There isn't enough time since the beginning of, well, *time* for the dumb luck scenario to play out.[242] The analogy is more like one monkey and one keyboard getting King Lear right the first time. While you can't logically prove that can't happen, we all know it won't.

> "To place one's confidence in neo-Darwinist cosmology (i.e. blind chance) and the unknowable existence of a virtually infinite number of universes is to commit a form of the gambler's fallacy, a logic error so blatant as to express irrationality. ... To bet that the universe fell together exactly the way it is, precisely suited for life, by innumerable quirks of fate...makes even less sense than to bet [on a coin toss that it will come up heads on every toss for 10,000 tosses]."[243]

People who assert this minimize the level of fine-tuning needed for life. The odds against it are so incomprehensibly great that it cannot be reasonably faced. They would never embrace such a hypothesis if they had to bet their rent or grocery money, much less their lives.

One response to this is that improbable things happen every day, such as winning a lottery: the chance of someone winning is improbable, yet someone has to win. The winner no doubt appreciates how lucky they were.

But this is a false analogy. The correct analogy is more like the *same person* winning the lottery every time, *millions* of times or more in a row. Of course, no one will just brush that off as luck. Police investigations and lawsuits would

---

[242] See Lennox, *God's Undertaker*, chapter 9 'The Monkey Machine'. Lennox is a mathematician who goes to great lengths showing in detail that it's mathematically impossible to get King Lear.
[243] Hugh Ross, *Why I Am a Christian*, p.142

ensue, and no doubt jail terms handed out because we all know that it had to be rigged.

What is at issue here is specified improbability: that what happened conforms to an independently discovered pattern. If the monkeys happen to type an English sonnet, we know this is not the result of blind chance because the letters conform to English grammar. It has meaning.

In the same way physics and biology tell us what is needed for life apart from any knowledge of the early conditions of the universe. The universe has that specified improbability. That's what theists mean when they talk about design. It appears to be *intentional*. The universe has every indication that someone rigged it.

"Where did God come from?"

Some atheists respond with the 'Who Made God' argument. The problem with this argument is that it posits the need for a series of ever increasingly complex gods. God created the universe, but an even more complex god would be needed to create the creator, and so on, with no logical end in sight. But this is not a rational rebuttal and is easily dispensed with:

God is a properly basic brute fact. He is the starting point. In this debate, we are trying to show that there is good evidence for God, such that it is rational to believe God exists. Throwing up questions about where he might have come from does not refute His existence. For instance, if you are trying to prove the existence, say, of some alien life form, and have good evidence for it, questioning where the aliens came from is not a proper rebuttal or a defeater for the evidence. If you can show that there is evidence for the existence of the alien life form, questioning who or what made them is not proof against their existence.

The Christian position, as that of the Jew and Muslim, is that God is uncaused. He has no beginning. He is a brute fact, the starting point. All that is necessary is to show evidence for his existence.

Atheism of the Gaps: The Multiverse Argument.

This is the 'billions of monkeys on keyboards' argument dressed up in a fancy scientific looking suit. Given enough monkeys hammering away on enough typewriters, perchance one will eventually come up with King Lear. Given enough universes, eventually one will come up with all the right ingredients for life.

The multiverse argument says that we aren't the only universe, and that there are potentially an endless number of universes, millions if not billions. This allows for endless trial and error until time and chance gets it right. Given enough universes we would eventually get the right one and we just happen to be in it – ergo, no need for God.

The multiverse theory is more indicative of the over all weakness of atheist's position, rather than any kind of rational argument. There is no evidence for the multiverse. That atheists are forced to retreat into such wild imaginary speculations to try and get around the obvious signs of design shows just how powerful the theistic design argument is.

Nor is it a scientific theory, since there is not one shred of evidence for it, even if it does make for interesting sci-fi. There is as much evidence for fairies at the bottom of my garden as there is for the multiverse.

But that aside, even if it turns out to be true, so what? All it does is push the design problem up into a higher level. It does not dispense with the evidence for design we see all around us, in the universe, solar system and Earth's biosphere.[244]

Many Christians are very comfortable with science fiction ideas like this. If our God is big enough to create the universe, he is certainly big enough to create more that one universe, as well as life on more than one planet. The multiverse idea, far from being a threat to Christianity, is more telling of the weakness of the atheist position.

"An important question is whether the multiverse inherently conflicts with the Bible. In principle, the answer is no. Although scripture does not directly address the concept of a multiverse, several passages provide hints that support the idea of multiple worlds. The Bible refers to an angelic realm that exists beyond our universe, … as well as the creation of a new physical world… these other realms imply that the existence of other universes represents no conflict with Scripture."[245]

The Grand Unifying Theory (GUT).

Many atheists are betting the family farm on this one. The idea here is that there is as yet some undiscovered unifying principle that ties all the cosmological constants together, so that the relative values would be determined. This would, they argue, remove the need for a designer since the GUT principle would drive out all the various values once the show got started.

---

[244] Jeffrey Zweerink, Ph.D., *Who's Afraid of the Multiverse?*
[245] Ibid, p. 49.

Like the multi-verse, this is entirely speculative. But the biggest problem with this argument is that all it really does is move the 'design problem' up into a different level. It doesn't really dispel design, it just locates it in a different place. It is still just as inconceivable that such a fundamental law would happen to have all the right parameters to drive out the design necessary for life.

Atheists often dismiss Christian arguments as a 'God of the gaps.' That we are basing our arguments on what we don't know. But that's not the case – the design argument is based on what we do know. It seems to me, however, that the multiverse argument is an 'atheism of the gaps', because they are basing their argument on something we have no evidence for and very likely can never know: multiverses and unifying theories.

The Other Life-Forms Objection

Atheists object that we are presupposing that intelligent life has to be like us. If the parameters of the universe had been different, then different forms of life could have arisen. So what we view as wonderful design in the universe is just a form of observational bias. If the parameters of the universe had been different, it could have produced very different forms of life, and those forms of life would have seen the universe as wonderfully designed for them.

But most cases of fine-tuning are not presupposing life has to be like us. Most of the fine-tuning we observe is required for *any* form of advanced life. It is difficult to imagine life forming without stable stars or planets. It is hard to imagine life arising in a universe composed entirely of hydrogen gas. Robin Collins has a good response: "Consider, for instance, the case of the fine-tuning of the strong nuclear force. If it were slightly smaller, no atoms could exist other than hydrogen. Contrary to what one might see on *Star Trek*, an intelligent life-form cannot be composed of merely hydrogen gas: there is simply not enough stable complexity: So, in general the fine-tuning argument merely presupposes that intelligent life requires some degree of stable, reproducible organized complexity. This is certainly a very reasonable assumption."[246]

The Weak Anthropic Principle

This is a flavour of the blind luck theory: If the laws of nature were not fine-tuned, we wouldn't be here to talk about it. So fine-tuning isn't really improbable at all, but simply follows from the fact that we exist and are here to wonder about it.

There are a few reasons why this objection can be discounted. For one thing, at bottom, it's really just a form of question-begging in a fancy dress. The best way to respond to this objection is to recast the argument: our existence is highly improbable given atheism, but not at all improbable under theism. Therefore our existence strongly confirms theism over atheism.

John Leslie makes the following analogy:[247] I am to be executed by firing-squad. When the moment comes, all fifty sharpshooters miss me. The natural response to such an unlikely event would not be: "They all missed me by accident. If they hadn't missed me, I wouldn't be alive to think about it, so I shouldn't be surprised at my luck."

---

[246] *Reason for the Hope Within*, p.56-57
[247] John Leslie, "How to Draw Conclusions," p. 304.

This is not an adequate explanation. A much more reasonable explanation is that there must be some reason they all missed, such as they never intended to shoot me. My continued existence is much more probable under the theory that they intended to miss me, rather then all fifty sharpshooters just happened to miss by chance.

Conclusion: We Are Not an Accident.

Our universe is unfathomably unlikely. The constants of the universe have extremely precise settings. When you calculate the odds of just one coming out right, you get a number in the trillions. When you calculate the odds of just 5 coming out right, you get a number that exceeds the number of atoms in the known universe. There are many more than just 5, so the odds of us coming about by chance is really beyond imagination and unreasonable to entertain.

Such precision is mind-boggling. The coincidences are simply too amazing to be the result of mere happenstance. The fine-tuning of the universe is scientific fact, not just a theory or an interpretation.

William Lane Craig summarizes it nicely:

"There are about 50 such quantities and constants that had to be precise. And not just fine-tuned themselves, but fine tuned in their ratios to each other. So the odds by chance are literally incomprehensible. We are confronted by improbability upon improbability until our minds reel with incomprehensible numbers."

Astronomer Hugh Ross:

"Thirty-five years of research on the Anthropic Principle (the universe's tendency to provide every necessity for human life and sustenance) has built an expanding rather than diminishing body of evidence for divine design. What we see is the opposite of the 'God of the Gaps' notion. As knowledge and understanding of the natural realm has advanced, the need to invoke a supernatural explanation has only increased. The trend line moves so conclusively in one direction that nontheistic astronomers must own up to the non-scientific basis for their position. As cosmologist Ed Harrison says, an honest look at the cosmos's finely tuned features leads to a moment of truth: 'Here is the cosmological proof of the existence of God...The fine tuning of the universe provides prima facie evidence for deistic design. Take your choice: blind chance that requires multitudes of universes, or design that requires only one'...Many scientists, when they admit their views, incline toward the teleological or design argument."[248]

There is strong support in science for faith. Enough so that it is very reasonable to conclude there is a Creator. The evidence is there. Atheists, naturally, have come up with alternative explanations for the evidence. We can choose not to believe in God – God made us free agents, after all. *But it can't be argued that there's not enough evidence for God.*

There are sufficient clues that it is reasonable for a rational, thinking person to believe in God. Contra Dawkins,

---

[248] Hugh Ross, *Why I Am a Christian*, p. 141-142

287

et al, who claim there is no evidence that a rational person will accept, therefore making belief in God equivalent to joining the flat earth society.

"The community of believers has no reason to fear and every reason to anticipate the advance of scientific research into the origin and characteristics of the cosmos. The more we learn, the more evidence we accumulate for the existence of God and for his identity as the God revealed in the Bible."[249]

Some will point out that even if science points us to a Creator, this doesn't prove the Christian God. Richard Dawkins mentioned once in a debate that even if there is a god, how do we know any of our religions on Earth got it right?

This is a valid objection. Science can only take us as far as deism:[250] God created the universe and got things started, but he's not necessarily a personal God who is involved with human affairs or hears prayer. He might be an all-powerful deity, but he's off somewhere else in the universe entirely unconcerned with us here on Earth. Given such a God, there is no reason to expect that any of our religions on Earth have it right.

Where do we go from here, and how do we get from an all-powerful Creator to the Christian God – the personal God of the Bible who loves us and revealed Himself to humanity? Science alone will not take us all the way to the Christian God, so we must look to other grounds, and this is

---

[249] Hugh Ross, *Why I Am a Christian*, p. 142
[250] Also referred to as Einstein's God, or the God of the scientists. Einstein believed in God, but as far as we can tell his view was deistic.

where the argument gets really interesting. That's the subject of the next two chapters.

Further Reading

Barrow, John & Tipler. *The Anthropic Cosmological Principle* (1986).

Behe, Michael. *The Edge of Evolution: The Search for the Limits of Darwinism* (2007).

_____. *Darwin's Black Box: The Biochemical Challenge to Evolution* (2006).

_____. *Darwin Devolves: The Science of DNA That Challenges Evolution* (2020).

Berlinski, David. *The Devil's Delusion: Atheism and Its Scientific Pretensions* (2009).

Collins, Francis. *The Language of God* (2006).

Collins, Robin. "A Scientific Argument for the Existence of God." *Reason for the Hope Within,* ed. Michael Murray (1999).

Flew, Anthony. *There is a God: How the World's Most Notorious Atheist Changed his Mind* (2008).

Glynn, Patrick. *God: The Evidence* (1999).

Gonzalez, Guillermo and Jay Richards. *Privileged Planet* (2004).

Lennox, John. *God's Undertaker: Has Science Buried God?* (2009).

_____. *God and Stephen Hawking: Whose Design is it Anyway?* (2011).

_____. *Gunning for God: Why the New Atheists Are Missing the Target.*

McGrath, Alister. *A Fine-Tuned Universe* (2009).

_____. *Why God Won't Go Away* (2010).

Rees, Martin. *Just Six Numbers* (2001).

Swinburne, Richard. *The Existence of God* (2004).

11

Is Right and Wrong Relative?

THE PROBLEM OF EVIL is the classic argument against the existence of God because of the evil in the world. If a good and powerful God exists, then He would not allow pointless evil. Because there is so much pointless suffering and injustice, then God could not exist.

It's a fair question, and the presence of evil is often cited by people as a major reason for not believing in God. Entire books have been written on this subject, and I won't be able to settle the question in the few pages I have here.[251] But, as Tim Keller relates, "Many philosophers have identified a major flaw in this reasoning. Tucked away within the assertion that the world is filled with pointless evil is a hidden premise, namely, that if evil appears pointless to me, then it must be pointless. This reasoning is, of course, fallacious. Just because we can't see or imagine a good reason … doesn't mean there can't be one. Again we see lurking within the supposedly hard-nosed skepticism an enormous faith in one's own cognitive faculties."[252]

The so-called 'problem of evil' is a much bigger problem for atheists, because you can't really talk about evil without

---

[251] Please see the list of recommended reading at the end of this chapter.
[252] Keller, *Reason for God*, p.23

acknowledging the moral standards by which we are enabled to judge something as evil. Atheism just can't account for objective moral standards. Alvin Plantinga summarizes the problem for atheism:

> "Could there really be any such things as horrifying wickedness [if there were no God and we just evolved]? I don't see how. There can be such a thing only if there is a way that rational creatures are supposed to live, obliged to live... A [secular] way of looking at the world has no place for genuine moral obligation of any sort... and thus no way to say that there is such a thing as genuine and appalling wickedness. Accordingly, if you think there really is such a thing as horrifying wickedness, (and not just an illusion of some sort), then you have a powerful...argument [for the reality of God]."[253]

CS Lewis was an army Lieutenant in the First World War. He survived the war, but his experience of the horrors turned him into a convinced atheist. But later, as he continued to think it through, he changed his mind. Lewis wrote:

> "My argument against God [when I was an atheist] was that the universe seemed so cruel and unjust. But how had I got this idea of just and unjust? A man does not call a line crooked unless he has some idea of a straight line. What was I comparing this universe with when I called it unjust? Of course I could have given up my idea of justice by saying that it was nothing but a private

---

[253] Alvin Plantinga, "A Christian Life Partly Lived".

idea of my own. But if I did that, then my argument against God collapsed too – for the argument depended on saying that the world was really unjust, not simply that it did not happen to please my private fancies. Thus in the very act of trying to prove that God did not exist – in other words, that the whole of reality was senseless – I found I was forced to assume that one part of reality – namely my idea of justice – was full of sense. Consequently, atheism turns out to be too simple...If there were no light in the universe and therefore no creatures with eyes, we should never know it was dark. *Dark* would be without meaning."[254]

The Problem of Good

Atheists are fond of telling us life is meaningless and that there is no ultimate right or wrong or justice in the universe. As Dawkins said:

"The universe we observe has precisely the properties we should expect if there was, at bottom, no design, no purpose, no evil and no good, nothing but blind pitiless indifference. As that unhappy poet A.E. Housman put it:

'For Nature, heartless, witless Nature
Will neither know nor care.'

DNA neither knows nor cares. DNA just is. And we dance to its music."[255]

---

[254] C.S. Lewis, *Mere Christianity* (New York: Collier Macmillan, 1960, paperback), p.45.
[255] Richard Dawkins, *River Out of Eden*, New York: Basic Books, 1995, p.133.

Charming. Someone should put that into a Hallmark sympathy card. Arthur Leff, no friend of Christianity, points out the problem for atheism:

> *"Only if ethics were something unspeakable by us, could law be unnatural, and therefore unchallengeable. As things now stand, everything is up for grabs. Nevertheless:*
> *Napalming babies is bad.*
> *Starving the poor is wicked.*
> *Buying and selling each other is depraved.*
> *Those who stood up to and died resisting Hitler, Stalin, Amin, and pol Pot – and General Custer too – have earned salvation. Those who acquiesced deserve to be damned.*
> *There is in the world such a thing as evil.*
> *[All together now:] Sez who?*
> *God help us.* "[256]

The Salad Bar Ethics of Atheism

Arthur Leff hits the nail on the head. Darwinian evolution leaves us with free-floating ethics in which we are at liberty to pick and choose what we like, like making selections at a salad bar. As an atheist, he attempts to find some kind of solid ground for morals, but realizes that in a universe without God there can't be. At the same time he realizes that we inescapably know that there is real evil, right and wrong, and that these things are not – cannot be – determined by us. Only recognized by us.

---

[256] Arthur A. Leff, "Unspeakable Ethics, Unnatural Law", Duke Law Journal 6, 1979, p. 1249. Available online at http://bit.ly/leff.

Atheism, in order to attack Christianity, is forced to borrow values that can only come from a theistic universe, values that atheism can never provide intellectual grounds for. Genuine morality is not something we get to choose. We don't determine what's really right and wrong. We can only recognize it and seek to align our lives with that reality. This is a powerful clue to the existence of God. Not even atheists live consistently according to evolutionary values, which should tell us something. No one except a sociopath or moral monster could.

It is tragic when Christians behave badly. Unfortunately, not all Christians walk on water, but, alas, as it turns out we are as human as anyone else. The bad behavior of individual Christians is often used as an argument against Christianity, but it is a much more powerful argument the other way around: the moral outrage of atheists at injustice and wrong-doing is a good argument against atheism, because their insistence on morality gives the whole game away, whether they realize it or not.

This sets us up nicely for the next chapter, in which we'll explore this topic in more detail. For many believers it is the most compelling and emotionally satisfying argument for the existence of a personal God.

Further Reading

Howard-Snyder, Daniel. "God, Evil, and Suffering" in *Reason for the Hope Within*, (Eerdmans, 1999).

Keller, Timothy. *Walking with God Through Pain and Suffering* (2013).

Lewis, C. S. *Mere Christianity* (1952).

Volf, Miroslav. *Exclusion & Embrace* (1996).

Wood, David. "God, Suffering and Santa Claus: An Examination of the Explanatory Power of Theism and Atheism." *Evidence for God,* ed. William Dembski (2010).

Yancey, Philip. *Where is God When it Hurts?* (1990).

12

The Moral Arc of the Universe

"You are right in speaking of the moral foundations of science, but you cannot turn around and speak of the scientific foundations of morality."

Albert Einstein

IT WASN'T VERY LONG AFTER the publication of *On the Origin of Species* in 1859, that atheists began to extend the logic of Darwin's theory beyond the science of biology into every aspect of human existence. If our minds and bodies are the result of unguided evolutionary processes, they reasoned, then *everything* about human life and society must be as well.

Karl Marx brought evolutionary theory into economics and class struggle. Sigmund Freud brought it into mental health and psychology. Social Darwinism applied evolution to society and politics.

Fredrich Nietzsche was one of the first to grasp the implications of Darwinism for morality, and argued that there could be no moral absolutes, just power. All of our ideas of morality are just sentimental delusions, according to Nietzsche.

The eugenics movement in the first half of the 20th century drew heavily upon Darwinism. It advocated a scientific approach to improving the human gene pool by removing weak and inferior genetic traits and breeding superior ones. The eugenics movement promoted the forced sterilization of 'inferior' or 'defective' people, sought to ban or restrict inter-racial marriage, and advocated planned breeding between 'superior' members of the human race. These are all logical extrapolations of *unguided* evolution which assumes an atheistic view of the theory.[257]

My DNA Made Me Do It

Others sought to bring Darwinism into the practise of law. In 1924 Clarence Darrow, the lawyer for two men on trial for the thrill killing of a fourteen-year-old boy, argued that the killers couldn't be held responsible for their actions because they were just acting out what evolution had programmed into them. Darrow said in court: "Science has been at work...and intelligent people now know that every human being is the product of the endless heredity back of him and the infinite environment around him."[258]

As Dawkins famously said:

> "DNA neither cares nor knows. DNA just is. And we dance to its music."[259]

This gets to the heart of the problem for atheism: Darwinian evolution selects for survival fitness, not truth, much less moral truth. The entire process of evolution depends on the violence of the strong against the weak. The strong survive to pass on their genes, the weak perish and so inferior traits are eventually bred out of the species and the

---

[257] For more on Darwin's legacy, see the award-winning *Human Zoos:* https://www.youtube.com/watch?v=nY6Zrol5QEk
[258] Quoted in Behe, *Darwin Devolves*, p. 272
[259] Dawkins, *River Out of Eden*

species as a whole is strengthened – regardless of how right or wrong the actions of the strong are.

Therefore in a purely Darwinian world our ideas around social justice, fair treatment of other people, the evils of slavery, rape and racial bigotry, just happen to be our own feelings resulting from an accidental arrangement of chemicals in our brain. In which case there is nothing particularly right or wrong about such ideas and we are forced to concede, if we are to remain logically consistent, that there is no real good or evil in the world, and by extension no real moral obligation.

We've discussed previously that the science of evolution is completely compatible with Christian faith. The fossil record indicates some forms of evolutionary processes have been at work throughout the biological history of Earth. That's one thing, and fine at the level of biological processes.

The problem is that atheists elevated Darwin's theory into an all-encompassing worldview in order to use it as a lever by which to eject God from the universe. As an all-encompassing worldview it would explain everything about us without any need for God.

> "The Astonishing Hypothesis is that 'You,' your joys and your sorrows, your memories and your ambitions, your sense of personal identity and free will, are in fact no more than the behavior of a vast assembly of nerve cells and their associated molecules. As Lewis Carroll's Alice might have phrased it: 'You're nothing but a pack of neurons.'"[260]

---

[260] Francis Crick, *The Astonishing Hypothesis: The Scientific Search for the Soul*, 1994.

Along these lines, Richard Dawkins has this to say:

"In a universe of electrons and selfish genes, blind physical forces and genetic replication, some people are going to get hurt, other people are going to get lucky, and you won't find any rhyme or reason in it, nor any justice. The universe that we observe has precisely the properties we should expect if there is, at bottom, no design, no purpose, no evil, no good, nothing but pitiless indifference."[261]

Science versus the Darwinian Worldview

Darwinism as a term typically stands for certain philosophies that have developed which assumes an atheistic understanding of evolutionary processes.

Questioning Darwinism is not at all the same as questioning the *science* of evolution. The ancient bones and fossils exist. There are hominid skulls millions of years old. There is good evidence that some sort of evolutionary process over vast amounts of time is responsible for our present physical form.

That's fine as far as the physical evidence goes. What it may all *mean* is an entirely different question that isn't science, but philosophy.

Our philosophical view will be largely informed and shaped by our personal assumptions, biases, and other information we bring to the question. What certain facts of science might mean to me may be very different for you.

Personally, I see no compelling reason why the discovery of a 2-million-year-old human jawbone should

---

[261] Richard Dawkins, *River Out of Eden: A Darwinian View of Life*

299

disturb my Christian faith. And I'm in good company on that score, as I've discussed and shown throughout this book.

So whatever that 2-million-year-old human jawbone may mean, it doesn't mean there's no God.

Atheists, of course, insist that such facts means that there is no God, because in their view this puts God out of a job. But that's a very large assumption on their part, based heavily on another assumption they insist on: that any such biological processes throughout our past must have been unguided, undesigned, and accidental.

But those are philosophical assumptions, and I think it's very safe and reasonable to take another direction, a more theistic one.

The reason I say this is because there are other facts that weigh very heavily in on the question, both moral and scientific, that are extremely compelling.

We covered the very powerful evidence for intentionality behind the cosmos in chapter 10. This is positive, scientific evidence for the existence of a Creator.

For me, the most satisfying evidence for the existence of God is found within us – our internal moral compass pointing to an objective moral reality that is external to us, a moral law that seems to be written into the very fabric of the universe itself.

If unguided Darwinian evolution is the whole story, then everything about us, everything we think and believe about morality and justice, are also a result of evolution – an accidental arrangement of chemicals in our brains.

If that's the case, then Nietzsche was right: all of our ideas of morality are just sentimental delusions. Not only does Darwinian evolution destroy morality, but it also destroys any real moral obligation.

Is morality really just a delusion?

Darwinism as a philosophy is ultimately incompatible with our moral values. If all our moral values are just chemicals in our brains, by what obligation need I follow them? I can determine my own ethical rules, and why should I pay any attention to yours?

As such we would be free to ignore them or believe differently. However, I think we all know that we are not free to believe whatever we want about certain moralities. The moral outrage a normal person will rightfully feel at evil – child molestation, gassing Jews, rape, slavery – are not just "sentimental delusions".

Invoking rule of law or cultural convention doesn't help much here. If the only thing that determines our moral behavior is the law with its attendant fear of punishment, then what if I happen to live in a different culture with different laws?

We happen to live in a culture that says, for instance, rape is wrong, and convicted rapists will go to prison. Is that what makes rape wrong? Is it *really* wrong, or just our personal feeling or a societal convention? What if we lived in a rape culture, in which rape is acceptable as a legitimate method for a man to pass on his genes?

Most of us will easily see that such things are wicked, but we also need to recognize they are *objectively* wicked. By 'objective' I am using the term to denote something that is an external reality, an absolute truth that is independent of our feelings.

Objective truth means something is true whether or not we believe it. When we agree that such things as rape and genocide are evil, we are simply aligning ourselves correctly with an external moral fact. These things are not determined by us nor are they wicked because we believe so. They are wicked and remain so independently of our feelings. Moral truths are an objective reality whether or not we personally believe it.

Many people find this a very powerful and persuasive argument for the reality of God, because the moral truth we can all sense is not possible within the confines of evolutionary naturalism.

Just as the mountains in the distance are external physical facts, right and wrong are external moral facts. The mountains are there whether I see them or not, whether or not I happen to like skiing. They are there even if my vision is poor and I can't see them, or cloudy weather obscures them. I can't wish them away.

If I argued that I didn't believe in mountains, or that they're just illusions, such an argument would not be very convincing and would only manage to make me look irrational.

Right and wrong is like that. It is not possible to really believe otherwise, unless you are also prepared to argue that, ultimately, butchering the children of another 'inferior' race is just a culturally relative ethic.

The Mad Mad World of Darwinian Ethics

Which, of course, is exactly where many determined atheists, committed to their philosophical worldview, are heading. Recently a couple of bright sparks published *A Natural History of Rape: Biological Bases of Sexual Coercion*.[262] Their book presents an evolutionary justification for rape, which they see as a beneficial behavior since, from

---

[262] MIT Press, 2000

an evolutionary viewpoint, sexual coercion is just seeking to pass on genes to the next generation.

They argue that rape is not really wrong, not a pathology, just an evolutionary adaptation. Rape is "a natural, biological phenomenon that is a product of the human evolutionary heritage."[263]

Randy Thornhill, one of the authors of the paper, was of course heavily criticized. But he insisted that it is not debatable: "every feature of every living thing, including human beings, has an underlying evolutionary background. That's not a debatable matter."[264]

Richard Dawkins takes great delight in telling us that we're just dancing to our DNA. That there is no justice, no right or wrong.

"The naturalist must not destroy my reverence for conscience and morals on Monday and expect me to venerate it on Tuesday and live as if it did matter. There is no escaping along these lines."[265]

Try telling the rape victim that her rapist was just acting out his evolutionary programming.

This underscores the fatal flaw with atheism, because it leaves the atheist in an *impossibly absurd position, a place we all know can't be true:* that the moral outrage we feel at horrific acts such as rape, molesting babies, or the gassing of Jews during the Holocaust, is just a reflection of some subjective (relative) moral value we happen to possess – but not really wrong in an objective sense.

---

[263] Quote taken from Nancy Pearcey, *Total Truth*, p.211

[264] Pearcey, *Total Truth*, p. 211

[265] C.S. Lewis, *Miracles*, p.58

This is a defeater for atheism because evolution and evolutionary ethics are a package deal.

I see no way around this for the atheist, and I believe it's a deathblow for atheism. The atheistic worldview fails, quite dramatically, to accurately describe the universe of objective moral reality we find ourselves living in.

> *"But it is painfully clear … that literally any behavior that is practiced today can be said to have survival value – after all, it has survived to our own times. Evolution fails as a moral guide because it provides no standard for judging any existing practices."*[266]

In stark contrast to Darwinian ethics, we have the Christian ethic of love and self-sacrifice as expressed by Captain Kirk:

> **"Better to die saving lives than to live with taking them."** *~Captain James T. Kirk*

Militant atheists claim that religious feelings and ideas can be explained away in evolutionary terms. There is therefore no need to fool yourself into thinking there is a God. But this is an absurd argument that undercuts itself, because if our religious ideas are just the result of evolution – and therefore wrong – then so is everything else we think and believe, including our moral ideas of right and wrong.

As Richard Dawkins thoughtfully said, we are all just gene machines, dancing to our DNA. Real morality no longer exists, because everything about us is just so many chemical reactions within us.

---

[266] Nancy Pearcey, *Total Truth*, p. 216

How then can we be expected to take anything seriously?

> "You can't, except in the lowest animal sense, be in love with a girl if you know (and keep on remembering) that all the beauties of both her person and her character are a momentary and accidental pattern produced by the collision of atoms, and that your own response to them is only a sort of psychic phosphorescence arising from the behavior of your genes. You can't go on getting very serious pleasure from music if you know and remember that its air of significance is a pure illusion, that you like it only because your nervous system is irrationally conditioned that way."[267]

The same applies to our moral sentiments. And the moral outrage we feel at evil is also just an accident of evolution. Evolutionary theory, when followed through to its logical conclusion, leads to a dog-eat-dog existence in which the only thing that matters is strength. *A fascist paradise.*[268]

Annie Dillard spent a year living by a creek in the mountains of Virginia. She hoped to be inspired by getting close to nature. Instead, she came to see how nature is dominated by the violence of the strong against the weak.

> "There is not a person in the world that behaves as badly as praying mantises. But wait, you say, there is no right or wrong in nature; right and wrong is a human concept. Precisely! We are moral creatures in an amoral world...Or consider the alternative...it is only

[267] CS Lewis. Quoted in *The Reason for God* by Tim Keller, p. 146
[268] Fascism, boiled down, is essentially 'strong man' politics.

human feeling that is freakishly amiss...All right then –
it is our emotions that are amiss. We are freaks, the
world is fine, and let us all go have lobotomies to
restore us to a natural state. We can leave the library
then, go back to the creek lobotomized, and live on its
banks as untroubled as any muskrat or reed. You
first."[269]

It's impossible for anyone not a sociopath (or an ivory-
tower academic writing for MIT Press) to believe that the
anger we feel at outrages such as rape or gassing Jews is just
an evolutionary adaption, a product of our evolutionary
heritage. But that's where Darwinian evolution takes us. If
you accept naturalism, then it is rationally unavoidable.

A theory that can accommodate itself to any moral
behavior is useless and unfalsifiable, and as such cannot be
true.

It needs to be said here that the argument is *not* that
atheists are immoral, or will necessarily be immoral people.
The theistic argument is that atheism does not provide the
intellectual framework or rational grounds for the morals
that we all (atheists and theists) hold.

The Universe Bends Toward Justice

*The arc of the moral universe is long, but it bends
toward justice*, Martin Luther King said. There is an objective
moral reality that is easy to see in a wide range of issues:
slavery, racism, bigotry, murder, rape, genocide.

Some may argue that our moral ideas are just
something we are taught. It's what we learned from our

---

[269] Annie Dillard, *Pilgrim at Tinker Creek.*

parents or taught at school. People who say such things will also need to be prepared to argue that our feelings that slavery and racism are wrong are just something we are taught. They will also, as CS Lewis once quipped, be the first to complain if you steal their lunch money or cheat at a game of cards.

Our inner moral compass points to a moral 'magnetic' north pole, which is a reality external to us just as the real north pole is. Just because we are taught something in school – like the four points of a compass – doesn't mean it's not objectively true. We are also taught the periodic table of elements.

Now, it needs to be admitted that some things are social conventions and therefore just culturally relative. Like the length of a woman's dress. The Victorian's used to think that it was immoral for a woman to show her legs, and long dresses were considered the right thing to do.

Moral relativists shouldn't get confused at this point. The simple fact that some things are morally relative – culturally determined or something we get to decide for ourselves – doesn't mean everything is relative.

Even committed Darwinians, when it comes to morality, make a leap out of a strictly evolutionary worldview and into the realm of objective human values and morals. They would have to, because no decent person could remain sane in the strictly Darwinian world that atheism requires. If it's impossible to live consistently as a Darwinist, then it warrants serious skepticism of the accuracy of such a worldview.

We Can All See the Stars

Atheists try to get around this dilemma by saying that we don't need God to see what's right and wrong. Sam Harris has argued that we can have a basis for genuine moral values in atheism, because we can all recognize that some behavior is not good, or is harmful, and so we shouldn't do it.

According to Harris, we can all see that being nice is better than being bad, we are all capable of recognizing good and bad, therefore we don't need God.

This is simply illiterate question begging. Of course we can all see this. Any normally functioning person will recognize that the Holocaust, for instance, was pure evil and something we shouldn't do. That's the point behind the Christian argument.

The fact that we can all use our eyes, if they are sharp enough, to see the stars above or the mountains on the horizon, does not preclude the existence of God. It's like arguing, "I can use my own eyes to see the stars. I don't need to invoke a god to do that," and then claiming that such an 'insight' disproves God.

However, just as we see the stars with our physical eyes, our moral intuition perceives the metaphysical fabric of a moral universe around us.

The moral reality of the universe we see with our moral intuition are metaphysical facts, as real as the stars above. And just like the ancient navigator, we can all look up and guide our lives accordingly. We may be short-sighted, or refuse to look up, or develop ridiculous arguments about how the stars aren't real, but the moral 'stars' are still there.

Our moral intuition tells us something else very important: there is an obligation to behave accordingly. We all sense this obligatory moral 'ought' in the universe.

We know justice and equality are important and that we ought to treat each other accordingly, even if we often fail to do so, and that this moral 'oughtness' transcends culture and is true for all people for all times.

When we consider such questions, a reasonable, properly functioning person will admit that such things are objective moral truths and therefore transcend all culture, and that a culture is wrong if it decides to gas a minority group. If you accept that there is such a thing as real right and wrong, actual good and evil, then you have a powerful argument for the existence of God.

Given the external moral standards that we know exist, it makes much more sense that there is a God then not. One of the reasons I find theism more convincing than atheism as a worldview is that it would be impossible to live as a consistent atheist.

The existence of objective moral values makes infinite sense given the existence of God. The presence of a Moral Law in the universe with its moral obligation points us to a Law Giver who is concerned with human affairs. It doesn't, of course, prove Christianity. But it does strongly indicate that some theistic religion, *and not atheism*, must be the truth.

This brings us to the point where we need to take a closer look at Christianity.

The Reason for Christianity

The Moral Law in the universe brings us to the feet of a Law Giver and at the same time tells us something about what this Law Giver must be like.

Apparently, He or She is very concerned with personal relationships, because how we treat each other is *the* primary concern behind the Moral Law. It follows then that this Law Giver is very concerned personally with us. The Law Giver is therefore Personal, since an impersonal 'force' is unlikely to evince such concern for our personal relationships and how we treat each other. This seems to be a very safe take-away from the Moral Law.

Given that this Law Giver is a person concerned with relationships between people, it makes sense that this God is also concerned with our relationship to Him. It is very likely, then, that He would have made some sort of arrangement to make Himself knowable to humanity.

Therefore it follows that at least one of the religions on Earth comes from this Law Giver, and this religion would have to be *theistic* since we are looking for a personal Law Giver.

We will also be looking for a God who is transcendent since this Law Giver cannot be a part of nature. He is responsible for creation, so He cannot be a part of it. He must be outside of time and space, external to our universe, something Unnatural.

None of the pagan religions will do since pagan gods are not transcendent. They are created beings, very much a part of this universe. Pantheism will be totally out of the picture since those religions see 'god' and the world as one.

Deism[270] doesn't fit the picture either, because, as we've seen, the Moral Law points to a personal God who is very concerned with relationships. It makes sense then, that the God we are looking for is Personal, not Deistic.

Since the Moral Law brings us to a personal God, none of the religions promoting an impersonal 'force' or some sort of New Agey 'universal consciousness' will do.

---

[270] Deism is the belief in a Supreme Being as a Creator, but this God is distant and impersonal with little concern for human affairs.

Nor will any religion without a transcendent Deity. Buddha, for instance, never claimed to be god – only a man. He had some very laudable ideas, and a person can live an excellent life following his teachings, but that's not nearly good enough.

We can put Confucius in the same category. It wasn't a human philosopher behind the Big Bang or responsible for the existence of objective moral reality. We need much more than just good philosophy.

So we need an all-powerful Creator who is also, at the same time, extremely personal and concerned about us as individuals. It makes sense, then, that we can investigate the world's *theistic* religions with confidence that one of them will have it right.

The seeker shouldn't get confused at this point. This does not mean that a religion coming from God will need to be perfect. People often make the mistake of looking for perfection, and turn away when they discover imperfect people representing a religion.

Any religion that comes from God, however perfect He may be, will become very imperfect once people get involved. God has no interest in puppets on strings, or biological robots with no choice but to 'dance to their DNA'. He made us free moral agents; as a result we have genuine freedom, and our choices really do make a difference.

This makes perfect sense when you think about it. Christians believe that they are entering into a personal relationship with the Creator of the Universe through Jesus Christ. This aspect of encountering God in a genuinely personal way is the essence of Christianity.

But you cannot have a real relationship with a puppet on strings or a robot with no choice but to follow its programming. Apparently, God thought it was important enough to risk giving us *real* freedom. So we must not make the mistake of thinking that once we find the 'right religion', if I may use that term, all perfectly wonderful people will populate it.

The single most important question anyone will ever answer is whether or not they believe in God, and what they decide to do about it. Our eternal condition hangs in the balance, and the best thing a person can do is devote the time and energy required to look for the answers. I will end with these words from C.S. Lewis:

> "Christianity simply does not make sense until you have faced the sort of facts I have been describing (i.e. the moral law). Christianity tells people to repent and promises them forgiveness. It therefore has nothing (as far as I know) to say to people who do not know they have done anything to repent of and who do not feel that they need any forgiveness. It is after you have realized there is a real Moral Law, and a Power behind the law, and that you have broken that law and put yourself wrong with that Power – it is after all this, and not a moment sooner, that Christianity begins to talk. When you know you are sick, you will listen to the doctor. When you have realised that our position is nearly desperate you will begin to understand what the Christians are talking about. They offer an explanation of how we got into our present state of both hating goodness and loving it. They offer an explanation of how God can be this impersonal mind at the back of the Moral Law and yet also a Person. They tell you how the demands of this law, which you and I cannot meet, have been met on our behalf, how God Himself becomes a man to save man from the disapproval of

God... Christian religion is, in the long run, a thing of unspeakable comfort. But it does not begin in comfort; it begins in dismay...If you look for truth, you may find comfort in the end: if you look for comfort you will not get either comfort or truth – only soft soap and wishful thinking to begin with and, in the end, despair."[271]

Further Reading

Bannister, Andy. *The Atheist Who Didn't Exist* (2015).
Berlinski, David. *The Devil's Delusion: Atheism and Its Scientific Pretensions* (2009).
Brierley, Justin. *Unbelievable? Why After Ten Years of Talking to Atheists I'm Still a Christian* (SPCK Publishing, 2017).
William Dembski, Michael Licona (Editors). *Evidence for God: 50 Arguments for God* (2010).
Flew, Anthony. *There is a God: How the World's Most Notorious Atheist Changed his Mind* (2008).
Keller, Timothy. *The Reason for God* (2008).
_____. *Making Sense of God* (2016).
Lewis, C. S. *Mere Christianity* (1952).
_____. *Miracles* (1947).
McGrath, Alister. *Why God Won't Go Away* (2010).
_____. *Twilight of Atheism* (2006)
Pearcey, Nancy. *Total Truth: Liberating Christianity from its Cultural Captivity* (2005).
Wright, N.T. *Simply Christian: Why Christianity Makes Sense*.

---

[271] C.S. Lewis, *Mere Christianity*, p. 31-32.

Appendix 1

But they shall sit every man under his own vine

IN CHAPTER ONE, I made the claim that social justice saturates the Bible. Such a bold assertion needs to be backed up, and I am happy to do so. What follows is a survey of relevant biblical passages in addition to those already discussed in chapter 1.

This is by no means exhaustive, but I think it will serve to make the point that concern for the poor and practical support for others runs through the heart of the Gospel message. Notably, the biblical imperative to assist the poor is free of any anxiety over moral hazard.[272]

For the most part I will simply list the passages with little comment, as an introduction and invitation to further study.

Old Testament Passages

Exodus 22:5. Commands fair business practice.

Ex. 23:6. Do not pervert justice due the poor in a lawsuit.

Leviticus 19:13. You shall not oppress your neighbor; you are not to withhold workers pay.

Lev. 19:15. "do no injustice in court."

---

[272] When it comes to helping people, the term 'moral hazard' expresses the belief often held by those who resist social programs that assistance will only encourage laziness. This stems from our cultural myth that the poor just need to try harder to better their situation, and that social safety nets encourages moral degeneracy and undermines self-reliance.

Lev. 19:35-36. Do not cheat in your business dealings. Do no wrong in business. This is a picture of economic justice and honesty we are expected to apply in any economic system.

Lev. 12:8; 14:21-22. Accommodations are made for the poor by lowering the cost for them to participate in community worship services.

Lev. 19:14. "Do not curse the deaf or put a stumbling block before the blind." In other words, do not take advantage of any weakness or vulnerability in others.

Lev. 25:10. The year of jubilee in which sweeping land reform and redistribution of wealth was enacted on a regular basis. Preventing the rise of a class of super-wealthy and excessive concentration of wealth would be one of the positive results.

Lev. 25:35-36. Help the poor and don't charge interest.

Deuteronomy 15:1-3. "At the end of every seven years you must cancel all debts."

Deut.15:4. "There is to be no poor among you." This commandment to end poverty, along with the law to cancel debts every 7 years, would lay the groundwork for a just society in which all forms of oppression, including any form of slavery, would be impossible.

Deut. 16:18-20. Pursue justice and only justice.

Deut. 24:14-15. Do not oppress hired workers, whether citizens or foreign immigrants.

Deut. 25:13-15; Lev.19:35-36. Economic righteousness.

Deut. 32:4. Justice is a defining characteristic of God (also Ps. 37:28; Is.30:18).

Psalms 33:5; 37:28. The Lord loves justice and righteousness.

In the Psalms, 'justice' and 'righteousness' are often paired. It is fair to say that this typically means what we would call today 'social justice', not just personal piety. This is because the Hebrew words for justice and righteousness carry with them strong connotations of community behavior, righteousness in how we treat others and behave as a member of a community, not just personal abstinence from sin.

Psalms 72:1-4. God defends the cause of the poor and crushes the oppressor.

Psalms 72:12-14. Have pity and deliver the needy from oppression and violence.

Psalms 82:3. Give justice to the weak, and maintain the rights of the afflicted and destitute.

Psalms 97:2. Justice is foundational to God.

Psalms 106:3. Blessed are those who do justice.

Psalms 112:3-9. "He has distributed freely and given to the poor." Generosity to the poor is closely linked to righteousness.

Proverbs 19:17. "He who is kind to the poor lends to God." (See also 11:24),

Isaiah 3:14. "the plunder from the poor is in your houses." (NIV). Destruction is coming to the wealthy who have enriched themselves at the expense of the poor.

Is. 11:1-4. The poor are to receive fair treatment.

Is. 28:16-18. Righteousness and justice should be the standard, and any refuge in lies and falsehood swept away.

Is. 30:18. The Lord is a God of justice.

Is. 58:6-8. True religion is expressed in setting the oppressed free, sharing your bread with the hungry.

Amos 5:24. "Let justice roll on like a river, righteousness like a never-failing stream." (NIV).

Micah 4:3-4. "Every man will sit under his own vine and under his own fig tree, and no one will make them afraid." (NIV). This is a picture of everyone having their own means of secure income, unthreatened by the predations of the rich and powerful. (Israel was an agrarian society that lived off the land, and owning land was the primary means of supporting yourself. Vineyards and fig trees were commonly cultivated for food.)

Malachi 3:5. Judgment is coming upon those who "defraud laborers of their wages, who oppress the widows and the fatherless, and deprive aliens (immigrants) of justice..." (NIV).

New Testament Passages

Matthew 3:13-15; 5:10; 6:1-5,33. The Greek word for righteousness, *dikaiosune*, does not mean just personal piety. It has an expanded meaning into the public sphere that goes beyond simply avoiding personal sin. It stands for how we behave towards others as members of a community. It strongly connotes social justice. Therefore Matthew 3:13-15; 5:10 and 6:1-5,33, should not be understood as referring only to individual piety, but justice in the community.

Verse 5:10 says, "Blessed are those who are persecuted for righteousness' sake, for theirs is the kingdom of heaven."

People are rarely harassed for personal piety, as long as they keep their religion private. The world is happy to leave such pious people alone. It is only when they attempt to extend justice into society by changing public policy and law, and thereby becoming a threat to entrenched power interests, that they get into trouble.

Matthew 6:24-34. Don't be anxious for money; don't chase wealth. You can't serve God and money.

Mat. 10:10. The laborer deserves his pay.

Mat. 11:28-30. Christ's yoke is easy. We are to ease the burden of those who are weighed down with heavy labor.

Mat. 19:21. Sell your possessions and give to the poor.

Mat. 19:24. "I tell you the truth, it will be easier for a camel to pass through the eye of a needle than for a rich man to enter heaven."

Mat. 22:39. "Love your neighbor as yourself."

Mat. 25:40. Whatever you do to the least in society you've done to God.

Luke 4:18-19. Citing Isaiah 61:1-2, Christ defined his ministry as setting the oppressed free.

Luke 6:24-25. Woe to the rich and well-off.

Luke 10.7. The worker deserves his pay (also Mat 10.10).

Luke 12:13-21. The parable of the rich fool. Christ used this story of a successful businessman to warn us to "be on guard against all kinds of greed, for your life does not consist in the abundance of possessions."

Luke 16. In this parable, a rich man goes to hell. Not for oppressing the poor, indeed, not for anything he had done, but for what he *hadn't* done; for simply ignoring the beggar at his gate and doing nothing to alleviate his suffering.

John 13:34. I give you a new commandment, that you love one another.

Acts 4:32-33. Describes Christians who held everything in common. As a result, there were no needy among them, because those who had possessions and money shared with those who didn't.

2 Cor.9:6-9. Give generously.

Phil 2:3-4. "Do nothing out of selfish ambition or vain conceit, but in humility consider others better than yourselves. Each of you should look not only to your own interests, but also to the interests of others." (NIV).

James 1:27. The nature of "true religion" is to look after widows and orphans. (In James' day, widows and the fatherless were the most vulnerable members of society and often the poorest).

James 2:1-13. Showing favoritism towards the rich over the poor in social gatherings is harshly rebuked.

James 2:14-19. "Faith without action is dead." Genuine faith will be expressed in practical ways, notably in assisting "the hungry" (the less fortunate). Faith that does not express itself in practical ways is strongly denounced as useless and dead.

James 5:1-6. The rich are invited to weep and howl over their coming misery, because they've oppressed their workers and defrauded them of wages.

ABOUT THE AUTHOR

Mike Manto was a software developer and co-founded a technology start-up. Shortly after becoming a Christian he sold his stake in the company to take a few years off to study theology. He graduated seminary with a Master of Theological Studies degree in 2008.

He lives in SW Ontario with his wife. They like to get outdoors camping, canoeing and hiking. He also enjoys blacksmithing and writing sci-fi in his spare time.

michaelmanto.substack.com